Outlines of Christian Dogma

The Nature of God and Christ, and the Role of the Church in Christianity

By Darwell Stone

Principal of Dorchester Missionary College

PANTIANOS
CLASSICS

Published by Pantianos Classics

ISBN-13: 978-1-78987-474-7

First published in 1900

Contents

Preface

In the following pages the author has attempted to supply such an account of the Christian religion as may afford to those who are not students of technical theology a clear and systematic idea of the chief tenets of the Faith. It has been his aim to be, as far as possible, uncontroversial. He has sought to state facts rather than to defend theories. The book is the outcome of a conviction that one of the great needs of the present time is accurate knowledge, on the part of those who have not opportunity for deep study, of what historical Christianity really is. That the great Christian dogmas have been tried through many centuries and have stood the test of time, alike in relation to thought and as the support of life, is, to say no more, a most significant fact.

It is hoped that some parts of the book, and especially the notes which are printed separately at the end, may be of use to theological students also. For them, too, it may well be thought that, among the many demands which are made upon their time, knowledge of what is, and what is not, the historical religion of the Christian Church is not the least important of their needs.

Thanks are due to the Rev. C. O. Becker, of the Church of St. Barnabas, Pimlico, who has added to the many services of a long friendship that he has read the greater part of this book before it was in print. The responsibility for it belongs to the author alone, but he owes very much to the valuable suggestions which Mr. Becker has made.

Chapter One - The Approach to Dogma

The foundation of religion in human thought is belief in the personal God. This belief may come to be the possession of the soul in different ways. Probably very many who accept and act upon it have never seriously asked themselves what is the ground of their belief. By those who have really faced their own inner life, widely differing answers would be given to the question why they believe in God. Not only would the answers differ in matters of detail they would refer to different sides of life. In the case of one person, the answer would relate to spiritual needs. In the case of another, it would relate to moral claims. A third would base it on intellectual considerations. For some the intellectual, the moral, and the spiritual would all have their parts to play in the formation of conviction.

There are strong intellectual reasons for the conviction that God exists. Short of the work of a Creator, no satisfactory explanation of the existence of the world has ever been given. The researches of modern science, if they have changed the form, have increased the force of the argument which demands personality and mind in the maker of the universe. The general tendency of human thought to believe in God suggests a consideration which does not grow less impressive with the growth of knowledge about the religions of mankind. The intellectual reasons are supported by moral claims. It is acknowledged that the sense of duty is one of the finest elements in the character of man. When this sense is analyzed, it demands something more than the claims of the highest self-interest, irresponsibility towards kindred, or patriotism, or the good of the human race. All these have their place in it. Each one of them rests on something beyond itself; and the voice of conscience, alike in its imperative command to do what is right, and in its stern rebuke for wrong which has been done, is a witness to a power higher than human speaking with authority. In the last resort, to acknowledge the existence of duty is to acknowledge the existence of God.

There are spiritual faculties which yearn to be satisfied. The oft-quoted words, 'Thou, Lord, hast made us for Thyself; and therefore our hearts are restless until they rest in Thee,' [1] wake an echo among many whose intellectual thoughts are very few and poor and to whom any analysis of the sense of duty would be impossible. Human nature, even when it has fallen very low, craves to be able to pray. And if prayer, in its proper sense, is a possibility, God exists.

The heart of man cannot be satisfied with a God who should hold Himself apart from human life. Mind and conscience and love concur in demanding a God who is not only personal but also good. They claim, further, that the good God must be one who makes Himself known to His creatures and helps them in the battle of life.

Natural religion cannot stop with itself. If it is true at all, it leads on to fuller truths. It does not despise, even if it fails to understand, the tracks of the footsteps of God which are found all through the history of human thought. But it feels instinctively that these are but the preludes of something that is greater, the movements by which God Himself has formed and fostered the longing for that revelation which, it is reverently convinced, His goodness cannot fail to give.

The idea of revelation directs attention to the life of Christ. The Gospels contain the history of One who claimed to be sent from God and to reveal God. The moral grandeur of His life is in accordance with His claim. Here, if anywhere, it is felt by those whose thoughts are passing from natural to revealed religion, the revelation of God is to be found.

If the life of Christ is the revelation of God, the teaching contained in it is God's declaration to man. This teaching involves the Godhead of Christ Himself. Unless the record in the Gospels is to be made into a hopeless puzzle, He is Himself one with the Father in the sense that as the Father is God, so also is He. It involves also belief in the Old Testament Scriptures as a former revelation, and in the Christian Church as the work and organ of Christ.

The life of the Church, as seen in history, is the complement to the anticipations of the Christian society which are found in the teaching of our Lord. The Church herself calls for consideration by the very greatness of her claims; for she boldly says that she is the representative of Christ, and that, through her, God satisfies human needs.

The cry which comes from the depths of the soul of man is an entreaty to know the truth, to be freed from sin, to attain to righteousness. The Church answers the cry by pointing to herself, and, through herself, to the Son of God and the Holy Trinity. She bids man recognize that she brings the truth which Christ revealed; that she conveys the pardon which Christ won; and that she imparts the righteousness of Christ's own life. She takes him by the hand and tells him that, under the guidance and with the help which the Holy Ghost vouchsafes through her, he may pass in safety through the present life and attain to the eternal glory of the perfected kingdom of God.

Each step in this journey of human thought, from the first glimmer of natural religion to the theology of the Christian Church, involves many problems and great searchings of heart. To those problems and the questions they involve, this book does not attempt to give any direct answer. The author does not, indeed, depreciate their importance, or hide from himself their momentous character; and he is not unaware of the terrible pressure which they exercise on many minds. But he has taken as his task an attempt, not to establish the truth of the Christian religion, but to state and explain what the Christian religion is. Consequently, in the following pages he must take for granted fundamental positions which, at the right time and place, call for lengthy treatment. He will assume, that is, the existence of God, the reality of revelation, the trustworthiness of the Bible, and the divine guidance of the Church.

Yet the author is not without hope that this book may help some to grasp the inherent reasonableness of the Christian religion. In ordinary life we test the worth of things by using them. If the Christian religion can be seen to possess a great harmony of consistent thought, that will be to many minds as strong evidence of its truth as they think themselves likely to obtain.

It is for this reason, among others, that what may be called the logical order of theology will be followed in this book. The doctrines of God and the Holy Trinity will be taken as the foundation. The facts of Creation and the Fall will be treated as the outcome and the perversion of the work of God. The Incarnation and the Atonement will be viewed as the remedies designed by God for a fallen race. The Church, in her offices of teaching and sanctifying, will be regarded as springing out of the incarnate life of the eternal Son of God. The future of mankind will have its place as resulting from the response given, for good or for evil, to the loving purpose of Him who desires the blessing of all whom He has made, but, none the less, will not violate moral law by constraining human will.

This order, it is clear, has its disadvantages. To mention one of them, it assumes readers who already believe what is fundamental rather than those who have not attained to belief. For the present purpose, as it seems to the author, the advantages outweigh all that there is on the other side.

As dogmatic theology starts with fundamental positions which some deny, so it is incomplete if it ends with itself. The Christian religion has more to do than to formulate a true system of thought. Dogma misses its end unless it is used to mould life. And if the student of dogmatic theology has learned aright the inner truth of those facts and doctrines with which, of necessity, he is driven to deal in technical and systematic methods, he can but feel that those only have used dogma well who through it have been led to say, 'O veritas Deus, fac me unum tecum in caritate perpetua. Taedet me saepe multa legere et audire: in te est totum quod volo et desidero. Taceant omnes doctores, sileant universae creaturae in conspectu tuo: tu mihi loquere solus.' [2]

[1] St, Augustine, *Conf.,* i. 1.
[2] *De Imitation Christi,* I. iii. 2, God, the truth, make me one with Thee in abiding love. Often is it a weariness to me to read and hear many things: in Thee is all that I will and desire. Let all teachers be silent, let all creatures be quiet in Thy sight: do Thou alone speak to me.'

Chapter Two - The Nature and Attributes of God

It has been said in the preceding chapter that the standpoint from which dogmatic theology is to be treated in this work is the belief that God exists and has revealed Himself to man in the religion, first of the Jews and then of Christians. Thus, the aim which is here in view is not so much to prove the truth of Christian doctrine as to state and explain what Christian doctrine is.

Going through the Christian religion in the order which has been described, the first subject is that of God Himself. In writing on the doctrine of God there is very little to be done except to put the words in which Holy Scripture speaks of Him in such a systematic form as the teaching of the Church suggests. The truths about God are so far above our reason that we do best simply to take them as they are revealed, without much attempt at explanation, and to remember that the Scriptural utterances, especially those contained in the Psalms, have life and power which any mere technical statement must always lack. And on this subject the exhortation of the Preacher has a special meaning: 'God is in heaven, and thou upon; earth: therefore let thy words be few.' [1]

The Nature of God

It is revealed in both the Old and New Testaments that the nature of God is Spirit. In the Book of Deuteronomy Israel is exhorted: 'Take ye therefore good heed unto yourselves; for ye saw no manner of form on the day that the Lord spake unto you in Horeb out of the midst of the fire.' In the Book of Isaiah the prophet indignantly asks, 'To whom, then, will ye liken God? or what likeness will ye compare unto Him?' 'To whom then will ye liken Me, that I should be equal to him? saith the Holy One.' In St. John's Gospel our Lord Himself teaches, 'God is Spirit.' [2]

The Attributes of God

The attributes of God are not really distinct from His nature because they are the necessary results of His essential Being; but it is convenient for the purposes of thought and expression to consider them separately from His nature. Theologians distinguish between the absolute attributes of God and His relative attributes. The absolute attributes are those which are common to the Three Persons. The relative attributes are those which are personal to one or other of the Three Persons. The consideration of the absolute attributes therefore belongs to the doctrine of God. The consideration of the relative attributes belongs to the doctrine of the Holy Trinity.

The absolute attributes are generally divided into quiescent, operative, and moral. The quiescent attributes are -

1. Unity. It is revealed that God is One, that is, there is no other who is God. It was declared in the Book of Deuteronomy, 'Hear, O Israel: the Lord our God is one Lord;' and the comment of the scribe on these words, when quoted by our Lord, 'Master, Thou hast well said that He is one; and there is none other but He,' were approved as an answer which was discreet.

In the Book of Isaiah the prophet declares, 'Thus saith the Lord the King of Israel, and his redeemer the Lord of hosts: I am the first, and I am the last; and beside Me there is no God;' 'There is no God else beside Me; a just God and a saviour; there is none beside Me.' And in St. John's Gospel it is part of our Lord's prayer to the Father on the eve of His crucifixion, 'This is life eternal, that they should know Thee, the only true God, and Jesus Christ whom Thou hast sent.' [3]

Thus the unity of God has been revealed in the Bible. It may also be seen to be implied by other truths about God which have yet to be considered - His infinity, His perfection, the supremacy of His dominion, the facts that there is only one first cause of all things, and that the harmonies of the world point to the existence of one purpose and one ordaining mind. The craving of the human heart and spirit, and the demand of the human mind are alike, not for many gods, but for one God; and that which natural religion at its best desires is declared by revelation to be the truth.

2. Simplicity. It is revealed that the nature of God is simple. There are not in Him component parts as the body and soul in man. The assertion of this attribute is necessarily included in the truth of His essential Being, because His essential Being is Divine Spirit. Being such, He cannot be divided. Since He is such, there is in Him no possibility of conflict. As God is one, and is therefore distinguished from the many gods of some heathen systems, so also, in distinction from the divisible character of some false ideas of Godhead, He is simple. With regard to the attribute of simplicity, God differs from man because man's nature is compounded of body and soul; He differs from the angels because His nature, though it is like theirs in being spiritual, is unlike theirs in being divine.

3. Infinity. It is revealed that God is free from those limits which restrict created beings. His infinity may be best seen in the consideration of the operative attributes of knowledge and power. It includes also the truth that there is no limit to His presence. In the words of the Psalmist, 'Whither shall I go from Thy Spirit? Or whither shall I flee from Thy presence? If I ascend up into heaven, Thou art there; if I make my bed in Sheol, behold, Thou art there. If I take the wings of the morning and dwell in the uttermost parts of the sea, even there shall Thy hand lead me, and Thy right hand shall hold me.' [4]

In St. Augustine's language, 'He knows how to be everywhere in His whole Being and to be limited by no place. He knows how to come without departing from the place where He was; He knows how to go away without leaving the place whither He has come.' [5]

When it is asserted that God is infinite, it is not meant that He has not personal Being, or that there is no law in Himself or in His works. The personality of God is everywhere implied or insisted on in the Bible and in Christian thought. Belief in it underlies the utterances of the Psalmists. Its truth supplies the explanation of the words of our Lord, alike when He addresses the Father and when He instructs His disciples. It makes the possibility of Christian prayer. Moreover, God 'is a law both to Himself and to all other things besides.' [6] In His very Being there is law, as is shown by the doctrine of the Holy Trinity. In His works there is law imposed upon Himself by 'His own free and voluntary act.' [7] Nor does His infinity imply that He is to be identified with the universe. While, as St. Augustine says, 'He is everywhere in His whole Being, contained by no place, bound by no bond, divisible into no parts, mutable in no respect, filling heaven and earth with the presence of His power,' [8] He yet acts in all things in such a way as to transcend them. Man and nature everywhere are present to Him; yet He is to be distinguished from them in fact as well as in thought.

4. Eternity. The eternity of God necessarily follows from His infinity. As space cannot limit His presence, so time cannot limit it. He is present through all the ages before and after the creation of time. Abraham 'called on the name of the Lord, the everlasting God.' It was promised to Israel in the blessing of Moses, 'The eternal God is thy dwelling-place, and underneath are the everlasting arms.' Before the mountains were brought forth, run the words of the Psalm which is entitled, 'A prayer of Moses the man of God,' 'or ever Thou hadst formed the earth and the world, even from everlasting to everlasting, Thou art God.' In the Book of Isaiah it is proclaimed, 'Hast thou not known? Hast thou not heard? The everlasting God, the Lord, the Creator of the ends of the earth, fainteth not, neither is weary: there is no searching of His understanding.' St. Paul writes to the Romans, The in visible things of Him since the creation of the world are clearly seen, being perceived through the things that are made, even His everlasting power and divinity. The same Apostle exclaims in his First Epistle to St. Timothy, 'Unto the King eternal, incorruptible, invisible, the only God, be honour and glory for ever and ever.' [9]

5. Immutability. It is revealed that God does not change. He declares through the prophet Malachi, 'I, the Lord, change not.' It is part of the teaching of St. James: Every good gift and every perfect boon is from above, coming down from the Father of lights, with whom can be no variation, neither shadow that is cast by turning.' [10] Yet, though God Himself does not change, there are changes in what He does. As it is expressed by St. Augustine, 'Thou changest the works, but the design Thou dost not change;' 'All these things' (seasons of the year and times of life) 'are changed, but the plan of the divine Providence, whereby it comes to pass that they are changed, is not changed.' The same thought was tersely put by St. Thomas Aquinas: 'It is one thing to change the will; it is another thing to wish for the change of certain things.' [11] It is a part of the true immutability of God that under different circumstances He acts in different ways.

The operative attributes are

1. Knowledge. It is revealed in Holy Scripture that God is omniscient. The Psalmist sings, 'Great is our Lord, and mighty in power: His understanding is infinite.' In the Epistle to the Hebrews it is said, 'There is no creature that is not manifest in His sight: but all things are naked and laid open before the eyes of Him with whom we have to do.' [12] The omniscience of God is one aspect of His infinity. All things are present to His knowledge in consequence of the fact that He is unrestrained by the limits which are characteristic of created existence. Holy Scripture connects His omniscience and His omni-

presence. The verses from the Psalm already quoted to describe His omni-presence are immediately preceded by the passage, 'Thou knowest my down-sitting and my uprising, Thou understandest my thought afar off. Thou searchest out my path and my lying down, and art acquainted with all my ways...Such knowledge is too wonderful for me; it is high, I cannot attain unto it.' [13] Divine knowledge has special characteristics which distinguish it from the knowledge possessed by man. The know ledge of man, at any rate almost entirely in the present life, depends on his use of his senses; that of God is subject to no such restriction. Human knowledge is compelled to think of one thing after another, and possesses a very limited power of being sim-ultaneously conscious of more objects than one; the knowledge of God em-braces all things at one moment. Human knowledge is compelled to judge by what is outward and apparent; the knowledge of God penetrates to what is most inward. It is possible for the Psalmist to say with reality, 'Search me, God, and know my heart: try me and know my thoughts.' [14]

2. Will. The will of God is often referred to in Holy Scripture. God, it is de-clared in the vision recorded in the Book of Daniel, 'ruleth in the kingdom of men, and giveth it to whomsoever He will.' 'Thy will be done,' forms part of the prayer to the Father commanded by our Lord. The perfect freedom of the divine will is asserted by St. Paul in writing to the Ephesians of 'the purpose of Him who worketh all things after the counsel of His will.' [15] A distinction has been made by theologians between the antecedent will of God and the consequent will of God. The antecedent will refers to what He wills in the abstract, apart from conditions and circumstances. The consequent will re-fers to what He wills in view of particular conditions and circumstances. For instance, it is the antecedent will of God that every man be happy. It may be the consequent will of God that a particular man at a particular time should suffer in view of certain conditions and circumstances, whether the man's own need of discipline, or the man's own need of punishment, or the opera-tion of laws of cause and effect which have been set in motion outside the life of the man himself. There is a close relation between the distinctions neces-sarily made in the different methods of the operation of the divine will and the truth that, while God is Himself immutable, He may and does change par-ticular actions.

3. Power. Holy Scripture reveals God as almighty. 'Whatsoever the Lord pleased,' says the Psalmist, 'that hath He done.' In the Revelation of St. John the Divine it is said, 'I am the Alpha and the Omega, saith the Lord God, which is and which was and which is to come, the Almighty.' [16] In connexion with the omnipotence of God an apparent limitation has to be remembered. The meaning of the truth of God's almighty power is that He is able to do all things which are not inconsistent with His own attributes; for it would be a moral impossibility that God should do anything which would be incon-sistent with the attributes which are the necessary outcome of His essential Being. The divine attribute of holiness makes it impossible that God should

sin; and the divine attribute of truth makes it impossible that He should cause something which has happened not to have happened, or that He should contradict any of those necessary and fundamental truths which, as the elementary facts in mathematics and logic, are based upon His own consistency. Thus, St. Paul wrote to St. Timothy, 'He cannot deny Himself; and to St. Titus, In hope of eternal life, which God, who cannot lie, promised.' So, too, it is said in the Epistle to the Hebrews, 'That by two immutable things, in which it is impossible for God to lie, we may have a strong encouragement.' [17] In like manner, St. Clement of Rome writes, 'There is nothing impossible with God except to lie;' and St. Augustine, says, 'God is almighty; and, since He is almighty, He cannot die, or be deceived, or lie, and, as the Apostle says, He cannot deny Himself. How many things He cannot do, and yet is almighty, and is almighty for the very reason that He cannot do them. For if He could die, He would not be almighty; if He could lie, or be deceived, or deceive, or act unjustly, He would not be almighty, because if this should be in Him, He would not be worthy to be almighty. In short, our almighty Father cannot sin. He does whatever He wills: that is almighty power. He does whatever He well and justly wishes; but whatever is ill done, He wishes not. No one resists Him who is almighty so that He may not do what He wills.' [18]

The moral attributes are: -

1. Wisdom, which consists in the union of will and knowledge. The wisdom of God is referred to in the Song of Hannah in the First Book of Samuel: 'The Lord is a God of knowledge, and by Him actions are weighed;' and in the Epistle to the Romans, 'O the depth of the riches both of the wisdom and the knowledge of God! how unsearchable are His judgments, and His ways past tracing out! For who hath known the mind of the Lord? or who hath been His counsellor? Or who hath first given to Him, and it shall be recompensed unto him again?' [19] God not only knows all things; He also uses His omniscience in the exercise of His holy will.

2. Holiness. God is revealed as holy both in Himself and in His actions towards mankind. His own holiness is described in the Book of Leviticus: 'Speak unto all the congregation of the children of Israel, and say unto them, Ye shall be holy: for I the Lord your God am holy.' It is emphatically referred to in the vision which Isaiah saw: 'One cried unto another, and said, Holy, holy, holy, is the Lord of Hosts: the whole earth is full of His glory.' It is declared by the prophet Habakkuk, 'Thou art of purer eyes than to behold evil.' [20] The revelation of it was one great element in the conception of God which the Old Testament presents.

The holiness of God in relation to man is shown in His care. Much of the Old Testament deals with His care for the Jewish nation. His care for mankind was preached by St. Paul at Athens: 'Neither is He served by men's hands, as though He needed anything, seeing He Himself giveth to all life, and breath, and all things.' It is shown also in His mercy. St. Paul wrote to St. Titus, 'Not by works done in righteousness which we did ourselves, but according to His mercy He saved us. It is shown, again, in His love. 'We know and have believed,' says St. John, 'the love which God hath in us. God is love; and he that abideth in love abideth in God, and God abideth in him.' [21] In striking contrast to many of the deities of the heathen religions which in some ways afford strange resemblances to the religion of the Bible, the God who has been revealed to Jews and to Christians is a holy God.

3. Truth. It is a part of the holiness of God that He is true. He, sings the Psalmist, 'keepeth truth for ever.' 'Let God be found true, but every man a liar,' [22] wrote St. Paul to the Romans. The mind and conscience of man concur in requiring that the God who is to be worshipped must be a God of truth. The mind would not be satisfied with a being who could violate truth by teaching falsehood, or by making things which have been not to have been, or by contradicting primary laws of thought. The conscience would not be satisfied with a being who could deny Himself and be false to His word. Thus, the God who is revealed in the Bible has in this attribute, as in others, that for which human needs call.

4. Justice. It is another aspect of the holiness of God that He is just. The Psalmist says to Him, 'Righteous art Thou, Lord, and upright are Thy judgments.' St. Paul speaks of 'the righteous judgment of God; who will render to every man according to his works.' [23] Justice, no less than truth, is demanded by the moral sense. Men cannot reverence other men who are unjust. Much more is justice claimed in Him who is to be worshipped. The righteous God of whom Holy Scripture speaks answers to the felt needs of men.

In considering the attributes of God we must remember that the meaning of the words when applied to Him is greater than we can know. We form the highest conception of wisdom, and holiness, and truth, and justice which is possible for us in our present state; and thereby we have a notion, true indeed so far as it ; goes, but poor and imperfect, of the moral greatness of ; the Most High God.

In a passage of "great beauty St. Augustine has summed up one aspect of many of the attributes of God. 'Most merciful, yet most just; most hidden, yet most present; most beautiful, yet most strong; stable, yet incomprehensible; unchangeable, yet changing all things; never new, never old; renewing all things, yet bringing age upon the proud, though they know it not; ever at work, ever at rest; gathering, yet lacking nothing; supporting and filling and protecting; creating and nourishing and maturing; seeking, yet having all things. Thou lovest, yet Thou art not moved by passion; Thou art jealous, yet Thou art free from anxiety; Thou repentest, yet Thou dost not grieve; Thou art angry, yet Thou art calm; Thou changest the works, yet the design Thou dost not change; Thou receivest again what Thou dost find, yet Thou hast never lost; Thou art never in need, yet Thou rejoicest in gains; Thou art never covetous, yet Thou exactest usury.' [24]

[1] Eccles. v. 2.

[2] Deut. iv. 15; Isa. xl. 18, 25; St. John iv. 24.

[3] Deut. vi. 4; St. Mark xii. 32; Isa. xliv. 6; xlv. 21; St. John xvii. 3. Cf. Deut. xxxii. 39.

[4] Ps. cxxxix. 7-10.

[5] St. Augustine, *Ep.*, cxxxvii. 4.

[6] Hooker, *Laws of Ecclesiastical Polity*, I. ii. 3.

[7] *ibid.*, I. ii. 6.

[8] St. Augustine, *De Civ. Dei*, vii. 30.

[9] Gen. xxi. 33; Deut. xxxiii. 27; Ps. xc. 2; Isa. xl. 28; Rom. i.20; 1 St. Tim. i. 17.

[10] Mai. iii. 6; St. Jas. i. 17.

[11] St. Augustine, *Conf.*, i. 4; Ep. t cxxxviii. 2; St. Thomas Aquinas, *Summa Theol*, I. xix. 7. Cf. St. Thomas Aquinas, *In Heb.*, cap. vi. lect. 4; St. Gregory the Great, *Moral*, xvi. 14, 46.

[12] Ps. cxlvii. 5; Heb. iv. 13.

[13] Ps. cxxxix. 2, 3, 6.

[14] Ps. cxxxix. 23. On the differences between divine knowledge and human knowledge, see *Church Quarterly Review*, October, 1891, pp. 18-21.

[15] Dan. iv. 17, 25,32; St. Matt. vi. 10; Eph. i. 11.

[16] Ps. cxxxv. 6; Rev. i. 8.

[17] St. Tim. ii. 13; St. Tit. i. 2; Heb. vi. 18.

[18] St. Clement of Rome, *Ad Cor.*, i. 27; St. Augustine, *De Symb. ad Cat.*,2.

[19] 1 Sam. ii. 3; Rom. xi. 33-35.

[20] Lev. xix. 2; Isa. vi. 3; Hab. i. 13.

[21] Acts xvii. 25; St. Tit. iii. 5; 1 St. John iv. 16.

[22] Ps. cxlvi. 6; Rom. iii. 4.

[23] Ps. cxix. 137; Rom. ii. 5,6.

[24] St. Augustine, *Conf.*, i. 4. Cf. St. Bernard, *De Consid.*, v. 13-29.

Chapter Three - The Holy Trinity

The Old Testament affords slight indications that there are more Persons than one in the Godhead. In the account of creation contained in the Book of Genesis God is represented as using the plural number and saying, 'Let us make man in our image.' In the history of the Fall the Lord God is recorded to have said, 'The man is become as one of us, to know good and evil.' The words of the Lord at the building of the tower of Babel are, 'Let us go down.' In the vision which Isaiah saw, the Lord was heard to say, 'Whom shall I send, and who will go for us?' [1] Too much should not be made of this plural method of speech; but, at the same time, its remarkable character cannot rightly be ignored.

Reference is often made to the Angel of the Lord. The person so described was probably a manifestation of God the Son, who may have assumed the form of an angel in something the same way as that in which the Holy Ghost assumed the form of a dove at the baptism of our Lord, or may have been represented by a created angel. [2]

The Spirit of the Lord God is spoken of by the prophet Isaiah in the words, 'The Spirit of the Lord God is upon me;' and the use made by our Lord of this passage as a prophecy of His own preaching after He had received the gift of the Holy Ghost at the time of His baptism, shows that by them the Holy Ghost is denoted. [3]

Thus, there are hints scattered about in the Old Testament of more Persons than one who are God. There is no teaching about the Holy Trinity of any clearness. This fact is in accordance with what may be gathered as to the purpose of God in His different dispensations. In the Old Testament revelation it was necessary to impress the idea of the unity of God. Until the belief in Monotheism was firmly established, the teaching about God could not go to any marked extent beyond the truth of His unity without danger that those who received it might fall into polytheism and idolatry. Therefore, in the Old Testament the doctrine of the Trinity is scarcely to be seen. Yet there are dim indications of it because of the need of showing that both Testaments are the revelation of the one God, and to supply such a preparation for the teaching of this doctrine that, when it was taught, it would be recognized by those whose hearts were open to truth as being in harmony with, and affording the explanation of, what they had been taught all along. This is one of the many facts which illustrate the truth of the saying of St. Augustine, 'The New Testament lies hid in the Old, and the Old Testament is explained in the New.' [4] Thus, in the Old Testament preparation was made for the teaching of the doctrine of the Holy Trinity. In the New Testament it was clearly taught.

The doctrine of the Holy Trinity includes the following points:

1. There are Three the Father, the Son, and the Holy Ghost. They were mentioned by our Lord in His words to His disciples before His ascension: 'Go ye therefore and make disciples of all the nations, baptizing them into the Name of the Father, and of the Son, and of the Holy Ghost.' They were referred to by St. Paul in a passage which shows that at the time when he wrote the Second Epistle to the Corinthians, belief in Them formed an accepted part of the Christian faith: 'The grace of the Lord Jesus Christ, and the love of God, and the communion of the Holy Ghost, be with you all.' In an earlier epistle, probably written within fourteen years of our Lord's ascension, St. Paul speaks of God the Father, the Lord Jesus Christ, and the Holy Ghost: 'The Church of the Thessalonians in God the Father and the Lord Jesus Christ;' 'Ye became imitators of us, and of the Lord, having received the word in much affliction, with joy of the Holy Ghost.' St. Peter, in his First Epistle, makes mention of God the Father, 'the Holy Ghost sent forth from heaven,' and the Lord Jesus Christ, whose Spirit the Holy Ghost is. [5] These and similar passages show that the existence of the Three was revealed by our Lord and taught by His Apostles.

2. Each One of the Three is distinct from the Others. Our Lord distinguishes Himself from the Father, and distinguishes the Holy Ghost from both the Father and Himself when He says, 'I will pray the Father, and He shall give you another Comforter;' 'When the Comforter is come, whom I will send unto you from the Father, even the Spirit of truth.' [6]

3. Each of these Three is a Personal Being. That the Father and the Son are Personal Beings is shown by the way in which They are habitually spoken of. For instance, our Lord mentions the work of the Father and Himself: 'My Fa-

ther worketh even until now, and I work.' [7] That the Holy Ghost also is a Personal Being is shown in the following ways:

(a) Personal actions are attributed to Him. Our Lord speaks of Him, not only as abiding with the disciples, but also as teaching them and bringing to their remembrance all things which He had said unto them, as bearing witness of Him, as convicting the world in respect of sin, and of righteousness, and of judgment, and as coming, guiding, speaking, hearing, declaring. [8] In like manner, St. Paul describes the personal actions of the Holy Ghost in the Epistle to the Romans: 'The Spirit also helpeth our infirmity; for we know not how to pray as we ought: but the Spirit Himself maketh intercession for us with groanings which cannot be uttered; and He that searcheth the hearts knoweth what is the mind of the Spirit, because He maketh intercession for the saints according to the will of God.' [9]

(b) Personal dispositions are attributed to Him. St. Paul, writing to the Ephesians, speaks of His grief: 'Grieve not the Holy Spirit of God.' [10]

(c) The possibility of committing sin against Him is spoken of. Our Lord said to the Pharisees, 'Every sin and blasphemy shall be forgiven unto men: but the blasphemy against the Spirit shall not be forgiven.' [11] In the Acts of the Apostles St. Peter is recorded to have said to Ananias, 'Why hath Satan filled thy heart to lie to the Holy Ghost, and to keep back part of the price of the land?' In the same book, the words of St. Stephen are given: 'Ye stiffnecked and uncircumcised in heart and ears, ye do always resist the Holy Ghost: as your fathers did, so do ye.' In the Epistle to the Hebrews it is said, 'Of how much sorer punishment, think ye, shall he be judged worthy, who hath trodden under foot the Son of God, and hath counted the blood of the covenant, wherewith he was sanctified, an unholy thing, and hath done despite unto the Spirit of grace?' [12] In the proper sense of the word, sin cannot be committed against any but a personal being. The possibility, therefore, of sinning against the Holy Ghost shows that He is a Person.

Each one of the Three, the Father, the Son, and the Holy Ghost, is, then, a Person. It is necessary to use care about this word as applied to the Persons of the Holy Trinity. When it is so applied, it is used in a somewhat different sense from its ordinary meaning as applied to human persons. When applied to human persons, it means a separated individual; as applied to the Persons of the Godhead, it means that each of them has personal being, and that each of them is distinct; but not that they are separated from one another.

4. These Three Persons are One. Our Lord teaches, 'I and the Father are one;' 'He that hath seen Me hath seen the Father.' In the phrase used in St. Matthew's Gospel in the command for the teaching and Baptism of all the nations, 'In the Name of the Father, and of the Son, and of the Holy Ghost,' the singular noun 'name' denotes that the Father, the Son, and the Holy Ghost are One. [13]

5. The Unity of the Three Persons means more than that they share in the same Substance. It is taught that the Father and the Son are in the Spirit and

16

the Spirit in Them, the Father in the Son and the Son in the Father. 'Believe Me,' said our Lord, 'that I am in the Father, and the Father in Me.' 'Who among men,' wrote St. Paul, 'knoweth the things of a man, save the spirit of the man, which is in him? even so the things of God none knoweth, save the Spirit of God.' [14] This truth is technically known as περιχώρησις, or *circuminsessio,* or co-inherence.

6. Each of these Three Persons is God.

(*a*) The Father is described as God in many passages. For instance, our Lord said to St. Mary Magdalene, 'Go unto My brethren, and say to them, I ascend unto My Father, and your Father, and My God and your God;' and St. Paul wrote to the Romans, Grace to you and peace from God our Father, and the Lord Jesus Christ. [15]

(*b*) The Son is described as God. St. John's Gospel begins with the words, 'In the beginning was the Word, and the Word was with God, and the Word was God.' St. Thomas addressed our Lord after His resurrection, 'My Lord and my God.' St. Paul, writing to the Colossians, said, 'In Him dwelleth all the fulness of the Godhead bodily.' In the Epistle to the Hebrews the Son is addressed as God: 'Of the Son He saith, Thy throne, God, is for ever and ever.' [16]

(*c*) The Holy Ghost is described as God. St. Peter told Ananias that he had lied to the Holy Ghost, and immediately after that he had lied unto God. In the First Epistle to the Corinthians St. Paul refers to the indwelling of the Spirit in Christians as making them 'temples of God.' [17]

The Father

God the Father is so called as being the Father of God the Son. The generation of the Son is called in theology the Eternal Generation. [18] It is not an event which once happened and then ceased to happen, but an eternal relation which always exists. As God is always and has been always and will be always God, so the Father is always and has been always and will be always the Father. The term 'priority' is applied to the Father. It does not mean that He existed before the Son, or that His essence and attributes are greater than those of the Son; but simply that the Father has His nature of Himself, and the Son has His nature by the gift of the Father. In our Lord's words, 'As the Father hath life in Himself, even so gave He to the Son also to have life in Himself.' [19] In Hooker's phrase, 'The substance of God with this property to be of none doth make the Person of the Father.' [20] The Father possesses by reason of His deity all the absolute attributes of God. He possesses by reason of His Fatherhood these relative attributes

1. He is Himself begotten of none (ἀγεννησία: *innascibilitas*).

2. He is the Father of the Son (πατρότης: *paternitas*).

3. He is the Source of the Procession of the Holy Ghost (προβολή: *communis spiratio*).

17

The Son

The Son, who is eternally begotten of the Father, possesses because of His deity all the absolute attributes of God. He possesses because of His Person the relative attributes of being begotten (υἱότης: *filiatio*), and of a work in the Procession of the Holy Ghost (προβολή: *communis spiratio*). The term subordination is applied to the Son. It does not mean that He is less than the Father, or that He is not equally eternal. Of Them both the glory is equal, the majesty co-eternal. [21] It means that He is God of God, [22] that is, His life is derived from the Father. As it was expressed by Dr. Liddon, The Son's life was derived from, and, in that sense, subordinate to the life of the Father; [23] or by Bishop Pearson, The Father hath that essence of Him self; the Son, by communication from the Father; [24] or by Hooker, The very selfsame substance in number with this property to be of the Father maketh the Person of the Son. [25] Thus, there are two co-ordinate truths about the relation of the Son to the Father -

1. The Father is the Source (ἀρχή: *principium*) of Godhead. The Son derives His Being from Him.

2. The Son is co-eternal and co-equal with the Father. Time has nothing to do with the Eternal Generation.

The Holy Ghost

The Holy Ghost possesses all the absolute attributes of God because of His deity. The relative attribute which distinguishes God the Holy Ghost is that He proceeds (ἐκπόρευσις: *processio*). Hooker says, 'The same substance having added to it the property of proceeding from the other Two maketh the Person of the Holy Ghost.' [26] Our Lord teaches that the Holy Ghost proceeds from the Father: 'When the Comforter is come, whom I will send unto you from the Father, even the Spirit of truth, which proceedeth from the Father.' [27] The doctrine of the procession of the Holy Ghost from the Son has been a subject of much controversy, and it was one of the nominal causes which led to the separation of the churches of the East from Western Christendom. The truth of the statement that the Holy Ghost proceeds from the Father and the Son may be seen in the following ways:

1. The unity of essence in the Holy Trinity implies that the Son shares in every work of the Father, except that whereby He Himself is begotten; for it is implied in the truth of the co-inherence of the Three Persons that They work together in everything except in what constitutes the personal relations.

2. The temporal mission of the Holy Ghost is from the Son as well as from the Father. Our Lord speaks of Himself as sending the Holy Ghost: 'Behold, I send forth the promise of My Father upon you;' 'When the Comforter is come, whom I will send unto you from the Father, even the Spirit of truth, which

proceedeth from the Father;' 'It is expedient for you that I go away: for if I go not away, the Comforter will not come unto you; but if I go, I will send Him unto you.' It is probable that the temporal mission corresponds to a truth in the eternal relation of the Persons. Moreover, St. Paul calls the Holy Ghost the Spirit of the Son. [28]

3. In the undivided Church there was Eastern as well as Western teaching of what is called the double procession. The procession of the Holy Ghost from the Son, in the sense in which it has been taught by the theologians of the West, is implied by, among others, writers of so great authority as St. Athanasius and St. Cyril of Alexandria. [29] It is a mistake to describe the doctrine as merely Western.

The Western statement that the Holy Ghost proceeds from the Father and the Son must be maintained; but there is need of great care lest it be misunderstood, since it might be regarded in such a way as to detract from the truth that the Father is the one Source of the Godhead. It is a mistake of this kind which the Eastern Churches have feared. In reality the belief in the East has been essentially the same as in the West, though in the pressure of controversy Eastern writers have sometimes unduly minimized the work of the Son in the procession of the Holy Ghost, as, on the other hand, there have sometimes been unguarded assertions about the double procession in the West. The truth is that the Holy Ghost proceeds from the Father and the Son as from one principle of life. He possesses the one essence which is the substance of the Father and the Son; and the Son has part in the work of His procession; but the primary source of life in the Holy Ghost, as in the Son, is the Father. The Western phrase 'from the Son' has advantages over the Eastern phrase 'through the Son,' because the former guards more completely the truth of the co-inherence of the Three Persons in the God head; and is well fitted to be, in Dr. Pusey's words, 'a great preservative against heresy, which would not have been guarded against by the Greek formula.' [30] It is then to be asserted about God the Holy Ghost -

1. He proceeds eternally from the Father and the Son.

2. The ultimate source of His Being is the Father.

"The Lord our God," writes Hooker, "is but one God." In which indivisible unity notwithstanding we adore the Father as being altogether of Himself, we glorify that consubstantial Word which is the Son, we bless and magnify that co-essential Spirit eternally proceeding from both which is the Holy Ghost. Seeing, therefore, the Father is of none, the Son is of the Father, and the Spirit is of both, they are by these their several properties really distinguishable each from other.' [31] 'The Catholic faith is this,' says the hymn *Quicunque vult,* 'that we worship one God in Trinity, and Trinity in Unity.' [32]

---

[1] Gen. i. 26; iii. 22; xi. 7; Isa. vi. 8.

[2] On the Angel of the Lord, see note 1 in the concluding Notes.

[3] Isa. lxi. 1; St. Luke iv. 18.

[4] St. Augustine, *Quaest. in Exod.,* 73.

[5] St. Matt, xxviii. 19; 2 Cor. xiii. 14; 1 Thess. i. 1, 6; 1 St. Pet. i. 2, 3, 11, 12. On the significance of 2 Cor. xiii. 14, see Sanday in Hastings, Dictionary of the Bible, ii. 213, 214.
[6] St. John xiv. 16; xv. 26.
[7] St. John v. 17.
[8] St. John xiv. 16, 26; xv. 26; xvi. 8, 13.
[9] Rom. viii. 26, 27.
[10] Eph. iv. 30.
[11] St. Matt. xii. 31.
[12] Acts v. 3; vii. 51; Heb. x. 29.
[13] St. John x. 30; xiv. 9; St. Matt, xxviii. 19. The passage in 1 St. John v. 7, 'There are Three that bear record in heaven, the Father, the Word, and the Holy Ghost: and these Three are One,' is an interpolation probably due to a note of a scribe in the margin originally meant to be a comment on 'There are Three,' and subsequently written into the text by mistake. The right text is given in the revised version.
[14] St. John xiv. 11; 1 Cor. ii. 11.
[15] St. John xx. 17; Rom. i. 7.
[16] St. John i. 1; xx. 28; Col. ii, 8; Heb. i. 8.
[17] Acts v. 3,4; 1 Cor. iii. 16, 17.
[18] See note 2 in the concluding Notes.
[19] St. John v. 26.
[20] Hooker, Laws of Ecclesiastical Polity, V. li. 1.
[21] Quicunque vult.
[22] Nicene Creed.
[23] Liddon, The Divinity of our Lord and Saviour Jesus Christ, p. 431.
[24] Pearson, An Exposition of the Creed, article i.
[25] Hooker, Laws of Ecclesiastical Polity, V. li. 1.
[26] Hooker, Laws of Ecclesiastical Polity, V. li 1
[27] St. John xv. 26.
[28] St. Luke xxiv. 49; St. John xv. 26, xvi. 7; Rom. viii. 9; Gal. iv. 6. Cf. 1 St. Pet. i. 11.
[29] See note 3 in the concluding Notes.
[30] Pusey, On the Clause 'And the Son,' p. 179.
[31] Hooker, Laws of Ecclesiastical Polity, V. li. 1.
[32] For various forms of unbelief about the doctrines of God and the Holy Trinity, see note 4 in the concluding Notes.

Chapter Four - Creation

The doctrine of creation includes the creation of the angels, the material universe, and man. It is revealed that heaven and earth, with all which they contain, whether spiritual or corporal, were created by God out of nothing. The first two chapters of the Book of Genesis refer the origin of all things to God. It is said in the Psalms, with reference to the angels, the sun and moon, the stars, and the heavens, 'Let them praise the name of the Lord; for He commanded and they were created.' St. John teaches, 'All things were made by Him; and without Him was not anything made that hath been made.' [1] In a remarkable expression in the Revelation of St. John it is said, 'Thou didst create all things, and because of Thy will they were, and were created.' [2] The apparent meaning is that before creation the universe existed in the mind of God; and that, in creation, all things were made by God in accordance with the type which already existed in His own mind, so that the angels and the world and man, from having been as divine ideas, were made to be in fact under the limitations of time and space. [3]

The Universe

In considering the creation of the universe, a distinction, too often forgotten, must be made between what is clearly revealed in Holy Scripture and many matters about which no clear revelation of one kind or another has been made. It is included in the revelation contained in the Bible that
1. God is the one first cause and the ultimate maker of everything.
2. The Father made the universe through the Son by the working of the Holy Ghost. God, it is said in the Epistle to the Hebrews, 'hath at the end of these days spoken unto us in His Son, whom He appointed heir of all things, through whom also He made the worlds.' 'The Spirit of God,' it is declared in the Book of Genesis, 'moved upon the face of the waters.' [4]

On the other hand, revealed religion does not assert –
1. What is meant by the six 'days' upon which, in the Book of Genesis, the creation is described as taking place. So far as Holy Scripture is concerned, there is nothing to show whether the word 'day' in the first chapter of Genesis means a period of twenty-four hours, or an indefinite space of time; or simply distinguishes order or artificial arrangement without signifying anything about succession of time. Thinkers so orthodox as St. Augustine and St. Thomas Aquinas have not hesitated to allow that the last method of interpretation is probably right. [5]
2. What was the state of the universe before what are called the 'days' of creation. In the Book of Genesis it is said, 'In the beginning God created the heaven and the earth. And the earth was waste and void.' [6] Of these two statements, the first may be a summary of the account which follows, so that the rest of the chapter describes the first creation of material things; or it may narrate a different action from that which is described in the following verses, so that there is first a reference to an original creation of matter and then a description of the formation of this matter into the present world. And, on the latter supposition, there is nothing to show what happened between the original creation of matter and the state of the earth as 'waste and void,' or between this state and the work of God which the rest of the chapter describes.
3. Whether the distinct acts of the creative power of God produced their full effect at once or gradually. It follows from what has been already said about the days of creation that, so far as revelation is concerned, there is nothing to show, for instance, whether all the plants were completely formed before the beginning of the creation of the animals, or whether there was, to a certain extent, a concurrent development of both.
4. Whether intermediate agencies of any kind were employed by God. It is characteristic of Hebrew thought and language that they leave secondary

causes unnoticed and refer the result of a long process simply to the primary cause.

In this matter, as in many others, there has been a tendency to view an Eastern document of great antiquity as if it were a Western document written in modern times. [7]

The Angels

It is the usual belief that the angels are spirits without bodies of any kind. That this is true appears to be the natural inference from the way in which the angels are spoken of in Holy Scripture; and, with few exceptions, it has been taught by the theologians of the Church. [8]

The spiritual nature of the angels does not imply that they are everywhere present, or that they know all things. The most powerful and intelligent of them, including Satan, the chief of the angels who fell, are subject to the limitations of creaturely existence. The omnipresence and omniscience of God depend on His nature being divine as well as spiritual; and, while it is probable that the capacities of the angelic nature are so great as to be difficult for us to comprehend, the distinction between them and God Himself makes it necessary to deny that they are omnipresent or omniscient.

As to the time of the creation of the angels, it has been thought by some that they were created previously to, and independently of, the material universe. This opinion has been based largely on the words spoken by the Lord in the Book of Job: 'Where wast thou when I laid the foundations of the earth? declare, if thou hast understanding. Who determined the measures thereof, if thou knowest? or who stretched the line upon it? Whereupon are the foundations thereof fastened? or who laid the corner stone thereof; when the morning stars sang together, and all the sons of God shouted for joy?' [9] The phrase 'sons of God' has been interpreted to denote the angels, and it has been supposed that the passage describes them as having been present at the whole work of the creation of the universe. On the other hand, it has been held that they were created at the time of the creation of the world either just before the first 'day' or as the first act of creation on the first 'day.' Since there is nothing revealed on this subject, there is no good ground for the rejection of either opinion. [10]

Some of the angels fell into sin. The details of their fall are not known. Their sin has generally been supposed to have been some form of pride. St. Paul warns St. Timothy that a bishop is not to be 'a novice, lest being puffed up he fall into the condemnation of the devil'; and St. Jude writes of the 'angels which kept not their own principality, but left their proper habitation.' [11] Those who thus fell were condemned to eternal penalties. Our Lord speaks of 'the eternal fire which is prepared for the devil and his angels.' St. Peter refers to the fact that 'God spared not angels when they sinned, but cast them down to hell, and committed them to pits of darkness, to be reserved unto judgment.' [12]

No light is thrown by Holy Scripture on the darkness of the fall of the evil angels. No hint of their future restoration is anywhere given. [13] We cannot tell why their fall was irretrievable. It may be inferred from the analogy of the revealed dealings of God with mankind and from His attributes of mercy and love that, if redemption had been morally possible for the angels who sinned, they would have been redeemed. If it be so, sin in them must have been a final act setting a permanent seal on a completed character. [14] On such a subject, revelation does not encourage conjecture; and when it has been pointed out that the sin of the angels appears to have been a sin against a high degree of light; to have been self-originated, not the result of external temptation; and to have involved that choice of evil for its own sake which is apparently implied in their not possessing a bodily nature, it is well to say no more.

The angels most frequently referred to in Holy Scripture are those who remained in the service of God. From various lists of these angels it may be inferred that they comprise nine orders of differing ranks, with the names Seraphim, Cherubim, Thrones, Dominions, Powers, Authorities, Princedoms, Archangels, Angels. [15] Among the writers of the early Church there are differences as to the classification of the angels, but there is substantial agreement as to the existence of different orders. As time went on, very clear distinctions as to the ranks and work of the angels came to be made. At the end of the fifth century, the writer known as Dionysius the Areopagite gives the list of names which have been mentioned, and divides them into three groups, each containing three ranks. The first group consists of Seraphim, Cherubim, and Thrones; [16] these are occupied in drawing from the divine presence the direct revelation of the nature of God, each rank in the group allowing those below it to receive through it the contemplation of God. The characteristic of the Seraphim is that a holy fire consumes in them all thoughts except those of God. That of the Cherubim is the power akin to an intellectual power proceeding from the contemplation and knowledge of God. That of the Thrones is the supremacy which they have over every thing which might be in them which would not be of God. The second group consists of Dominions, Powers, and Authorities; these receive their knowledge from God less directly than the first group, because they are dependent upon the first group. Their characteristics are the control of the Dominions over vain attractions; the masculine courage of the Powers; the ordered sway of life subject to the authority of God in the Authorities. The third group consists of Princedoms, Archangels, Angels; these have to do with the relations of heaven and earth. The Princedoms overrule the history of nations; the Archangels carry the messages of God; the Angels attend to the needs of individuals. This third group is in dependence on the two higher groups in receiving the revelation of the nature of God, and in the contemplation of God. [17] In drawing up this system, Dionysius probably combined much which was really the teaching of the Church as to the existence of different ranks with much which was his own, parts of which may have been due to heretical influences. For instance, the particular way in which he makes the contemplation of God in the lower ranks to come through the higher ranks contains much that is akin to features of the Gnostic heresies of the second century. The list given by Dionysius is adopted a century later by St. Gregory the Great, but the names are placed in the different order of Seraphim, Cherubim, Thrones, Dominions, Princedoms, Authorities, Powers, Archangels, Angels. The previously mentioned order was followed by St. John of Damascus, and others. That stated by St. Gregory was adopted by St. Bernard and others. [18] While there is substantial agreement as to the existence of different orders, it is probable that the distinction between their offices is not so clearly denned as many theologians since the time of Dionysius have supposed. For instance, in the Book of Isaiah [19] the Seraphim are represented not only as worshipping God, but also as performing acts of ministration towards man; and in St. Luke's Gospel [20] Gabriel speaks of himself as standing in the presence of God as well as ministering to man. [21]

The names of two Archangels are given as Michael and Gabriel in various places in Holy Scripture. [22] The name Raphael is given in the Book of Tobit. [23] The names Uriel and Jeremiel are in the Second Book of Esdras. [24] Seven angels of equal rank, of whom Raphael is one, are referred to in the Book of Tobit; and a greater number are mentioned by name in the Book of Enoch and the Rabbinical writings. [25] All the names, except Michael, Gabriel, and Raphael, were rejected in Western Councils of the eighth century, and are now repudiated by the Church of Rome. [26]

The angels are described as worshipping God in the Books of Job, Isaiah, and the Revelation. [27] Passages in the Gospel according to St. Luke, and the Epistle to the Hebrews, [28] show both sides of the work of the angels. In the Gospel according to St. Luke, Gabriel refers to the worship of God when he says he stands in the presence of God, and to work for man when he says he is sent to speak to Zacharias. In the Epistle to the Hebrews the angels are spoken of as 'ministering spirits sent forth to do service for the sake of them that shall inherit salvation.' In this passage the phrase ministering spirits denotes spirits who minister in the worship of God, and the phrase 'sent forth to do service' refers to their work for man. The work of the angels for man is of the following kind:

1. Help in prayer. In the Book of the Revelation an angel is described as adding incense to the prayers of the saints which go up before God. [29]

2. Succour in life. The Acts of the Apostles record that St. Peter was delivered from prison through the instrumentality of an angel. [30]

3. Care after death. In the parable of the rich man and Lazarus, our Lord says, 'the beggar died,' and 'was carried away by the angels into Abraham's bosom.' [31]

For the purpose of helping man, guardian angels are assigned to individuals. Our Lord gives as a reason for not despising little children, 'that in heaven their angels do always behold the face of My Father which is in heaven.' In the Acts of the Apostles it is told that the Christians who were gathered together in 'the house of Mary the mother of John whose surname was Mark' imagined that it was the angel of St. Peter who came to them when that Apostle was miraculously released from prison. [32] The usual opinion in the Church has been that a guardian angel is assigned to each human being, not only to the baptized.

Besides thus worshipping God and helping man, the angels have some share in the work of the day of judgment, probably connected both with what they have to do towards God and with what they have to do towards man. Thus, it is said, 'He shall send forth His angels with a great sound of a trumpet, and they shall gather together His elect from the four winds, from one end of heaven to the other;' 'Whosoever shall be ashamed of Me and of My words in this adulterous and sinful generation, the Son of man also shall be ashamed of him when He cometh in the glory of His Father with the holy angels.' [33]

The holy angels also carry on war against evil angels. The Book of the Revelation describes the 'war in heaven' in which 'Michael and his angels' were 'going forth to war with the dragon; and the dragon warred and his angels; and they prevailed not, neither was their place found any more in heaven;' and the binding of 'the dragon, the old serpent, which is the Devil and Satan,' by an angel. [35]

Man

Man was created by God possessed of body, soul, and spirit. The Book of Genesis records, 'The Lord God formed man of the dust of the ground, and breathed into his nostrils the breath of life; and man became a living soul.' St. Paul refers to the 'spirit and soul and body' of the Thessalonians. [36] The word 'spirit' may denote a part of man separate from his soul and his body, or, as is more probable, the soul itself viewed in its higher aspect. [37]

Man was created in the image of God. 'God created man in His own image, in the image of God created He him; male and female created He them.' [38] As God is Spirit, it was in spiritual nature and in mind that man was formed in the image of God. Since God does not possess body, the body of man cannot be said to be in the image of God; but, since man's whole nature is closely united together, there can be little doubt that the body bears marks which are due to the divine image in the soul, so that the body is different from what it would be if the soul were not in the image of God. In the phrase of St. Thomas Aquinas, 'The likeness of God is in the mind of man after the manner of an image; in his other parts it is after the manner of a footprint.' [39] It is probably with some such meaning that St. Justin Martyr and St. Irenaeus say that the flesh of man is in the image of God. [40]

Man was created in the image of God, and the divine image was part of his being, so that he could not lose it without ceasing to be man. It is the essen-

25

tial feature which distinguishes man from the rest of creation. It is an illustration of this that fallen man is spoken of as having a position different from that of all other created beings, which belongs to him because he was made in the image of God: 'Whoso sheddeth man's blood, by man shall his blood be shed: for in the image of God made He man.' [41]

God added a further gift to man by virtue of which he was well-pleasing in the sight of God. The theological term for this gift is 'original righteousness.' It may be distinguished from the image of God by calling it the likeness of God. Adopting this phraseology, the image of God, as being part of the true natural condition of man by creation, cannot be lost, while the likeness? as being the gift added to the natural condition, could be lost. Free-will forms part of the true natural condition of man, because man by his creation was a moral being in a state of probation. The possession of free-will, therefore, as part of the image, was independent of the retention of the likeness.

The life of man after his creation is described as having been a life of work, thought, companionship, and probation. That it was of work is denoted by its being his task to 'dress' 'the garden of Eden,' and 'keep it.' The thought is indicated by his giving the beasts their names. The companionship was that of the woman, who was a 'help meet for him.' The probation is signified by the presence of the 'tree of the knowledge of good and evil,' and the command that he must not eat of it. In this life man was well-pleasing to God, and was able either to retain the favour of God by obedience, or to lose it by sin. [42]

[42] Gen. ii. 15-24. On the whole subject of the state of man before the Fall, see the discourse entitled *Concerning the First Covenant, and the State of Man before the Fall, according to Scripture and the Sense of the Primitive Doctors of the Catholic Church*, in Bull, *English Theological Works*, pp. 445-503 (Oxford, 1844).

[1] Gen. i., ii. 1-3; Pa. cxlviii. 5; St. John i. 3. Cf. 2 Mac. vii. 28.

[2] Rev. iv. 11.

[3] Cf. Westcott on Heb. xi. 3; Milligan on Rev. iv. 11 (Schaff's *Popular Commentary on the New Testament*, iv. 404).

[4] Heb. i. 1, 2; Gen. i. 2.

[5] See St. Augustine, De Gen. ad Lit., iv. 52; *De Gen. c. Manich.*, i. 20; *De Gen. Lib. Imperf.*, 19, 20; *De Civ. Dei*, xi. 6, 7; St. Thomas Aquinas, *Sent.* II. xii. 1 (2); *Summa Theol.*, I. lviii. 6, 7; lxviii. 1; lxix. 1; lxx. 1; lxxiv. 1, 2.

[6] Gen. i. 1.

[7] On this subject, see. further, note 10 in the concluding Notes.

[8] See note 5 in the concluding Notes.

[9] Job xxxviii. 4-7.

[10] See note 6 in the concluding Notes.

[11] 1 St. Tim. iii. 6; St. Jude 6.

[12] St. Matt. xxv. 41; 2 St. Pet. ii. 4.

[13] See, *infra*, concluding notes.

[14] On one aspect of this point, see St. Thomas Aquinas, *Summa Theol*, I. lxiv. 2. Cf. St. John of Damascus, *De Fid. Orth.*, ii. 3.

[15] For these names, see Isa. vi. 2, 6; Ezek. x.; St. Matt, xxviii. 2, 5; Eph. i. 21; Col. i. 16; St. Jude 9.

[16] Dionysius also places the ranks in this group in the order of Thrones, Cherubim, Seraphim.

[17] Dionysius the Areopagite, *De Cael. Hier.*, vi.-ix. Cf. Westcott, *Essays on the History of Religious Thought in the West*, pp. 162, 163.

[18] See St. Gregory the Great, *In Ev. Rom.*, xxxiv. 7; St. John of Damascus, *De Fid. Orth.*, ii. 3; St. Bernard, *De Consid.*, v. 4; *In Cant. Serm.*, xix. 6; St. Thomas Aquinas (who thinks each list has its own appropriateness), *Summa Theol.*, I. cviii. 5, 6.

[19] Isa. vi. 1-7.

[20] St. Luke i. 19.

[21] The explanations given to make these passages consistent with a clear-cut distinction of offices by, *e.g.*, St. Gregory the Great, *In Ev-Hom.*, xxxiv. 12, do not appear to be satisfactory.

[22] Dan. viii. 16; ix. 21; x. 13, 21; xii. 1; St. Luke i. 19, 26; St. Jude 9; Rev. xii. 7.

[23] Tobit xii. 15.

[24] 2 Esdras iv. 1, 36; v. 20; x. 28.

[25] Tobit xii. 15; Enoch ix. 1; xx.; xxiii. 4; xl. 9; liii. 6; lxvii. 4; lxx. 11, 16 (Michael, Gabriel, Raphael, Uriel, Phanuel, Suryal, Sarakiel, Raguel, Rakael). Cf. Fuller, *Introduction to Tobit*, pp. 174, 176 (*Speaker's Commentary*).

[26] Conc. Rom. (745 A.D.) actio iii.; Conc. Aquisgran. (789 A.D.) cap. 16. Cf. Vacant in Vigouroux, *Dictionnaire de la Bible*, i. 577.

[27] Job i. 6; ii. 1; Isa. vi. 1-3; Rev. viii. 1-4.

[28] St. Luke i. 19; Heb. i. 14.

[29] Rev. viii. 3, 4.

[30] Acts xii. 7-10.

[31] St. Luke xvi. 22.

[32] St. Matt, xviii. 10; Acts xii. 12-15. It is possible that a difficult passage in Eccles. v. 6 may refer to the guardian angel.

[33] See note 7 in the concluding Notes.

[34] St. Matt. xxiv. 31; St. Mark viii. 38.

[35] Rev. xii. 7, 8; xx. 1-3.

[36] Gen. ii. 7; 1 Thess. v. 23.

[37] See note 8 in the concluding Notes.

[38] Gen. i. 27.

[39] St. Thomas Aquinas, *Summa Theol*, I. xciii. 6. St. Thomas, however, ascribes likeness to God of the latter kind to all creatures.

[40] See note 9 in the concluding Notes.

[41] Gen. ix. 6.

Chapter Five - The Fall

In the Fall man was tempted and sinned. The Book of Genesis describes the agent in the temptation as 'the serpent,' the means of temptation as 'the tree of the knowledge of good and evil,' and the act of sin as the eating of the tree. [1] The phrase 'the serpent' may mean that the devil assumed the form of a serpent; or it may be a figurative description of the devil, as in the Book of the Revelation, where we read of 'the dragon, the old serpent, which is the Devil, and Satan.' [2] In the abstract it seems more likely that the word serpent is a figurative description than that the devil assumed the form of a serpent. On the other hand, the terminology in the Revelation is likely to be derived from the passage in Genesis; and the words to the serpent, 'Because thou hast done this, cursed art thou above all cattle, and above every beast of the field; upon thy belly shalt thou go, and dust shalt thou eat all the days of thy life,' [3] are less easy to explain if there is simply a figurative description of the devil than if the form of a serpent had actually been assumed. The theological import of the narrative is not affected by a difference of interpretation as to the meaning of the word 'serpent.' There is a similar question about the word 'tree.' There is nothing either in the history itself or elsewhere to show whether the word is used to denote a tree or is an allegorical description of some thing else. Thus, in the narrative of the Fall, as in the narrative of the Creation, there is room for considerable difference in interpretation. What is clear is that man was in the favour of God, and by an act of sin lost that favour. [4]

In the account of the Fall, in the Book of Genesis, it is stated that the woman was the first to sin; and St. Paul says, with evident reference to her words to God about the serpent, that she was 'beguiled.' The man afterwards sinned also. [5] It may perhaps be the meaning of St. Paul that the man had a clearer idea than the woman what he was doing. Probably, the sin of the woman in its essence included all sin. St. John summarizes all sin when he says, 'All that is in the world, the lust of the flesh, and the lust of the eyes, and the vainglory of life, is not of the Father, but is of the world.' [6] The three heads which he mentions are all in the sin of the woman as described in the Book of Genesis. The lust of the flesh was in the tree being 'good for food.' The lust of the eyes was in the tree being 'a delight to the eyes.' The vainglory of life was in the tree being 'desired to make one wise.' [7] From one point of view the sin committed in the Fall differed in enormity from all sins subsequently committed, because it was a sin in an unfallen nature the tendency of which was towards good, while subsequent sins have been in a nature disturbed by evil, and therefore prone to it.

The Book of Genesis recounts the results of the Fall as being that man loses the favour of God and is driven out of the garden of Eden. [8] This loss of the favour of God has extended to all men. St. Paul wrote to the Corinthians, 'In Adam all die.' [9] By the Fall man lost his original righteousness, the likeness of God, that is, the supernatural gifts whereby he was pleasing to God; and he incurred the distortion of original sin; but he still retained the image of God in which he was naturally made. Sin is the distortion of the nature which God created. The nature itself, although become sinful, is still the same nature which it was. Free-will, being part of the natural condition of man, and not one of the supernatural gifts, was retained after the Fall; and Holy Scripture everywhere regards fallen man as a being who has the power of choice which brings moral responsibility. In considering the fact that the consequences of the first sin of man extend to all the human race, it is well to observe that, while man as an individual is accountable to God for what he himself does, and is judged because of it, it is also true that every man, as a member of the organism of the human race, is intimately connected with the other members of the race.

The condition of man after the Fall may therefore be summarized as follows: -

1. He was deprived of the favour of God by the loss of original righteousness.

2. He was not simply in a negative condition, but had in his nature the distortion of original sin. He was therefore under the wrath of God, which is the necessary attitude of the holiness of God towards sin.

3. He was capable of restoration if the guilt of original sin could be removed, because he was able, by the use of his free-will, with the help of the grace of God, to choose what is good.

On the subject of original sin there has not been complete agreement among representative Christian theologians. St. Justin Martyr, writing before the middle of the second century, takes pains to assert the co-ordinate truths that by his natural birth man is, in consequence of the Fall, under the dominion of sin, and that each man commits sin by his own fault. [10] St. Irenaeus [11] and Tertullian [12] are somewhat later witnesses to the belief in original sin. The theology current at Alexandria in the third century made less of it than has been customary in the Church. Clement of Alexandria, if he did not deny it, gave it no prominent place in his system. [13] Origen, after some hesitation, came to believe in it. [14] At the beginning of the fifth century, the genius of St. Augustine did much to impress his strong doctrine of original sin on the Western Church, [15] though a section of the schoolmen by no means followed much which he taught. [16] In the East, the emphasis on original sin has been less marked than in the West. Yet St. John of Damascus in the eighth century, representing the traditional teaching of the East in this, as in much else, regarded the whole human race as affected by the Fall. [17] In spite of considerable differences on matters of detail, it may be truly said that historical Christianity is committed to the belief that man fell from a state of holiness to a state of sin, that the effects of sin are part of the inheritance of the human race, and that a state of holiness must now be the result of restoration and new gifts. Since 'in Adam all die,' [18] there is need of a gift of life which God alone can bestow. Since 'in Christ' 'all' 'shall be made alive,' [19] there is need of the will of man associating itself with the work of Christ and receiving His grace.

'Death,' says St. Paul, 'entered into the world through sin.' [20] Revelation does not tell us the exact meaning of the word 'death' in such a context. It does not explain by what means man, if he had not sinned, would have been raised from that high state in which he already was to the glory which was his true destiny. It has been suggested that he would have been exalted without anything corresponding to what we call death. It has been thought, again, that he would have died; but that the process, being painless and altogether unlike the death which we now know, would not rightly be called by this name, since, in that case, there would have been a gentle and happy transition from one state of existence to another. Because of sin, death is a cruel tyrant, the king of terrors, who, in St. Paul's phrase, 'reigned.' [21] All which revelation bids us say is that, if man would have passed through anything corresponding to death without the Fall, the process of transition would have been the work of a welcome friend. 'The transgression of the commandment,' wrote St. Athanasius, 'turned them back to their natural state that, just as from not being they had come to be, so also, as was reasonable, they might look for corruption into nothing by the lapse of time...Man is by nature mortal, since he came to be out of what is not; but, because of this likeness to Him who is, and if he had guarded this likeness by contemplating Him, he would have destroyed the force of the corruption which is according to nature and remained incorrupt.' [22] 'If Christ has abolished death,' [23] says a modern writer, 'then there is at least a certain sense in which sin has been the cause of death. The essence of death, according to this use of the word, lies not in the physical transition from one state of existence to another, which is no more death than it is birth. Death means destruction, ruin, and collapse...In the moral sense, then, in which Christ abolished death, sin certainly introduced it for man.' [24] Death, as we know it, is the result of sin. More than that, revelation does not lead us to say.

[1] Gen. iii. 1-7.

[2] Rev. xx. 2; cf. xii. 9.

[3] Gen. iii. 14.

[4] See note 10 in the concluding Notes.

[5] Gen. iii. 6, 13; St. Tim. ii. 14.

[6] 1 St. John ii. 16.

[7] Gen. iii. 6.

[8] Gen. iii. 9-24.

[9] 1 Cor. xv. 22.

[10] St. Justin Martyr, Apol., i. 43, 61; ii. 7; *Dial. c. Tryph.*, 88, 93, 95, 116, 124. Cf. H. S. Holland, in Smith and Wace's Dictionary of Christian Biography, iii. 579, 580.

[11] St. Irenaeus, C. Haer., III. xxii. 3; V. xix. 1; xxiii. 2.

[12] Tertullian, De Anim., 41.

[13] See Bigg, *The Christian Platonists of Alexandria,* pp. 80, 81. Dr. Bigg possibly exaggerates the extent to which a doctrine of original sin would be inconsistent with Clement's theology; but it is clear that Clement's teaching does not require it.

[14] See Bigg, *ibid.,* pp. 202-206.

[15] See Mozley, *A Treatise on the Augustinian Doctrine of Predestination,* pp. 116-126.

[16] See note 60 in the concluding Notes.

[17] St. John of Damascus, on Rom. v. 12, 13; *Hom. in Fie. Aref.,* 3; *Hom. in Sanc. Parasc.,* 2.

[18] 1 Cor. xv. 22.

[19] *ibid.*

[20] Rom. v. 12.

[21] Rom. v. 14.

[22] St. Athanasius, *De Incarn.,* 4.

[23] 2 St. Tim. i. 10.

[24] Gore, *St. Paul's Epistle to the Romans,* i. 198. Cf. Westcott on Heb. ii. 15.

Chapter Six - The Incarnation

The results of the Fall placed man in bondage to sin. Yet he was capable of being restored to a state of blessedness in the favour of God. The Incarnation accomplishes this restoration. The word 'Incarnation' denotes the union of human nature with divine nature in the one Person of God the Son.

It is important to observe how long and fully God prepared for the Incarnation. Immediately after the Fall He gave a promise of help. The first promise was merely that a human being should crush the power of the devil, though He should Himself suffer in so doing. The seed of the woman, it was said to the serpent, 'shall bruise thy head, and thou shalt bruise his heel.' [1] The promise was frequently renewed. It was given in different ways. Some of the anticipations of the Redeemer were in the general idea of a great deliverance in which man should be taught by God and given the power of further service. Other anticipations were in typical lives and actions which in the providence of God were the foreshadowings of Him who was to come. Others were by means of direct prophecy. In these ways, as the Old Testament Scriptures grew, the picture of the Redeemer who was to come became more distinct and more complete. The promise was fulfilled in the life of our Lord, who made it possible for man to be perfectly delivered from sin, who revealed God and His truth, through whom man possesses the power of serving God. His life was the fulness of which the various types of the Old Testament supplied parts. In the phrase of St. Irenaeus, 'He summed up man into Himself,' [2] He was, that is, a perfect representative of the true idea of manhood, of which there had been partial representatives in the typical lives of the Old Testament; and He exhibited that presentation of divine attributes and power in a human life which was possible because man was made in the image of God. He fulfilled the direct prophecies. As foretold by Micah, He was born at Bethlehem. As foretold by Isaiah, He was the Son of a virgin, and was anointed with the Holy Ghost. As foretold by Zechariah, He entered into Jerusalem riding on an ass. He was betrayed by one who should have been a friend, the price being thirty pieces of silver. He was mocked and pierced in His death. [3] He Himself claimed to be the Messiah whom the Jews expected; [4] and the only reasonable explanation of all the facts of His life lies in the truth of this claim.

To the Jews of our Lord's time, with their acceptance of the Old Testament and their expectation of a deliverer who should fulfil the prophecies, the recognition of our Lord, where it came at all, would come largely because the Old Testament prophecies were fulfilled in His life and death. This explains the prominent place which is given to the fulfilment of prophecy in the Gospels and the Acts. The recognition of our Lord at the present time necessarily in most cases comes by a different process, because at the present time there are not, to any large extent, besides the Jews, those who accept the Old Testament as a divine revelation and yet have not accepted our Lord. In most cases now the process in religious truth would be a reverse one from what it was to many Jews in the first century. Such a reverse process would begin with regarding our Lord as a true Teacher; would pass from His own claims to His God head; would work back from His teaching to the Old Testament as a divine revelation and to prophecy as a real fact; and would only then see in our Lord's fulfilment of the prophecies a corroborative proof of the truth

31

about Him which had already been accepted. The argument from prophecy to the position of Christ as Teacher and Redeemer has in itself the same value which it had in the days of the Apostles. Its practical utility, however, is of a widely different kind.

Prophecy formed one part of the work by which the human race was made ready for the coming of the promised Redeemer. St. Paul taught the Galatians that 'God sent forth His Son' 'when the fulness of the time came.' [5] This time was fitting both because it was the 'term appointed of the Father.' [6] and because man had now been prepared. Here, as elsewhere, the decree of God and what is best for man are bound together. There was preparation for the Incarnation both among the heathen and among the Jews. Among the heathen, whenever there was any movement towards what was good in a religion, or a code of law, or material progress, there was to a certain extent preparation for the Incarnation, since any such movement towards good was a witness to the possibility of the restoration of man. The providential help which heathenism afforded towards the preaching of Christianity was in some ways great. Greek commerce and philosophy and language, Roman law and provincial government, and the great Roman roads, all had their parts to play. While there was thus preparation of a positive kind, that among the heathen was mainly negative. The failure of anything in heathenism to satisfy man was a witness to the need of help from outside man. Among the Jews the preparation was carried out by the sense of sin and need which was formed and deepened by the law and the sacrifices; the longing for help which was fostered by the prophecies of the Messiah; and the training of the discipline of the Mosaic law. [7]

It has often been discussed why there was so long an interval between the Fall and the Incarnation. It is not possible for any complete answer to be given. Man cannot enter fully into the plans of God. Such explanation as is possible has been well put by St. Thomas Aquinas: 'God first left man in the freedom of his will under the natural law, so that he might in this way come to know the strength of his own nature. Then, when he had failed, he received the law. On the law being given, the disease gathered strength by the fault, not of the law, but of man's nature, so that when his own weakness was thus made known, he might cry out for the Physician, and seek the help of grace.' [8]

The Relation of the Incarnation to the Fall

It has been asked to what extent the Incarnation was independent of or dependent upon the Fall. This question does not appear to have presented itself in any definite way to the minds of Christians for a very long time; and the point is nowhere discussed until the middle ages. Here and there one of the Fathers, in speaking about some other subject, says briefly in passing, that if man had not sinned, God would not have become man. [9] Such brief cursory statements make up all that there is on the subject in the patristic period. During the middle ages, in the formation of great systems of theology, when an attempt was made to arrange all Christian doctrine on a methodical plan, every hypothesis of which the schoolmen could think was raised and discussed. In the discussion of this question, two distinct schools of thought came to be formed. That known as the Scotist, from the name of Duns Scotus, [10] maintained that the Incarnation formed part of the eternal purpose of God independently of human sin; that the object of it was not simply or primarily to be a remedy for sin; and that therefore it would have taken place even if there had never been any human sin. That known as the Thomist, from the name of St. Thomas Aquinas, [11] maintained that the Incarnation was the remedy designed by God for the restoration of man from sin; that it was eternally purposed only as sin was foreseen in the foreknowledge of God; and that therefore, if there had been no human sin, there would have been no Incarnation. Both schools of thought long existed side by side. Then the Scotist view seemed almost to die out; for the last three or four hundred years it has probably been held by very few; in the present century it has been revived by many, especially in the English Church.

The main arguments which have been used on both sides are the following:

1. In support of the Scotist theory, it has been urged that in the Epistle to the Ephesians, St. Paul speaks of Christians being chosen in Christ 'before the foundation of the world,' and of 'the eternal purpose which' God 'purposed in Christ Jesus our Lord;' [12] that, speaking generally, the Incarnation is the centre of St. Paul's teaching; and that, if the Incarnation happened because of the Fall, the sin of Adam eventually brings man to be in closer union with God than he would have been without sin; and it is inconceivable that so great a blessing should be the result of sin.

2. In support of the Thomist theory, it has been urged -

(a) The arguments used to support the Scotist theory are not satisfying. The passages in the Epistle to the Ephesians do not necessarily mean more than that in any case the full blessing of man by God would have been through God the Son; and we cannot know how far this was possible without the Incarnation. The line of argument which has been used with regard to these passages might also be used to show from the words of St. Peter in his first Epistle [13] that the death of Christ was independent of the Fall, a position it would be impossible to maintain. It is true that the Incarnation is central in St. Paul's teaching; but sin is central also. St. Paul everywhere treats man as he is, that is, in view of the facts of the Fall and sin. The argument that, if the Incarnation took place because of the Fall, sin produced good, goes beyond the limits of our knowledge, because we cannot tell in what ways God might have blessed man under conditions different from those which actually exist, or to what degree the divine method of bringing good out of evil may extend.

(b) While the arguments in support of Scotism are insufficient, there are positive arguments on the other side. The general tone of Holy Scripture is represented in St. Paul's words to St. Timothy that 'Christ Jesus came into the world to save sinners,' [14] and regards the Incarnation as taking place as a remedy for the state of things which sin produced. Though the statements in the Fathers are only cursory, and do not amount to any thing like the teaching of the Church, yet when the Fathers say anything at all, it is always, as has already been pointed out, that if man had not sinned, God would not have become man.

On a mystery so profound we may well be content to say with Dr. Bright, 'Attractive as such speculations may be, they would seem to be precarious, and in some hands they might be perilous...Man *has* fallen, and God *has* become incarnate; that may well suffice "until the shadows flee away."' [15]

The Conception of the Blessed Virgin

The question whether the mother of our Lord was herself immaculately conceived, that is, conceived with out incurring original sin, was not, so far as is known, raised in the patristic period. It came to be discussed in the middle ages because devotion to the Blessed Virgin had led some to assert her immaculate conception. It was agreed by almost all in the West, in the middle ages, that at the time of her birth she was free from all sin, original as well as actual. St. Anselm was an exception, and taught that she had original sin both when she was conceived and when she was born. Among those who accepted this usual mediseval Western teaching, that when born she was free from original sin, there were two schools of thought

1. Those who asserted that from the first moment when the Blessed Virgin Mary was conceived she was free from original sin, so that there never was any moment of her existence either before or after her birth in which she had original sin. This opinion was thought probable by Duns Scotus. It came to be associated with the Franciscan Order.

2. Those who taught that the Blessed Virgin Mary was conceived like all others, except our Lord, with original sin, but that she, as well as Jeremiah and St. John the Baptist, was freed from original sin before her birth. This opinion was held by St. Bernard and St. Thomas Aquinas. [16] It came to be associated with the Dominican Order.

These two opinions remained for a long time the subject of controversy. By the time of the Council of Trent in the sixteenth century, the Franciscan opinion had become the most prevalent among the theologians in communion with Rome. Most of those who were present at the Council of Trent were in favour of the Franciscan theory; but in order to avoid any breach with the Dominicans, who still held their traditional view, the question was shelved. It remained open in the Church of Rome until 1854, although for a long time before that date the Franciscan opinion had practically crushed out the other. [17] In 1854, Pope Pius IX. removed the matter out of open questions and made the Franciscan opinion binding upon all in communion with Rome by a decree stating, 'The doctrine that the most Blessed Virgin Mary was in the first instant of her conception preserved free from all stain of original sin by the singular grace and privilege of Almighty God in view of the merits of Christ Jesus, the Saviour of mankind, has been revealed by God, and is therefore to be firmly and stedfastly believed by all the faithful.' [18]

The subject does not appear to have been fully discussed in the East at any time. The Eastern formularies do not except the Blessed Virgin from the general truth that all incur original sin. Some Eastern theologians have expressly condemned the doctrine of the immaculate conception. [19]

As to the theological aspect of this question it is to be noticed

1. There is nothing in Holy Scripture definitely on the point. The passages which have been cited by controversialists to support the doctrine of the immaculate conception have nothing to do with the subject. The chief of these are the passages in the Book of Genesis and the Book of Job: 'It' (translated 'She' in the Vulgate) 'shall bruise thy head'; 'Who can bring a clean thing out of an unclean? not one.' [20] The general tendency of Holy Scripture is to regard the whole human race, as merely human, as being denied with sin. For instance, St. Paul says in the Epistle to the Romans, 'As through one man sin entered into the world, and death through sin; and so death passed unto all men, for that all sinned.' [21]

2. There is no discussion of the subject in the Fathers. The Blessed Virgin is compared with Eve in somewhat remarkable language by St. Justin Martyr, St. Irenaeus, and later writers. Occasionally in the Fathers, and frequently in the Liturgies, she is spoken of in general terms as undefiled, or as free from all stain of sin, or as all-holy. There are also passages in the Fathers in which it is asserted in general terms that all human beings are touched by sin, as when St. Leo says that the nativity of Christ 'has no concern with what we read in regard to all men: "No man is clean from defilement, not even an infant whose life on earth is but one day old."' St. Augustine often declares that of all human beings our Lord alone was conceived free from sin: in one place he says that he will not speak about the relation of the Blessed Virgin Mary to sin. This last passage has been differently interpreted by different writers, to mean that she was in one way or another free from sin, or that St. Augustine did not think so. The assertions of some of the Fathers, as St. Chrysostom, that faults were committed by the Blessed Virgin imply that those Fathers did not hold the immaculate conception. [22]

3. The schoolmen were divided on the subject, though agreeing that when born the Blessed Virgin was free from original sin.

4 The doctrine of the immaculate conception does not appear to have been affirmed at any time in the East. In the West it was not made a dogma at Borne until 1854.

5. The main grounds on which the doctrine has been advocated are subjective, namely, that the fitness of things suggests that she who was to be the mother of the Lord was never in any way touched with sin; and that the per-

fect holiness of our Lord demands that she who supplied His human nature was always perfectly holy from the first moment of her conception. Obviously arguments of this kind will strike different minds in very different ways. They do not afford grounds for dogmatic assertions.

It may well be regretted that the question whether the Blessed Virgin Mary was conceived without original sin was ever raised. Having been raised, it may be expected that, in the absence of authoritative teaching, there will be disagreement about it; and it does not appear to be of supreme importance that an individual should either reject or accept it. There can be no justification short of the supposition of the infallibility of the Pope for making such a matter a necessary part of the faith, as it was made for Roman Catholics in 1854. It was well said by the late Dean Church, 'The dogma is itself an opinion which any one might hold, if he thinks that there are materials in the world from which to form an opinion about it. In itself there is not much to object to it, except its ground - which is absolutely nothing, not even a tradition, not even a misinterpretation of a dislocated text, nothing but the merest inferences from suppositions about a matter of which we know nothing - and its end, which is to give a new stimulus to a devotion which wanted none.' [23]

The Person of Our Lord

There are four great truths which make up the doctrine of the Person of our Lord. Firstly, He is truly God. Secondly, He is perfectly Man. Thirdly, He is only one Person. Fourthly, there are in Him two distinct natures, the divine and the human.

The Deity of Our Lord

The first great truth about our Lord is that He is truly God. In Holy Scripture His deity is taught in many ways. It is implied in prophecy, which the New Testament says He fulfilled. Isaiah foretold, 'The virgin shall conceive, and bear a Son, and shall call His name Immanuel.' St. Matthew quotes these words as applying to our Lord and adds the explanation of the name 'Immanuel' – 'God with us.' [24] The doctrine is asserted in express terms in the New Testament. St. John writes, 'The Word was God,' and then adds, with reference to our Lord's life, 'The Word became flesh.' In the Epistle to the Hebrews, the coming of our Lord is thus described: 'God' 'hath at the end of these days spoken unto us in His Son, whom He appointed heir of all things, through whom also He made the worlds;' and, a little later, the Son spoken of is addressed in the words, Thy throne, God, is for ever and ever.' [25] In the teaching of our Lord Himself His deity is declared. He said to the Jews, 'I and the Father are One,' a statement understood by the Jews to be a claim to Godhead, for they 'took up stones' 'to stone Him,' and said to Him, 'For a good work we stone Thee not, but for blasphemy; and because that Thou, being a man, makest Thyself God.' [26] In many different ways it is implied. The obvious differences between our Lord's own miracles and those of the Apostles recorded in the Acts indicate that, while He was working as the Son of man, yet He Himself possessed powers other than human. The claims which He made were such as could not be justified unless He was God. He claims to speak with an absolute authority by which, in the Sermon on the Mount, He can revise even the law of Moses. [27] He claims to be able to supersede the highest and holiest human relations, so that the most imperative earthly duties must give way if the fulfilment of them conflicts with the call to obey Him. [28] He claims to be the Judge of the world; [29] to have the power to establish the spiritual kingdom of the Church; [30] to be able to promise that He Himself will be permanently present with His Church; [31] and that belief on and union with Him are the means of receiving the gift of eternal life. [32] These different kinds of claim taken together show that, if the attitude which our Lord took up is to be morally justified, He must be regarded as God. The resurrection, more over, is a further indication of His Godhead, since, while it is represented as being the act of God the Father, it is also spoken of as our Lord's own act. Thus He says of His life, 'No one taketh it away from Me, but I lay it down of Myself. I have power to lay it down, and I have power to take it again. This commandment received I from My Father.' So St. Paul says, He 'was declared to be the Son of God with power, according to the spirit of holiness, by the resurrection of the dead,' [33] This teaching is borne out by the whole tone of the Epistles and the Revelation. In the Revelation the slain Lamb is adored as God. [34] In the Epistles our Lord is associated with the Father in salutations and benedictions. [35] St. Paul speaks of Him as the Judge of mankind. [36] He is made the centre of St. Paul's teaching and is there represented as the centre of man's whole religious life, since He is regarded as the Object of the belief which gives to man justifying faith. 'I determined not to know anything among you, save Jesus Christ, and Him crucified.' 'Other foundation can no man lay than that which is laid, which is Jesus Christ.' 'Christ Jesus, whom God set forth to be a propitiation, through faith, by His blood' that God 'might Himself be just, and the justifier of him that hath faith in Jesus.' 'Knowing that a man is not justified by the works of the law, save through faith in Jesus Christ, even we believed on Christ Jesus, that we might be justified by faith in Christ.' [37] These are but a few out of many passages in which the whole conception of our Lord is that of a Person who is God. An even stronger argument to many minds than that based on the express statements of His deity is derived from the fact that the whole theology and the whole way of regarding life which are found in the New Testament become meaning less on any other hypothesis than that our Lord is truly God. [38]

The doctrine of our Lord's Godhead is part of the teaching of the whole Church. Before the Council of Nicaea, in A.D. 325, the belief of the Church in His Godhead is shown both by statements which call Him God and by worship which is offered to Him as God. [39] The truth was unmistakably asserted at the Council of Nicaea by the declaration that the Son of God is of the same essence as the Father; and the decision of the Council was eventually accepted by the whole Church as a necessary part of the true faith.

As the truth of the deity of our Lord is taught and implied in Holy Scripture, and in the statements and practice of the Church, so also the whole Christian idea of the work of Christ implies that He is God. That which is central in the revealed aspect of Christ's ministry and work is that He reconciles man to God, and that through Him God and man are united. The possibility of His being in such a relation to God as to be able to do this depends on Himself being truly God. [40]

Our Lord being truly God, He is by His divine nature the Second Person of the Holy Trinity. Being truly God, again, He possessed in His divine nature all the absolute attributes of God. Whatever humiliation there may have been in His human life, our Lord in His Godhead of necessity retained all that belongs to the nature of God; and the divine attributes cannot be distinguished from the divine nature except in thought. To suppose that God the Son on becoming incarnate could relinquish His divine attributes would ultimately imply the possibility of change in God. It is true that He exercised His divine powers under the conditions of human life; but of the powers themselves He must have been, as God, always possessed.

In two striking passages St. Paul refers to the condescension of the Son of God in becoming man. 'Ye know,' he wrote to the Corinthians, 'the grace of our Lord Jesus Christ, that, though He was rich, yet for your sakes He became poor, that ye through His poverty might become rich.' [41] To the Philippians he wrote, 'Have this mind in you, which was also in Christ Jesus: who, being in the form of God, counted it not a prize to be on an equality with God, but made Himself low by taking the form of a servant, being made in the likeness of men: and being found in fashion as a man, He humbled Himself by becoming obedient unto death, yea, the death of the cross.' [42] As the context shows in each case, the poverty and lowliness refer, not to any loss in the divine nature of the Son of God, but to the humiliation which He underwent in His human life. In a clear statement by Dr. Bright, 'If we take ἑαυτὸν ἐκένωσε [43] in logical connexion with what precedes and follows, we shall see that practically it means, "He became inferior to the Father as touching His Manhood."' [44] That is, in the Incarnation the Son of God took to Himself the weakness of man; He did not abandon the strength of God. [45]

The truth of our Lord's Godhead has been denied by the early heretics known as the Ebionites, by the Arians in the fourth century, and by Socinians in modern times. Arianism was a transitory form of opinion which could not last, [46] but was certain to lead to a further departure from the truth, such as now exists in Socinianism; but it is well to notice that, while Arianism was on the incline which leads to Socinianism, there is a difference between the heresies themselves. Socinianism regards our Lord as possessing only one nature, namely, the nature of man that is, He is man, and He is nothing more than man, although some Socinians would admit that there was something out side the ordinary course of nature in His birth. Arianism, while denying the truth of Christ's Godhead, looked upon Him as being more than man. The Arians held that our Lord had, in addition to His human nature, a spiritual nature of great power and dignity, which had existed before the Incarnation, and even before the world, which possessed everything that was high and glorious, short of His being in the full sense the Eternal Son of God. One way of summing up the difference between the two would be to say: To the Socinian our Lord had no existence before His existence as man; to the Arian He existed in His higher nature before the world.

The Catholic faith asserts that our Lord in His higher nature existed from eternity, and is God in the same sense as that in which the Father is God.

The Arian said that in His higher nature our Lord had existed for ages, and had been made to be God.

The Socinian says that our Lord's only nature is the human nature wherewith He was born into this world.

The Manhood of Our Lord

The second great truth about our Lord is that He is perfectly man. This is clearly taught in the New Testament. It is directly asserted. St. John says, 'The Word became flesh, and dwelt among us.' St. Paul writes, 'The gift by the grace of the one man, Jesus Christ, did abound unto the many,' [47] It is implied in the general statements which are made about our Lord's life on earth. He was born of a woman. [48] He was circumcised. [49] He ate. [50] He slept. [51] He was weary. [52] He wept. [53] He suffered and died. [54]

The truth of our Lord's manhood has been declared with great clearness by the teaching of the Universal Church. The reality of it was asserted by early writers in controversy with the heretics who denied it; and the clearness with which St. Ignatius and St. Irenaeus declare that the humanity of Christ was real forms a very striking feature in their works. Thus, St. Ignatius says in his *Epistle to the Trallians,* 'Be ye deaf, therefore, when any one speaks to you apart from Jesus Christ, who was of the race of David, who was the Son of Mary, who truly was born and ate and drank, truly was persecuted in the time of Pontius Pilate, truly was crucified and died in the sight of those in heaven and those on earth and those under the earth; who also truly was raised from the dead, His Father having raised Him, who in like manner will raise us also who believe on Him His Father, I say, will raise us in Christ Jesus, apart from whom we have not true life;' [55] and St. Irenaeus writes, 'If any one, then, says that the flesh of the Lord is different from our flesh in this respect that it indeed sinned not and that no guile was found in His soul, but that we are sinners, he speaks rightly. But if he imagines that the Lord had a different substance of flesh, no longer is the word of reconciliation his. For that which was once in enmity is reconciled. But if the Lord had flesh of a different substance, no longer has that been reconciled to God which through transgression had become at enmity.' [56]

As time went on, and it was the completeness rather than the reality of the humanity of our Lord which was attacked, it was clearly taught that He possessed all the parts of human nature. The completeness of His manhood was definitely affirmed by the Council of Constantinople in A.D. 381, when the Apollinarians, who denied that He possessed a rational human soul, were condemned in the first canon of the Council, Seventy years later the following statements were made in the decree affirmed in the fifth session of the Council of Chalcedon: 'Following, therefore, the holy fathers, we all teach with one accord one and the same Son, our Lord Jesus Christ, perfect in Godhead and perfect also in manhood, truly God and also truly man, being of a reasonable soul and body, of one essence with the .Father as touching His Godhead, and also of one essence with us as touching His man hood, being like unto us in all things except sin, begotten of the Father before all times according to his Godhead, and also in the last days born for our sake, and because of our salvation, of Mary the Virgin, the Mother of God, according to His manhood, one and the same Christ, the Son, Lord, only begotten, of two natures,' [57] The statements of Constantinople and Chalcedon clearly affirmed what had always been the belief of the Church; and they were accepted by the whole Church as rightful ways of stating the truth.

The doctrine of our Lord's manhood is also involved in Christian teaching about the work of Christ. As it is necessary that He who is to reconcile man to God must Himself be truly God, so also it is necessary that He must be really and perfectly man.

While our Lord is thus in a true and proper sense man, the method of His human birth differed from that of other men. He derived His human substance from a mother only. That mother remained a virgin when He was conceived and born. The conception took place in her through the operation of God the Holy Ghost.

The fact of our Lord being born from a virgin is asserted with great clearness in Holy Scripture. [58] It is uniformly affirmed by representative Christian teachers from the earliest times, both in the East and in the West. St. Ignatius, at the beginning of the second century, makes mention of the three mysteries of the 'virginity of Mary,' 'her child-bearing,' and 'the death of the Lord,' which God prepared in silence and Christians preached, and describes our Lord as 'having been truly born of a virgin.' [59] A little later, Aristides placed in his declaration of the Christian faith the fact that the Lord Jesus Christ 'took flesh' 'of a virgin.' [60] A little later, again, St. Justin Martyr refers to the birth of our Lord from a virgin mother, and says expressly that 'Jesus Christ our teacher was born without the intercourse of man with woman.' [61] Before the end of the second century, St. Irenaeus bears witness, 'The Church, though scattered throughout the whole world to the ends of the earth, yet having received from the Apostles and their disciples the faith...in the Holy Ghost, who through the prophets proclaimed the dispensations, and the comings, and the birth from a virgin;' states that this belief was held by the Churches in Germany, Spain, Gaul, the East, Egypt, and Italy; and elsewhere speaks of 'Christ Jesus the Son of God, who submitted to be born of a virgin.' [62] The truth thus expressed in the earliest Christian writings passed into the doctrinal formulae of the Universal Church. [63]

In the perfection of His manhood Christ possesses all the parts of human nature. That He possesses a body is implied in all His bodily acts. He possesses a human soul, including the higher part of the soul, the spirit. He marvelled at the faith of the centurion; [64] and wonder implies the possession of the higher faculties of the soul. He 'advanced in wisdom;' [65] and wisdom belongs to the higher faculties of the soul.

That our Lord possessed a rational human soul or spirit was declared to be of faith in the condemnation of Apollinarianism at the Council of Constantinople in A.D. 381, already mentioned.

The possession of a human spirit is involved both in the work of our Lord and in the reality of His man hood. If He is to redeem the whole nature of man, it is necessary that He should take the whole nature of man; and, if He is to be really human, He must take that part of man's nature which separates man from the beasts.

Christ also possessed a human will. He Himself spoke of His will as man: 'Not as I will, but as Thou wilt;' 'Not My will, but Thine, be done;' 'I seek not Mine own will, but the will of Him that sent Me.' [66]

The Council of Constantinople of A.D. 680, the decision of which has been accepted by the Universal Church, asserted, against the Monothelites, who said that in Christ there was only one will, that He possessed a human will as well as a divine will. [67]

The completeness of the manhood of our Lord caused Him to be capable of experiencing suffering and passing through death, because the capacity for both is in human nature. This capacity of suffering and death was not taken away or diminished by the fact that He is also God. Care must be taken to keep it clear that the suffering and death were not in His divine nature, but in His human nature. There is, to a certain extent, a parallel in ordinary men. The soul of man acts and suffers through the organs of the body in many matters in which the action or the suffering can only be in the bodily organs, not in the spiritual faculties. For instance, the soul knows through the sight of the bodily eyes, and we speak of the soul seeing; but the actual process of sight is in the bodily organs. So, our Lord Himself suffered and died, the suffering and death being in His manhood.

As He was capable of suffering and death, so our Lord, by virtue of His manhood, felt the pressure of human necessities. He ordinarily acted under the same conditions of life as those under which we act. For instance, His human life and strength were preserved by food; His mind was kept clear by sleep; His spiritual relation to the Father was maintained by prayer and thanksgiving. Thus, ordinarily, body, mind, and spirit were all acting under the same conditions of life as our own.

It is involved also in His complete possession of human faculties that He was able to feel the force of temptation. He had the faculties which temptation aims at making instruments of sin; and He had the faculties by which, with the aid of grace, temptation is overcome in us. The fuller treatment of the subject of His enduring temptation belongs to the consideration of the unity of His Person.

The reality of Christ's manhood was wholly denied by early heretics, as the Docetic Gnostics, who asserted that the body of Christ and all its acts existed in appearance only. The Apollinarians, in the fourth century, denied that He possessed a higher human soul or spirit. The Monothelites, in the seventh century, denied that He possessed a human will.

The Union in Our Lord of the Two Natures of God and Man

The third great truth about our Lord is that He is only one Person. Being both God and man, He possesses two natures. Yet He is one Person only, and this one Person is God. This truth is implied by the language of Holy Scripture. It supplies the explanation of the passages in which Holy Scripture asserts, in relation to our Lord, what is human about God and what is divine about man. In St. John's Gospel it is said, 'The Word dwelt' - literally 'tabernacled' – 'among us.' [68] Here there is mention of the Logos, the eternal Word, Who is God, performing the human action of tabernacling among men. In St. Paul's speech at Miletus he spoke of 'the Church of God, which He purchased with His own blood.' The expression 'His own blood' asserts what is human of God. [69] In the First Epistle to the Corinthians St. Paul wrote, 'They would not have crucified the Lord of Glory,' [70] thus ascribing to God human suffering. On the other hand, in our Lord's discourse with Mcodemus He spoke of 'the Son of man, which is in heaven,' [71] thus predicating what is divine of the man Jesus Christ. In the First Epistle to the Corinthians St. Paul says of our Lord, 'The second man is of heaven,' [72] thus predicating of the man Jesus Christ that which is divine. The explanation of these two sets of passages is that, while the divine acts are in the divine nature, and the human acts in the human nature, both the divine and the human acts may be predicated of the one Person of Christ, in Whom the two natures are united. [73] This truth of the union of the two natures in the one Person is known as the hypostatic union, that is, the union in personality. The Scriptural use of language which depends upon it, and has been referred to here, is known in Latin as the *communicatio idiomatum,* and in Greek as the κοινοποίησις or ἀντίδοις.

The difference between this hypostatic union of the two natures in the one Person of our Lord, and the union between ourselves and God should not be for gotten. The union of the two natures in our Lord is a personal union, so that there is only one Person. The union between God and ourselves is a mystical union, so that the Person of God is distinct from the person of the soul which is united to Him.

This union of the two natures in the one divine Person of our Lord was implied throughout the teaching of the earliest Christians. At the beginning of the second century St. Ignatius wrote to the Ephesians, 'Our God, Jesus the Christ, was borne in the womb by Mary,' [74] a statement which implies that the manhood of our Lord was the manhood of the one Person of the Son of God. This doctrine was asserted with great distinctness at the Council of Ephesus in A.D. 431. In the second letter from St. Cyril of Alexandria to Nestorius he had said, 'The Godhead and the manhood complete for us the one Lord and Christ and Son by their unutterable and unspeakable concurrence into unity;' 'We do not worship a man conjointly with the Word, but we worship one and the same Person.' This letter of St. Cyril was ratified by the Council of Ephesus as rightly expressing the truth on the subject; and the decision of the Council has been accepted by the whole Church. [75]

As in the case of the two former points of the doctrine of the Incarnation, so also in this third point, the truth may be seen to be necessary to the work of Christ. The reality of the work of redemption requires that our Lord in both His natures is one Person. If we could divide Christ, and say there are in Him two Persons, a divine Person and a human person, the divine acts would not be the acts of the human person, and the human acts would not be the acts of the divine Person. Thus the whole idea of reconciliation would be lost, since it depends on the truth that one Person is acting both in the divine acts and in the human acts, and especially that in the death on the cross it is God wljo dies in human nature. If in the death of our Lord it was a human person who was dying, and not the Person of the Son of God, the death could not be of any value as an act of atonement, but would he, at the most, simply an example of self-sacrifice. [76]

It was to safeguard the truth of the one Person of our Lord that emphasis was laid on the title 'Mother of God' applied to the Blessed Virgin Mary. It was asserted by the Nestorians that there were in our Lord two Persons, a divine Person and a human person; and it had been further inferred from this by some of them that a human person was conceived by the Blessed Virgin Mary and was born from her, and that a divine Person was subsequently added to this human person. This opinion was a natural inference from the denial of the single Personality of Christ; and it is obvious that it was destructive of the whole truth of the Incarnation. St. Cyril of Alexandria and the divines of the Council of Ephesus saw that the crucial point was whether He who was conceived and born of the Blessed Virgin Mary was God at the time of His conception and birth. To his third letter to Nestorius, St. Cyril appended twelve anathemas, which, as well as many passages from earlier writers affirming the same truth, were read at the Council of Ephesus as a prelude to the condem nation of Nestorius. Of these anathemas the first was, 'If any one does not confess that the Emmanuel is in truth God, and that therefore the

43

holy Virgin is the Mother of God, for she gave birth after a fleshly manner to the Word of God made flesh, let him be anathema.' [77] It was as part of the vital truth that the manhood of our Lord was always in personal union with His God head, that St. Cyril of Alexandria and the Council of Ephesus, as well as the Council of Chalcedon twenty years later, deemed the Blessed Virgin Mary rightly called Θεοτόκος, the Mother of God, that is, the mother, not of the divine nature, but of Him who in all that appertains to both His natures is personally God. [78]

The truth that our Lord is only one Person, and that His one Person is divine, implies that His human nature has no independent centre of personality. If there had been a human person to whom the divine Person was added, there would have been an independent centre of human personality; but the human nature of our Lord never existed apart from His Godhead. At the first moment of the existence of His human nature, when it was conceived in the womb of His mother, it was in personal union with His Godhead, that is to say, the human nature in the first moment of its existence had its personality in the personal life of God the Son. This truth that there was in the humanity of Christ no independent centre of personality is a distinction which, when properly considered, is seen to unite our Lord closely with ourselves. That which divides men from one another is the possession of separate personalities; that which unites men to one another is the common possession of the same human nature. Our Lord took that which is the means of union, the possession of the same human nature. He did not take that which is the means of division, the possession of an independent centre of human personality.

The doctrine of the single Personality of Christ implies His impeccability. He is incapable of sin. To use technical language, it is necessary to assert of Him *non posse peccare,* 'not to be able to sin,' as well as *posse non peccare,* 'to be able not to sin.' The capacity of suffering lies in the nature; the essence of the act of sin is in the person. Sin is impossible for God because it is inconsistent with His own attributes; and it is the law of the Being of God that He cannot do anything which is inconsistent with His own attributes. There is in our Lord one Person only, and that one Person is God. Since, then, the essence of the act of sin is in the person, it follows that if our Lord could be capable of sin, God could sin. Thus, while our Lord, as being perfectly man, possessed all the faculties of human nature, and therefore possessed the instruments with which man sins, He could not sin because the choice of sin by His human will must have been either the choice of sin by His divine Person, which is impossible, because God cannot sin, or the choice of sin by a human person, which is again impossible, because there was in His manhood no independent centre of personality. Thus, one of the necessities of the Catholic faith is that our Lord was impeccable.

Nevertheless, temptation was real to our Lord. He completely possessed human nature. Since He possessed it completely, He possessed its needs. For instance, the sense of hunger gave Him pain, as it gives us pain. To remain hungry, when by a miracle He could have provided Himself with food, required in Him mastery over the human desire for food, as it would require selfmastery in us if we had the same possibilities. It needed in Him effort and action of the will, as it would need effort and will in us. Temptation is real, and to overcome it needs effort, when the will is immovably set on what is right. In one sense, temptation is harder to bear to a person whose will has never wavered than it is to another, because the fact of the will having never wavered means that the strain upon it has never been removed, and that the tension of the will on a hard course has never been relaxed, so that there has been necessarily continuous pain. When sin begins it has pains of its own; but the pain which is distinctive of temptation has for the time ceased. The effort and pain which the human will thus endures in mastery over temptation which is continuous and unbroken were in our Lord. For instance, to remain hungry when He could have satisfied His hunger was a painful effort, a continual tension of His human will.

The doctrine of the impeccability of Christ does not impair the value of His human example. It has some times been urged that the resistance of Christ to temptation is of no value to us as an example, if it was impossible that He should fall. This argument rests on a failure to grasp the true nature of the example of Christ. If the example of Christ was that of a mere man, or if it was the example of one who possessed an independent centre of human personality, the objection would probably be of weight, because in that case any example to us of Christ's life would simply be a kind of book or a kind of picture, and would be separated from ourselves. In such a case, the value of the example might depend on there being in it the same element of peccability which there is in us. The example of Christ is not of this kind. It is the example of one who not only shows the right course, but also imparts to men union with the life in which the example was given. Christ, as the second Adam, as the source of the life which is in those who are sacramentally united to Him, gives the strength wherewith His own victory was won. Therefore, the example is to be judged from a wholly different point of view from that from which a merely human example would be judged. [79]

The doctrine of the impeccability of Christ does not lessen His human sympathy. He felt fully the pain of temptation so far as the exertion of the will in overcoming it is concerned; and He has therefore fully the human sympathy of experience with all the sufferings of the tempted which proceed from the effort of maintaining the will fixed on what is right. In ordinary human temptations there is also the pain of the fear of falling. This, of course, could not be in our Lord, and in this respect His temptation was on a different level from the temptations of ordinary men; but it should be noticed that the fear of fall is the painful element in temptation chiefly at lower stages of the spiritual life. To those who are approximating in any degree to the pattern of Christ, the pain of temptation lies chiefly in two respects, the strain upon the will, and the horror of the idea of sin. The first of these, as we have seen, our Lord had in the fullest possible way. The second He had to an extent greater than is possible to any mere man, because the pain of the horror of the idea of sin is a pain which grows with every stage of growth in the spiritual life; and the more perfect any soul is, the more acutely it feels this element of pain. Consequently, it may be said truly that the reality of the human sympathy of Christ with the tempted exists co-ordinately with His impeccability. [80] That He should have been without what is usually an element of pain in temptation no more destroys His sympathy of experience than that sympathy is destroyed by the fact that He was without sin. He is not like us in not having experienced the fear of fall. He is not like us also in not having had to experience repentance.

It remains to consider the bearing of Christ's impeccability on the freedom of His human will. The impossibility of Christ committing sin is best thought of as a moral impossibility; that is to say, it was an impossibility which came, not from any restraint or external necessity, but from the perfect completeness with which His human will was fixed on that which is right. In the case of merely human beings, we may believe that even in this life there are moral impossibilities of real failure. We may believe that the will may become so strengthened in good, and so fully and permanently directed towards good by faith and grace, that it would be morally impossible for it really to choose to depart from God; that is to say, morally impossible to choose any course which it clearly saw to involve disobedience to God. It is this moral impossibility of fall which, in a still higher sense, is in the holy angels, and will be in all the saved in heaven. Yet in such cases the will makes a real act of choice. It does not cease to choose to serve God because the choice between good and evil is, practically speaking, at an end. It is in this higher sense of choice that the human will of Christ might be said to choose, and, in the higher sense of freedom which is associated with it, that the will of Christ is said to be free. Moralists distinguish two kinds of freedom of the will the lower kind whereby it is free to choose evil as well as good, the higher kind whereby, having definitely chosen good, it makes the choice of good a permanent act, and, more over, chooses between different means which are all free from evil. In this higher sense the human will of Christ was free. The moral impossibility of His committing sin is perhaps best realized by asking whether it is conceivable that He who was personally the Son of God should apostatize against God.

The infallibility of our Lord is the necessary consequence of a true conception both of what He came to do and who He is. He came to be the messenger of the Father to men, to bestow on men the revelation which St. John described in the words, 'The only begotten Son, which is in the bosom of the Father, He hath declared Him.' [81] The character which is thus assigned to His teaching implies special requirements as to His own knowledge. That these are supplied may be seen from the doctrine of His single Personality. Since He is Himself personally God; His teaching cannot be mistaken. [82]

With the doctrine of Christ's infallibility the subject of His knowledge is closely connected. It is certain that everything which He asserted must be true. It is a necessary consequence also of the immutability of the divine attributes that His divine knowledge did not undergo any change because of the Incarnation, and that, therefore, His knowledge as God, when He was incarnate, was all-embracing. Any idea that His knowledge as God was within the sphere of the Incarnation limited because of the humiliation of the Incarnation must be rejected. Such a view is unsupported by Holy Scripture; contradicts the practically unanimous teaching of the Fathers and the general tradition of the Church; and is inconsistent with the immutability of the divine nature. [83]

The question then presents itself whether it follows that our Lord's human knowledge was complete on all subjects, both on matters about which He made assertions, and on matters about which He asserted nothing. To this question different answers have been given, and widely different opinions, with regard to the human knowledge of Christ, are held by theologians who assert His infallibility both as God and as man. On this subject dogmatism is out of place. The evidence from Holy Scripture is not all in one direction. The Fathers are not all agreed. If, on the one hand, there is some difficulty in grasping the idea of a human mind without limitations as to matters of fact and in other ways, it is not easy, on the other hand, to suppose that, the nature of knowledge being such as it is, any knowledge could be excluded from the human mind of one who is personally God. Provided the omniscience which He possessed as God is declared to have remained unimpaired by the Incarnation, and throughout the lowest humiliation of the incarnate life, there is room for considerable difference of opinion as to the nature and extent of the knowledge of His human mind. While, in view of the unity of His Person and the nature of knowledge, it appears highly probable that His human knowledge embraced all things which a human mind is capable of receiving, it would ill beseem any who desire to limit their dogmatic assertions to the teaching of Holy Scripture and the Universal Church, to deny that any other opinion can be true. [84]

The Distinction of the Two Natures of God and Man

The fourth great truth about our Lord is that there are in Him two distinct natures, the divine and the human. It has been seen that His two natures are united in one Person. None the less, the divine nature remains wholly divine, and the human nature remains wholly human. They are not so intermingled either that one of them annihilates the other, or that a single nature not wholly divine or wholly human, but a mixture of both, results. The teaching of Holy Scripture in passages which speak of our Lord as truly God and as truly man are inconsistent with any other doctrine.

47

This doctrine has been implied also from the earliest times by the writers of the Church in their references to our Lord being truly God, and perfectly man. It was definitely asserted at the Council of Chalcedon in A.D. 451, which asserted that 'the distinction of the natures is in no way destroyed because of the union, but rather the peculiarity of each nature is preserved,' [85]

That this doctrine could not be denied without destroying what is necessary to the work of our Lord, may be seen by considering the result of each possible way of denying it.

1. If the human nature absorbed the divine nature, the link with God, which is necessary for the act of reconciliation, would be lost.

2. If the divine nature absorbed the human nature, the union with man, which is also necessary for the act of reconciliation, would be lost.

3. If a third nature, neither divine nor human, but a mixture of both, resulted, there would be no true link with either God or man. [86]

Further, it is only the permanent existence of our Lord's manhood which makes His ascension into heaven intelligible; and makes possible His continued inter cession, His continued sympathy as man, and the sacramental union of man with God through His humanity. The belief in the distinctness and permanence of our Lord's humanity, then, is necessary to the doctrines of the Atonement, the priestly work of Christ in heaven, and the Sacraments.

The correlative truths of the unity of the Person and the distinction of the natures received eloquent expression in the fifth century from the Eastern St. Proclus, Patriarch of Constantinople, and the Western St. Leo, Bishop of Some. Preaching in the Cathedral of St. Sophia, St. Proclus exclaimed, 'He, the Same, was in the bosom of the Father and in the womb of the virgin; the Same was in the arms of His mother and on the wings of the wind; the Same was worshipped in heaven by the angels and was sitting at meat with publicans on earth; the Seraphim held back from gazing at Him and Pilate was questioning Him.' [87] Writing to Flavian, St. Leo said, 'He who is true God is also true man; and there is no deceit in this union, while the lowliness of man and the loftiness of Godhead are united. For as the God is not changed by the compassion, so the man is not consumed by the dignity. For each nature in communion with the other does that which belongs to it, the Word, that is, performing what belongs to the Word, and the flesh accomplishing what belongs to the flesh. The one of these shines out in miracles; the other succumbs to injuries. And as the Word does not depart from equality in glory with the Father, so the flesh does not abandon the nature of our race. For He is one and the same, as must often be said, truly Son of God, and truly Son of man... He whom as man the craft of the devil tempts, is the same to whom as God the offices of angels minister. To be hungry, to be thirsty, to be weary, and to sleep is plainly human. But to satisfy five thousand men with five loaves, and to bestow on the woman of Samaria living water, a draught of which prevents one who drinks it from thirsting again, to walk on the surface of the sea with feet that sink not, and by chiding the storm to quell the swelling billows, is unquestionably divine...For although in the Lord Jesus Christ there is one Person of God and man, yet that whereby contumely is common to both is one thing, and that whereby glory is common to both is another. For from our nature He has manhood inferior to the Father; from the Father He has God head equal with the Father.' [88]

Summary of the Doctrine of the Incarnation

The Catholic doctrine of the Incarnation makes four statements
1. Jesus Christ is truly God. This was affirmed at the Council of Nicaea in A.D. 325 against the Arians, who denied the true deity of Christ.
2. Jesus Christ is perfectly man. This was affirmed at the Council of Constantinople in A.D. 381, against the Apollinarians, who impaired the perfect manhood of Christ.
3. Jesus Christ is one Person. This was affirmed at the Council of Ephesus in A.D. 431, against the Nestorians, who divided Christ into two Persons.
4. In Jesus Christ there are two distinct natures. This was affirmed at the Council of Chalcedon in A.D. 451, against the Eutychians, who confounded the natures of Christ.

These four truths are generally denoted by the four words, ἀληθῶς, truly; τελέως, perfectly; ἀδιαιρέτως, indissolubly; ἀσυγχύτως; without confusion. [89]

[1] Gen. iii. 15.
[2] St. Irenaeus, C. Haer., V. xiv. 2.
[3] Cf. Mic. v. 2 with St. Matt. ii 1; Isa. vll. 14 with St. Matt. i. 18-25 and St. Luke i. 34; Isa. lxi. 1, 2 with St. Matt. iii. 16 and St. Luke iv. 18-21, etc.; Zech. ix. 9 with St. Matt. xxi. 1-16; Psalm xli. 9 and Zech. xi. 12, 13 with St. Matt. xxvi. 14, 15; Psalm xxii. 7, 8, 16 and Zech. xii. 10 with St. Matt. xxvii. 39-43 and St. John xix. 37.
[4] St. John iv. 25, 26; St. Matt. xvi. 16, 17.
[5] Gal. iv. 4.
[6] Gal. iv, 2.
[7] See Lightfoot, St. Paul's Epistle to the Galatians, on iv. 4, 11; Church, Discipline of the Christian Character; Wordsworth, Church History, i. 12-33. While it is necessary to dissent from many of Dr. Hatch's conclusions, there are lines of thought in his Hibbert Lectures on The Influence of Greek Ideas and Usages upon the Christian Church which need consideration.
[8] St. Thomas Aquinas, Summa Theol., III. i. 5. Cf. Bright, Sermons of St. Leo on the Incarnation, pp. 144, 145 (edition 2).
[9] See note 11 in the concluding Notes.
[10] See note 12 in the concluding Notes.
[11] See note 13 in the concluding Notes.
[12] Eph. i. 4; iii. 8-11.
[13] 1 St. Pet. i. 18-20.
[14] 1 St. Tim. i. 15.
[15] Bright, Sermons of St. Leo on the Incarnation, p. 218 (edition 2). The history of the discussion of this question is given with greatfulness and fairness in Westcott, Epistles of St. John, pp. 273-315.
[16] See note 14 in the concluding Notes.

[17] The letters from Roman Catholic Bishops quoted by Pusey (*Eirenicon*, pt. i. pp. 127-145, 351-407) are against the opportuneness of a decree, or against the doctrine being made of faith, not against the truth of the doctrine.

[18] See note 15 in the concluding Notes.

[19] See note 16 in the concluding Notes.

[20] Gen. iii. 15; Job xiv. 4.

[21] Rom. v. 12.

[22] See note 17 in the concluding Notes.

[23] Church, *Occasional Papers,* i. 354, 355.

[24] Isa. vii. 14; St. Matt. i. 23.

[25] St. John i. 1, 14; Heb. i. 2, 8.

[26] St. John x. 30, 31, 33.

[27] St. Matt. v. 22, 28, 32, 34, 39, 44.

[28] St. Matt. viii. 21-2; x. 32-7.

[29] St. Matt. xxv. 31-33.

[30] St. Matt. xvi. 18.

[31] St. Matt, xxviii. 20.

[32] St. John vi. 40, 51, 54, 58.

[33] St. John x. 18; Rom. i. 4.

[34] Rev. v. 6-13.

[35] Rom. i. 7; xvi. 20, etc.

[36] 1 Thess. iv. 16, 17; 2 Thess. i. 7, 8; ii. 8.

[37] 1 Cor. ii. 2; in, 11; Rom. iii, 25, 26; Gal. ii. 16.

[38] See Liddon, *The Divinity of our Lord and Saviour Jesus Christ,* pp. 100-359.

[39] *ibid.,* pp. 387-435.

[40] See Newman, *Parochial Sermons,* vi. 5, 6 ('Christ the Son of God made Man,' 'The Incarnate Son a Sufferer and Sacrifice'); Wilberforce, *The Incarnation of our Lord Jesus Christ,* chap. vii.

[41] 2 Cor. viii. 9.

[42] Phil. ii. 5-8.

[43] *I.e.,* the words translated above 'made Himself low.' The authorized version has 'made Himself of no reputation.' The revised version has 'emp-tied Himself.' The other passages in the New Testament in which the verb occurs are Rom. iv. 14; 1 Cor. i. 17; ix. 15; 2 Cor. ix. 3. They do not support the assumption sometimes made that it must be used in its literal sense in Phil. ii. 7.

[44] Bright, *Waymarks in Church History,* p. 393.

[45] On these passages, see *Church Quarterly Review,* October, 1897, pp. 168-172; January, 1900, p. 377. On the subject generally, see also note 18 on page 291.

[46] For the completeness of the overthrow of Arianism, and the sig nificance of it, see Sanday, *The Oracles of God,* pp. 84, 108.

[47] St. John i. 14; Rom. v. 15.

[48] St. Matt. i. 25; Rom. i. 3; Gal. iv. 4.

[49] St. Luke ii. 21.

[50] St. Mark ii. 16; St. Luke vii. 36.

[51] St. Matt. viii. 24.

[52] St. John iv. 6.

[53] St. John xi. 35.

[54] St. Matt. xvi. 21; xxvii. 50.

[55] St. Ignatius, *Ad Trall.,* 9.

[56] St. Irenaeus, *C. Haer.,* V. xiv. 3.

[57] See note 19 in the concluding Notes.

[58] St. Matt. i. 18-25; St. Luke i. 31-35.

[59] St. Ignatius, *Ad Eph.,* 19; *Ad Smyr.,* 1.

[60] Aristides, *Apol.* (*Texts and Studies,* I. i. 29, 36, 110).

[61] St. Justin Martyr, *Apol.,* i. 21; Cf. *ibid.,* 22, 31, 32, 33, 46, 63; *Dial c. Tryph.,* 43, 63, 66, 84, 85.

[62] St. Irenaeus, *C. Haer.,* I. x. 1, 2; III. iv. 1.

[63] This subject is treated with great accuracy and fairness by Swete, *The Apostles Creed: its Relation to Primitive Christianity,* pp. 42-55; Gore, *Dissertations on Subjects connected with the Incarnation,* pp. 3-68.

[64] St. Matt. viii. 10.

[65] St. Luke ii. 52.
[66] St. Matt. xxvi. 39; St. Luke xxii. 42; St. John v. 30.
[67] See note 20 in the concluding Notes.
[68] St. John i. 14.
[69] Acts xx. 28. For a different reading see margin of revised version.
[70] 1 Cor. ii. 8.
[71] St. John iii. 13. For a different reading, see margin of revised version.
[72] 1 Cor. xv. 47.
[73] See an admirably clear note in Bright, Sermons of St. Leo on the Incarnation, p. 130 (edition 2).
[74] St. Ignatius, Ad Eph., 18.
[75] See note 21 in the concluding Notes.
[76] See Wilberforce, The Incarnation of our Lord Jesus Christ, chap. vi.
[77] St. Cyril of Alexandria, Ad Next. Ep., iii.
[78] See note 22 in the concluding Notes.
[79] See, on this point, Church Quarterly Review, July, 1883, pp. 291, 292.
[80] See, on this point, Church Quarterly Review, January, 1892, pp. 280-282.
[81] St. John i. 18.
[82] See Liddon, The Divinity of our Lord and Saviour Jesus Christ, pp. 461-480; Bright, The Incarnation as a Motive Power, pp. 299, 300 (edition 2); Gore, The Incarnation of the Son of God, pp. 153-154.
[83] See note 18 in the concluding Notes.
[84] See note 23 in the concluding Notes.
[85] See note 24 in the concluding Notes.
[86] See note 25 in the concluding Notes.
[87] St. Proclus, Orat., i. 9.
[88] St. Leo, Ep., xxviii. 4.
[89] See Hooker, Laws of Ecclesiastical Polity, V. liv. 10.

Chapter Seven - The Atonement

The Fall deprived man of the grace of the supernatural gifts which God had bestowed upon him; the privilege of future glory which God meant to give him; and the happiness which God had allowed him to possess. It brought upon man the wrath of God as the necessary attitude of perfect holiness towards sin; slavery to the devil and sin, which resulted from the loss of the super natural gifts, but could be removed by divine grace because of man's continued possession of free-will; and the penalty of temporary and eternal punishment as the necessary consequences of a sinful state.

The work of our Lord was to remedy the mischief which was caused by the Fall by restoring to man what he had lost, and removing what sin had brought upon him. This work was accomplished by our Lord potentially for the whole human race by His death. It is accomplished actually for individuals by the application to them, and their reception of, the merits of His death, together with the powers of His life, a union with Christ the results of which are the possession of man in this life and after death.

Holy Scripture shows with great clearness the main points of the fact of the Atonement. The source of the reconciliation of man to God is in the death of Christ. [1] This reconciliation is called redemption, that is, the paying of a

51

price whereby man is set free. [2] It is for all men. [3] It is for all sins, original and actual. [4] Its results are freedom from the penalties of the Fall and restoration to the promises forfeited by the Fall. [5]

There was careful preparation in the history of the Jews recorded in the Old Testament for the place which the fact of the Atonement was to fill in the work of our Lord and in Christian theology. A main idea of the Jewish religion was that of the value of sacrifice. Sacrifice was the means whereby Abel was acceptable. [6] It was offered by Noah in thanksgiving, but served the further purpose of eliciting the promise and blessing of God. [7] By it the covenants which God made with Abram [8] and Jacob [9] were ratified. The building of an altar was associated with patriarchal acts of worship. [10] A ram was offered on the mountain in the land of Moriah because of a special revelation from the angel of the Lord. [11] The blood of the Passover lamb was the token whereby the Israelites were delivered when the Egyptians were smitten. [12] Under the Mosaic law sacrifices were the means of propitiation, thanksgiving, and worship. [13]

In all the stages of the development of sacrifice the idea of substitution occurred. In the simplest forms it was the special dedication to God of a part where the whole, as being His gift, was really His possession. [14] The ram offered by Abraham was a substituted offering, because of which a human life was spared. [15] The regulations about the first-born commanded that human children should be redeemed by another offering. [16] In all the sacrifices that which was offered was given to God as a symbol of the personal and moral surrender of self on the part of him who offered it. The presenting of blood signified the dedication of life. [17]

The gift to God in the sacrifices of the Old Testament was a type of the offering of Christ. The preparation for His death emphatically taught its sacrificial character. The language of the prophets teaches the same lesson as the services enjoined in the Mosaic law. [18] St. John the Baptist described Him as the Lamb of God, [19] a phrase which to those to whom he spoke could only denote a sacrificial victim.

Our Lord Himself showed by word and act that His work was a sacrifice on behalf of and in the stead of others. [20] The sacrificial efficacy of His death is emphasized by St. Paul [21] and St. Peter, [22] the writer of the Epistle to the Hebrews, [23] and St. John. [24] Even in the vision of the unseen there is a place for the sacrifice of Christ. [25]

Holy Scripture thus states with great definiteness the fact of the Atonement accomplished by the death of Christ. As to the details of the method, it says nothing. 'I do not find,' wrote Bishop Butler, 'that the Scripture has explained it.' [26]

Similarly, the Church has always taught that man is set free from the evils produced by the Fall and recovers the good lost through the Fall by means of the death of Christ. There is no authoritative decision or consensus of teaching which commits the Church to any theory about the details of the method of the Atonement. But throughout Christian teaching it is affirmed that Christ's death was a sacrifice for human sin. In the Epistle of St. Clement of Rome the 'blood of Christ' is described as 'precious to His Father,' as 'shed for our salvation,' as having 'won for the whole world the grace of repentance;' it was typified by the scarlet thread in the house of Rahab as the means of redemption; it was 'given for' Christians 'by the will of God.' [27] St. Ignatius wrote, Christ 'suffered for our sakes,' 'judgment awaiteth' those who 'believe not in His Blood,' His 'flesh suffered for our sins.' [28] St. Polycarp declared that 'our Lord Jesus Christ endured to face even death for our sins,' and 'died for our sakes.' [29] In the *Epistle of Barnabas,* a book possibly written in the last quarter of the first century, [30] it is said that the 'Son of God suffered in order that the stroke inflicted on Him might give life to us,' that 'He could not suffer except for our sakes,' and that in fulfilment of the type of the sacrifice of Isaac He was destined 'to offer the vessel of His Spirit as a sacrifice for our sins.' [31] The *Letter to Diognetus,* which may have been written about A.D. 130, [32] teaches that He was given by the Father as 'a ransom for us,' because nothing but 'His righteousness' was 'capable of covering our sins,' and because we could not be justified by any other than the 'Son of God.' [33] St. Justin Martyr describes the blood of Christ as the means of the deliverance of Christians, and compares it with the type of the Passover lamb and the scarlet thread in the house of Rahab. [34] According to St. Irenaeus, Christ died and shed His blood for us, and redeemed us by His blood, and by His passion reconciled us to God. [35] Clement of Alexandria declares that the fleshly blood of Christ redeemed us from corruption; that the blood of the Word was the means of salvation for the spirit of man; and that Christ gave Himself as our ransom. [36] Tertullian regards our Lord as represented by the types of Isaac, the brazen serpent, and the scapegoat; and teaches that He redeemed man by His blood,' and restored by the cross that which Adam had lost by the tree. [37] According to St. Cyprian, Christ overcame death by the trophy of the cross, redeemed the believer by the price of His blood, and reconciled man to God the Father. [38] Origen believed that the 'soul of the Son of God was given as a ransom for us,' and that His death was for the healing of our wounds. [39] St. Gregory of Nazianzus, [40] St. Gregory of Nyssa, [41] St. Basil, [42] St. Cyril of Jerusalem, [43] St. Cyril of Alexandria, [44] St. Ambrose, [45] St. Leo, [46] and St. Athanasius, [47] agree that the death of Christ is an act of redemption. St. Augustine, whether he is exhorting in a sermon, or quietly working out a theological treatise, or passionately outpouring the devotion of his eager soul, regards our Lord as the Victim because of whom the Father is well pleased with man. [48] To select a few instances out of many, St. Gregory the Great, [49] St. John of Damascus, [50] St. Bernard, [51] and St. Anselm, [52] bear witness that this was the belief of the Church in later times.

Very serious objection has been taken at different times to this main fact that the death of Christ obtains forgiveness for man from God. The crucial points underlying the various forms of objections have been these:-

1. The exaction of such a penalty for sin has been regarded as implying that God is cruel.

2. The punishment of the Son of God because of the sin of man has been regarded as implying that God is unjust.

3. The fact that man receives benefit because of the sufferings of the Son of God has been regarded as implying that God is immoral on the ground that true morality requires that a person should receive benefit only because of what he himself is and does.

It cannot be questioned that the whole idea of Atonement contains much which is perplexing; but as the true nature of the Atonement, so far as it can be ascertained from Holy Scripture and Christian theology, is realized, the perplexities are lessened, and there are considerations which make the very real difficulties which have been felt about it less. Among these considerations the following are some of the chief:

1. Sin in itself, as being a terrible offence, requires a terrible penalty. If the righteousness of God is not a mere phrase, but a reality, and if sin in man is a reality also, and not merely on the surface, but penetrating deeply into his moral being, a great act of atonement is objectively necessary because of the nature of God and the sinfulness of man.

2. The necessity of maintaining among men a true conception of the righteousness of God and of the heinousness of sin requires a terrible penalty. If sin had been lightly forgiven, it might easily have been regarded as a light offence.

3. Christ who suffers is God. He is the merciful Judge who endures the penalty in order that He may not have to inflict it. The Atonement in the terrible character of the penalty reveals the righteousness and wrath of the Son as well as of the Father. The Father in His love appoints the acts of the Son. The Son in His love willingly bears the penalty of sin. The Father willingly accepts the atoning sacrifice of the Son. It is the love of the Father which appointed the sacrifice and accepts it, as it is the love of the Son which offers it. In both the Father and the Son there is necessary wrath against sin, and there is love which provides the remedy for sin. Any view of the Atonement which leaves out of sight either the wrath against sin on the part of the Son, or the love for those who have committed sin on the part of the Father, tends towards such a separation in the Holy Trinity as would ultimately mean the denial of the co-essential Godhead of the Father and the Son. In the language of St. Leo, 'Because by the envy of the devil sin entered into the world, and the captivity of man could not be loosened in any other way than by His taking up our cause who without loss of His majesty could both become man and be alone free from the contagion of sin, the merciful Trinity made division of the work

of our restoration, so that the Father should be propitiated, the Son should propitiate, and the Holy Ghost should enkindle.' [53]

4. Christ in offering the sacrifice does not stand out side the human race. The sacrifice is in one sense vicarious. In it Christ, being one, makes an offering for many. In another sense it is not vicarious. Christ, the one who offers, is not separated from the many for whom the sacrifice is offered. Christ's human nature makes Him truly representative of man, and the absence of an independent centre of personality in His humanity enables Him to be truly representative of all men. Moreover, as He joins Himself to the whole race of man in the Incarnation, so Ho joins Himself to separate individuals in the Sacraments. The destiny of the forgiven soul, which with poor, imperfect movements struggles towards the light, and with weak, faltering touch lays hold of the work and Person of our Lord, and in hope and fear turns away from the wrong which allures, is to attain by the grace of God to that perfect holiness towards which even now the divine foreknowledge sees that it begins to grow. The word 'substitution' has often been used of the bearing of the penalties of sin by Christ. As so applied, it may be used in a right sense or in a wrong sense. It is used in a right sense when it is taken to mean that if Christ had not died we should have suffered eternal loss, and that because of His death we have been saved from eternal loss. It is used in a wrong sense if it is taken to mean that the sufferings of Christ were instead of any action or condition of our own in such a way that His work is separate from us and that no penalties of any kind rest any longer on the redeemed. The same distinction is to be made with regard to the phrases 'satisfaction' and 'in our stead.' Christ's death satisfied for the salvation of men. It was an offering on behalf of man of that which man owed and could not pay; but at the same time it is required from man that he allow the results of Christ's work to be in his own life if he is to be benefited by the satisfaction of Christ. The phrases 'vicarious,' 'substitution,' 'satisfaction,' 'in our stead,' have all been used in wrong senses; in their proper meanings they express most valuable truth, and they ought not to be abandoned because of the false meanings which some have attached to them. To quote St. Leo again, 'It was right that those who were to be saved should also do something for themselves, and by the conversion of their hearts to the Redeemer should depart from the dominion of the enemy; for, as the Apostle says, God sent the Spirit of His Son into our hearts, crying, Abba, Father. Now, where the Spirit of the Lord is, there is liberty. No one can say that Jesus is the Lord but by the Holy Ghost.' [54] "Vicarious," "substitution," "satisfaction" - we must not give up the use of these terms in a sense which is neither immoral nor arbitrary, but consonant to our Saviour's office as Second Adam, and involved in the very perfection of His own miraculous love.' [55]

To sum up, then, this line of thought, the key to the doctrine of the Atonement, so far as it is revealed, appears to be found in two truths -

1. The essential oneness of Christ with the Father. The Atonement is the vindication of the righteousness of God who made man, against whom sin was an outrage, by His own willing enduring of punishment in order that He might not have to inflict it. Thus, it is not a punishment on an unwilling victim, but a voluntary act of self-surrender.

2. The communicated oneness of ourselves with Christ. The victim who suffered takes us into His own life. He suffered as the Head of the body, and we being of the body are partakers in His sacrifice.

For a long time a theory was prevalent within the Church that the death of Christ was a ransom which was paid, not to God, but to the devil. This opinion was held by many of the Fathers. It was evidently the result of pressing too far the details of an illustration. Holy Scripture represents the death of Christ as an act of redemption. Obviously, redemption implies captivity and release from captivity. Obviously, too, the person who was regarded as holding men in captivity was the devil. The argument was then formed that, since in a natural captivity the ransom is paid to the captor, therefore in the Atonement the ransom must have been paid to Satan. This line of argument had much plausibility; but it was contrary to the well-understood rule that illustrations can only be used to furnish arguments about the matters which they are definitely used to illustrate, and not in all the details associated with them. For instance, if all the details in an illustration were necessarily to be pressed, our Lord's parable of the unjust steward would be made to mean that injustice is a virtue. The illustrative use of the phraseology connected with the word ransom does not require the inference which some thought to be bound up with it; and the theory referred to is open to very grave objections. It really implied, as many of those who held it saw, that God acknowledged the possession by Satan of certain rights over man, and that God either made a bargain with Satan or deceived Satan by a trick. The theory was emphatically rejected by St. Gregory of Nazianzus; and teaching about the Atonement which was inconsistent with it was common among the Fathers. [56] It appears to be contrary to the passages in Holy Scripture which represent the death of Christ as a triumph over the evil powers. [57] The true doctrine that the ransom was paid to God was re-asserted by St. Anselm in the eleventh century and has since been universally held in the Church.

The reality of the Atonement depends upon the God head of our Lord. The sacrificial character of His death has been denied by those who have denied His deity; and as far as there has been a tendency in any to approach humanitarian views about Him, so far there has been a tendency also towards denying the atoning efficacy of His death. Grave errors about the Atonement of a different kind have been found in those who have not questioned the deity of Christ. For instance, there appear to have been some in the fifth century who anticipated Calvin in the sixteenth century and Jansen in the seventeenth century by denying that Christ died for all men, and, while regarding His death as a sacrifice, said that it was so only for the elect. An error existed in some quarters in the latter part of the middle ages that the sacrifice of the cross was a sacrifice for original sin only, and that all actual sin was atoned for by the sacrifice of the Mass as a separate sacrifice. [58] Calvin, in addition to limiting the efficacy of our Lord's death to a selected few, exaggerated and distorted the wrath of God to such an extent that, on his views, it would be truer to say God hated the world than, in the words of Holy Scripture, 'God so loved the world that He gave His only begotten Son, that whosoever believeth on Him should not perish, but have eternal life.' [59]

[1] Eph. ii. 16; Col. i. 20-22; Heb. ix. 11-14; x. 10, 19; 1 St. Pet. i. 18, 19; ii. 24.

[2] Eph. i. 7; Col. i. 14; 1 St. Tim. ii. 6; Heb. ix. 12.

[3] 1 St. Tim. ii. 6; iv. 10.

[4] St. Titus ii. 14; 1 St. John ii. 1, 2.

[5] St. John iii. 16.

[6] Gen. iv. 4; cf. Heb. xi. 4. ˋ

[7] Gen. viii. 20-22.

[8] Gen. xv. 7-18.

[9] Gen. xxxv. 14.

[10] Gen. xii. 8; xxvi. 25.

[11] Gen. xxii. 11-13.

[12] Ex. xii. 13.

[13] E.g., Lev. i.-vii.

[14] E.g., Gen. iv. 4; cf. Lev. xxiii. 10; Num. xviii. 17-19.

[15] Gen. xxii. 13.

[16] Exod. xiii. 2, 12, 13, 15; xxxiv. 20; Num. xviii. 15, 16.

[17] See Westcott, Epistles of St. John, pp. 34-37; Epistle to the Hebrews, pp. 293-295.

[18] See, e.g., Isa. liii. 4-6, 10-12. (Cf. with the Hebrew of verses 4 and 12; Lev. x. 17; xvii. 16; xxiv. 15; and with the Hebrew of verse 10; Lev. v. 6; 1 Sam. vi. 3.) Cf. e.g., Job. xxxiii. 24; Ps. xxii.; Zech. xiii. 7-9.

[19] St. John i. 29, 36.

[20] See Dale, The Atonement, pp. 67-92; Christian Doctrine, pp. 111,112.

[21] E.g., Acts xx. 28; Rom. iii. 24, 25; 1 Cor. xv. 3; Gal. iii. 13; Eph. i. 7; ii. 16; 1 Thess. v. 9, 10.

[22] 1 St. Pet. i. 19; ii. 21-24; iii. 18.

[23] Heb. vii. 27; ix. 11-18; x. 1-20, 29; xii. 24; xiii. 11, 12.

[24] 1 St. John i. 7; iii. 16; iv. 10.

[25] Rev. v. 6-14.

[26] Butler, Analogy of Religion, II. v. 18.

[27] St. Clement of Rome, Ad Cor., i. 7, 12, 21, 49.

[28] St. Ignatius, Ad Smyr., 2, 6.

[29] St. Polycarp, Ad Phil., 1, 9.

[30] For the date, see Lightfoot, Apostolic Fathers, I. ii. 503-512.

[31] Ep. Barn., 7.

[32] For the date, see Lightfoot, Apostolic Fathers, I. i. 5; II. i. 517.

[33] Ep. ad Diogn., 9.

[34] St. Justin Martyr, Dial. c. Tryph., 95, 111.

[35] St. Irenaeus, C. Haer., III. xvi. 9.

[36] Clement of Alexandria, Paed., i. 5; ii. 2; Quis Dives salv., 37.

[37] Tertullian, Adv. Jud., 10, 13, 14; De Fug. in Persec., 12.

[38] St. Cyprian, Ad Demet., 26.

[39] Origen, In Mat., xvi. 8; In Joan., xxviii. 14.

[40] St. Gregory of Nazianzus, Orat., xlv. 22.

[41] St. Gregory of Nyssa, Cat. Orat., 23.

[42] St. Basil, Hom. in Ps. xlviii., 3, 4.

[43] St. Cyril of Jerusalem, Cat., xiii. 33.

[44] St. Cyril of Alexandria, Adv. Nest., iii. 2; De Rect. Fid. (p. 7, cd. Aubert).

[45] St. Ambrose, De Fug. Saec., 44.

[46] St. Leo, Serm., lxiv. 3; lxviii. 3.

[47] St. Athanasius, De Incar., 20.

[48] St. Augustine, *Serm.*, ccxv. 4, 5; *De Trin.*, xiii. 15; *Conf.*, x. 69.

[49] St. Gregory the Great, *Mor.*, xvii. 46.

[50] St. John of Damascus, *De Fid. Orth.*, iii. 27.

[51] St. Bernard, *De Err. Abael*, 22.

[52] St. Anselm, *Cur Deus Homo*, passim.

[53] St. Leo, *Serm.*, lxxvii. 2.

[54] St. Leo, *Serm.*, lxxvii. 2.

[55] Bright, *Morality in Doctrine*, pp. 330, 331.

[56] See note 26 in the concluding Notes.

[57] Col. ii. 13-15; Heb. ii. 14, 15.

[58] Vacant, *Histoire de la Conception du Sacrifice de la Messe*, p. 40, and in *Revue Anglo-Romaine*, November 21, 1896. Cf. *Church Quarterly Review*, April, 1896, pp. 40-42.

[59] St. John iii. 16.

Chapter Eight - The Resurrection and Ascension of Our Lord, and the Coming of the Holy Ghost

The central feature in our Lord's work is the Atonement. The incarnate life is also a revelation of the Father, and an example for man. Our Lord by His death removed the barrier between God and man which sin had set up, and in His life exhibited the perfect standard of human life by showing what God is and what man ought to be. In order that the work of redemption may be completed, it is further required that man be so united to God that, being forgiven, he may be able to live according to the pattern set by God. The work of the life of Christ is not completed in the mere forgiveness of sins. In human nature God the Son offers to the Father the sacrifice which is the means of the forgiveness of all sins original and actual, exhibiting in the sacrifice thus offered the wrath against sin and love for mankind of the Holy Trinity. In human nature, also, God the Son presents the example of a perfect life. It is, further, true that through His human nature God the Son conveys to man the power of His own life. It follows that there is an intimate connexion between the doctrine of the Atonement and the doctrine of the Church and the Sacraments; and it is not possible to have a proper appreciation of either of these doctrines in all its bearings if it is dissociated from the other. Between the death of Christ and the doctrine of the Church and the Sacraments, it is necessary to consider the descent of our Lord's soul into the place of the dead, the resurrection of our Lord's body from the tomb in its re-union with His soul, the ascension of our Lord into heaven, and the descent of the Holy Ghost upon the first Christians.

The Descent into Hell

Intervening between our Lord's death and His resurrection is the descent into hell, that is, in the old sense of the word hell, hades, or the unseen world. Our Lord told the penitent thief that he would be with Him on that day in Paradise. In St. Peter's speech in the second chapter of the Acts of the Apostles, he said that the soul of our Lord was not left in hades. In St. Peter's First Epistle reference is made to a work accomplished by our Lord in the unseen world which is described as preaching. [1] The Fathers differ as to the details of this work of our Lord. They substantially agree that He declared the accomplishment of redemption to the souls of the patriarchs and caused them to be in some higher state than that in which they were before. [2] Thus, during the time which elapsed between His death and His resurrection, our Lord's soul was separated from His body. His body lay in the tomb. His soul continued His work in the unseen world. His body was still the body of God, and His human soul was still in very deed the soul of God, since, though body and soul were separated from one another, neither body nor soul could be separated from His deity because of the indissoluble union between His two natures in His one divine Person.

The Resurrection

In the resurrection the body and soul of our Lord were re-united, and He rose from the dead possessing the same body which He had possessed before His death. [3] Though it was the same body it was not in the same condition as when He died. It was now a spiritual body endued with new powers. The chief of these new powers which make up the spiritual character of the risen body of Christ have been summarized as follows: -

1. The body has become inherently immortal so as to be incapable of suffering death. 'Christ being raised from the dead dieth no more; death no more hath dominion over Him.' [4]

2. It has become independent of the laws of space. In His body He passed through the closed doors of the room where the disciples were assembled. [5]

3. It has become independent of the laws of time. In a moment He vanished out of sight. [6]

4. It has become glorious. This glory appears to have been veiled by our Lord in His appearances after His resurrection because of man's incapacity in his present state. His possession of it is shown by St. Paul's teaching in the First Epistle to the Corinthians. [7] St. Paul is there speaking of the future resurrection of men, but he obviously means that anything which men will possess in their resurrection was possessed by our Lord in His resurrection.

Because of these new powers the resurrection of Christ was more than the restoration of life to His body by reason of its reunion with His soul. In His resurrection our Lord rose to new life. The body which He now possesses is no longer natural but super-natural. 'The resurrection,' says St. Bernard, 'is a journey and a passage. For Christ did not fall back, but rose; He did not return, but journeyed on; He passed over, He did not come back.' [8]

St. Paul describes the resurrection of our Lord as an essential part of the Christian faith. 'If,' he says, 'Christ hath not been raised, then is our preaching vain,' [9] That the resurrection of Christ is essential to Christianity may be seen from the following reasons:

1. If our Lord had not risen from the dead, it would be implied that His humanity had not been personally united with His deity. It is involved in the personal union that the body of Christ is so fully associated with Himself that it could not be left to corruption. There fore, if Christ had not risen from the dead, the reality of the Incarnation would be impaired.

2. Our Lord's teaching during His ministry would have been falsified if He had not risen. [10]

3. If Christ had not risen, there would not be the true means of union between Him and Christians which the Incarnation makes possible, because it is the body of Christ which affords the possibility of the sacramental means of union.

There is very convincing evidence for the historical reality of the resurrection of our Lord. It can only be rejected by setting aside the express testimony of the four evangelists and of St. Paul. There is no doubt that all these alike regarded the resurrection as a literal fact, and believed that the body of our Lord was restored to life. Nor can the evidence for the resurrection be rightly depreciated on the grounds sometimes alleged that the age was a credulous one, and any marvel would be readily believed, and the temperament of the Apostles would lead them to easily imagine such an event as the resurrection. On the contrary, the temperament of the Apostles was not imaginative. During our Lord's ministry, so far from being quick of apprehension, they were very slow, and after His death, so far from being ready to imagine the resurrection, they were unwilling to believe it. Their testimony was borne in the face of the Sadducean sceptics, whose influence was great. [11]

The evidence for the bodily resurrection of our Lord is not confined to that contained in the New Testament. The belief that, in the literal meaning of the words, He rose from the dead has been from the first an integral part of the Christian faith. It is not without significance that in the first century the heretic Cerinthus, who denied the birth of our Lord from a virgin, nevertheless acknowledged the fact of His resurrection. [12] St. Clement of Rome, writing to the Corinthians about A.D. 96, referred to the resurrection of our Lord in terms which leave no doubt that both he himself and those whom he was addressing regarded it as an historical fact. [13] St. Ignatius mentions the resurrection repeatedly in the course of seven short letters, and in one of the passages speaks of it in these definite words: 'I know and believe that He was in the flesh even after the resurrection; and when He came to Peter and his company, He said to them, "Lay hold and handle me, and see that I am not a demon without body." And straightway they touched Him, and they believed, being joined unto His flesh and His blood...After His resurrection He both ate with them and drank with them as being in the flesh, though spiritually united with the Father.' [14] St. Polycarp, writing like St. Ignatius at the beginning of the second century, refers to 'our Lord Jesus Christ, who endured to face even death for our sins, whom God raised;' 'Him who raised our Lord Jesus Christ from the dead;' 'Him who died for our sakes and was raised by God for us;' and 'His Father who raised Him from the dead,' [15] The *Apology* of Aristides includes our Lord's resurrection in the creed of Christians. [16] A passage in the so-called Second Epistle of St. Clement of Rome to the Corinthians,' which was probably written in the first half of the second century either at Rome or at Corinth, [17] implies that our Lord rose from the dead in His body. [18] St. Justin Martyr refers explicitly to the resurrection. [19] St. Irenaeus mentions it as forming part, like the virgin birth, of the creed of the Universal Church which the churches of Germany, Spain, Gaul, the East, Egypt, and Italy concurred in holding. [20] Like the virgin birth, again, it found a place in the statements of belief acceptance of which was necessary for share in the fellowship of Christians. [21] So clearly did this belief refer to the bodily resurrection of Christ, that St. Irenaeus and Tertullian thought it necessary to explain its consistency with St. Paul's words, 'Flesh and blood cannot inherit the kingdom of God,' [22] by saying that they denote 'the flesh in itself,' 'apart from the Spirit of God,' [23] without the spiritual gifts of 'incorruptibility and immortality.' [24] As part of the immemorial faith, it has sustained the belief of Christians in the reality of the life of the world to come and has given force to the best energies of the Church. [25]

The Ascension

Our Lord ascended into heaven forty days after His resurrection with His body in which He had lived and died and risen. [26] His humanity ascended into heaven in order that in it He might carry on His work in heaven. In the Epistle to the Hebrews this work is represented as a work of intercession, [27] and the whole argument of the Epistle shows that a comparison is to be made between the offering of the sacrifice of our Lord and the offering of the Jewish sacrifices. In the Jewish sacrifices the culminating point was the presentation of the victim to God after it had been slain. The culminating point in the sacrifice of Christ is the offering of His manhood to the Father in heaven after being slain and restored to life. Our Lord's present work of inter cession consists of His presentation to the Father of His living and glorified manhood after having passed through death.

The Descent of the Holy Ghost

The first result of the presentation of the sacrifice of Christ to the Father in heaven was the gift of the Holy Ghost. Our Lord received the Holy Ghost in His manhood when He was conceived, at the time of His baptism, and at His ascension. [28] Having received anew the Holy Ghost in His ascension, our Lord poured Him forth, so that, eleven days after the ascension, the Holy Ghost descended upon the Apostles to dwell in the Christian Church and in individual Christians. [29] Before His crucifixion our Lord connected the possibility of His sending the Holy Ghost with His ascension. [30] So far as we are able to discern the reasons for this connexion, they appear to have been that His sacrifice must be presented in heaven before the Holy Ghost was sent forth; and that He must Himself receive in His manhood the ascension gift of the Holy Ghost before the Holy Ghost could create and be communicated to His mystical body.

[1] St. Luke xxiii. 43; Acts ii. 24-31; 1 St. Pet. iii. 18, 19; iv. 6.

[2] See note 27 in the concluding Notes.

[3] St. Luke xxiv. 38-43; St. John xx. 26-29.

[4] Rom. vi. 9, 10.

[5] St. John xx. 19, 26.

[6] St. Luke xxiv. 31

[7] 1 Cor. xv. 43.

[8] See note 28 in the concluding Notes.

[9] 1 Cor. xv. 14: cf. 17.

[10] See, *e.g.*, St. Matt. xvi. 21.

[11] See Acts v. 17; Gore, *The Incarnation of the Son of God,* pp. 74-77.

[12] St. Irenaeus, *C. Haer.,* I. xxvi. 1; Hippolytus, *Ref. Haer.,* vii. 33.

[13] See note 29 in the concluding Notes.

[14] St. Ignatius, *Ad Smyr.,* 3. Cf. *Ad Eph.,* 20; *Ad Magn.,* 11; *Ad Trall.,* 9; *Ad Philad., init.,* 9; *Ad Smyr.,* 1, 2, 6, 7, 12.

[15] St. Polycarp, *Ad Phil,* I, 2, 9, 12.

[16] Aristides, *Apology (Texts and Studies,* I. i. 29, 37, 110).

[17] See Lightfoot, *Apostolic Fathers,* I. ii. 191-208.

[18] See note 30 in the concluding Notes.

[19] St. Justin Martyr, *Apol.,* i. 45; *Dial c. Tryph.,* 106-108.

[20] St. Irenaeus, *C. Haer.,* I. x. 1, 2. Cf. III. iv. 1; xix. 3.

[21] See, *e.g.,* Lumby, *History of the Creeds,* p. 188.

[22] 1 Cor. xv. 50.

[23] St. Irenaeus, *C. Haer.,* V. ix. 3.

[24] Tertullian, *De Resur. Carn.,* 50.

[25] See Church, *Cathedral and University Sermons,* pp. 147-150.

[26] St. Mark xvi. 19; St. Luke xxiv. 51; Acts i. 3-11.

[27] Heb. vii. 25.

[28] St. Luke i. 35; iii. 22; Acts ii. 33. See note 31 in the concluding Notes.

[29] Acts ii. 1-4, 33.

[30] St. John xvi. 7.

Chapter Nine - The Nature of the Church

The Christian Church is a visible society. Its earliest history is recorded in the Acts of the Apostles. It is there represented as a definite body consisting of baptized persons who continued in the fellowship of the Apostles and joined in hearing the word, receiving the Sacraments, and worshipping God. [1] This representation of the Church as a visible society fulfils the indications given by our Lord during His ministry. It was evidently His intention to call out from the world a body of men gathered round the Apostles. This intention is shown in the training given to the Apostles to fit them to be the nucleus of the future society. It is expressed in the promise to St. Peter that upon the rock of which our Lord speaks an ἐκκλησία, that is, a congregation called together, is to be built. [2] By instituting the Sacraments of Holy Baptism and the Holy Eucharist our Lord showed that the Church was to be known by outward tokens. Moreover, He expressly described His Church as a kingdom, especially in his parables; [3] and this appears to imply that it may be known by external marks.

There are similar indications that the Church is a visible society in the description given of it by St. Paul in his Epistles. In them he describes the Church as a body, [4] as a temple, [5] as containing good and bad members, [6] and as having a visible organization. [7]

The Church, then, is to be regarded as a visible society. As such, it has characteristics which are summed up in the enlarged form of the Nicene Creed 'One, Holy, Catholic, Apostolic.' These are known as the four marks or notes of the Church.

The Unity of the Church

In the New Testament the word Church is used in different senses. It denotes -

1. A congregation regarded as itself forming a Church. [8]

2. A number of congregations in one place regarded as forming the Church in that place. [9]

3. A united group in a city or country. [10]

4. These different bodies united together and together forming the one Church. [11]

Thus, the Church is regarded as one body. A separate congregation may be called the Church; but it is only so called because, for those of whom it consists, it is the representative of the whole body; and, strictly speaking, there is only one Church, namely, the Church which comprises the whole body. This aspect of the Church is found also in the Fathers. To quote one instance out of many, St. Leo, in describing the work of the Son of God, says, 'He it is who, having of the Holy Ghost been brought forth from a virgin mother, by the same inspiration makes fruitful His undefiled Church, so that by means of the baptismal child-bearing an innumerable multitude of children of God is produced, of whom it is said, "who were born, not of blood, nor of the will of the flesh, nor of the will of man, but of God." He it is in whom the seed of Abraham is blessed by the adoption of the whole world to sonship, and the patriarch becomes a father of nations, while the sons of promise are born by faith, not of flesh. He it is who, making no exception of any nation, forms out of every people under heaven one flock of holy sheep, and daily fulfils that which He promised when He said, "And other sheep I have which are not of this fold; them also I must bring, and they shall hear My voice; and there shall be one flock and one Shepherd."' [12]

The unity of the Church is generally defined as consisting in five points the worship of one God, the holding of one faith, the possession of one sacramental system, the looking for the realization of one hope, and the being animated by one Spirit.

These five points are collected from the teaching of St. Paul in his Epistles to the Ephesians and the Corinthians. [13] In each of them there is an ideal which ought to be aimed at, and there is a minimum which cannot be departed from without passing outside the unity of the Church. To take the second point as an example, the ideal is the holding in all fulness the complete body of the revealed faith, together with all the inferences which are rightly derived from it. The minimum is the holding such necessary truths as those without which the faith would not be. As a religious body ceases to possess that which is necessary, it ceases to be within the unity of the Church. As it approximates towards the ideal, it gains, so far as this matter is concerned, in strength at each approximation.

The unity thus far described is that known as objective unity. Objective unity is essential for the Church's life because it is the means whereby the Church is held in union with its Head, our Lord Jesus Christ. [14] Subjective unity is the external unity of inter-communion. Subjective unity is highly desirable. It existed in the early days of the Church. It is a means of much strength. It aids the development of life. Yet it is not essential to the being of the Church, because without it there can be that union with our Lord which makes essential unity. Thus, at the present time, the Roman, English, and Eastern portions of the Church, all possess objective unity. They all share in the essential unity of the Church, since they are in union with the one life of Christ, and are consequently inwardly united to one another. Each of them possesses subjective unity only to a limited extent, since each of them has it only with a part of the Church, instead of, as would be desirable, with the whole. It was well said by Bishop Alexander Forbes, 'Objective unity is that in wrought by our Head, Jesus Himself, through union with Himself. It is wrought on His side by the communication of the "one Spirit," and by the Sacraments, making us all one body in Him. It requires, on our part, continuity in the commission which He gave to His Apostles, and perseverance in the faith which He committed to the Church. Subjective unity is unity of will, and intercommunion with one another. Subjective unity may be suspended, while objective unity is maintained. Subjective unity was suspended during the schism at Antioch, yet objective unity is maintained, for the blessed Meletius is a saint. Subjective unity was suspended between the British and Western Churches in the Saxon times, yet nobody doubts of the salvation or sanctity of St. Aidan or St. Cuthbert. Subjective unity was suspended during the struggles of the antipopes, yet no one considers the followers of Peter de Luna as either heretics or schismatics. And this must also apply to the mighty dissension between the East and the West, and between ourselves and the rest of Christendom. It is deeply to be deplored that the state of the Church is as it is; but let us hope that the evil is not so great as it seems, and that there is a fund of unity, if men only understood each other; that the fissures are only surface ones; that the disorder is functional, not organic.' [15]

There are two theories of the unity of the Church which are, in one case fundamentally, in the other case to a considerable extent, opposed to what has been said here. The first of these theories is that the unity of the Church is wholly unseen, wholly independent of any thing material or external. According to this view, it consists simply in the union of heart and soul between those who are spiritually united to God, so that the union between believers and one another, and the union between believers and God are alike wholly spiritual. This theory has its attractive side because it emphasizes the value of the spiritual relations of the soul, and marks the need of the soul being in a state of friendship with God. But it fails to allow for counter-balancing truths, and is altogether inconsistent with considerations of great weight. Thus, Holy Scripture teaches, as has been seen, that the Church is a visible society, with its unity marked by the common possession of external means of grace, the Sacraments. The historical conception of the Church is that of a body for whose life the possession of valid Sacraments is necessary, so that any who are outside the sacramental working of God are outside the unity of the Church. It is one of the consequences of the resurrection and ascension of our Lord that a characteristic of the dealings of God with souls under the Christian dispensation is that the channel of covenanted grace between God and man is the glorified humanity of the risen and ascended Christ.

This theory, then, while it is at first sight attractive, will not bear to be brought to the test of Holy Scripture and the facts of the history of the Church.

The second of the two theories referred to is that of the Church of Rome. There is no difference between this view and all which is positive in the doctrine which has been stated here. It lays down the necessity of the five points which have been mentioned. But it adds to them another point, the necessity of unity of external organization, which includes intercommunion of all the parts with one another; and it asserts that for this there must be external communion with the Bishop of Rome, who is the one head on earth of the one Church. This theory, again, has an attractive side. It carries out in the most complete and logical way the idea of the Church as a visible society. It emphasizes to a peculiar extent the Scriptural aspect of the Church as a kingdom. It possesses great definiteness, and gives great practical strength. But it fails to make out positions which are essential to it in the following ways: -

1. There is nothing in Holy Scripture to support an opinion that communion with the See of Rome is necessary for the lawful and beneficial use of the covenanted means of salvation. Scripture nowhere asserts or implies that the rule of one head on earth is of the essence of the unity of the Church. On the contrary, Scripture implies that the Head who completes the body is our Lord in His glorified humanity, who by virtue of the reality of His humanity is a Head in the same order of thought and life as the Church is a body; and that, since the visible Church on earth is only a part of the Church, which includes the departed as well as the living, it is not necessary that the part of

the Church which is on earth should possess such a head as this theory demands. It is illogical to say that, because there cannot be a body without a head, therefore there cannot be a part of a body without a head. Western theology has, as a rule, failed to give sufficient emphasis to the truth that the living form part only of the mystical body of Christ, the Church.

2. In the undivided Church communion with the See of Rome was not regarded as a necessity for being within the unity of the Church. The primacy which the See of Rome unquestionably possessed was not of such a kind as to be a necessary centre of unity, and to make all those outwardly separated from it consequently outside the unity of the Church. [16]

Thus the Roman theory of the unity of the Church, so far as it goes beyond the doctrine which has been stated already, cannot be maintained. It is true that an ideal condition of the Church would include external intercommunion of all the different parts with one another, and that this would carry with it external inter communion of all the parts with the Bishop of Borne, who would naturally, under such circumstances, fill the place of the Primate of Christendom; but there are solid reasons for saying that this ideal condition is not the necessary unity which is a note of the Church, and that a particular religious body no more ceases to be part of the Church because it is externally separated from the See of Rome, than a part of the Anglican Communion, for example the Church in South Africa, would cease to be within the unity of the Church if it was separated from the See of Canterbury.

The Holiness of the Church

The Church is holy because its doctrines, laws, and Sacraments are holy, and because its aim is to make men holy. As in the case of unity, so in the case of holiness, it is necessary to distinguish that which is objective from that which is subjective. Objective holiness is the holiness of the Church's system. Subjective holiness is the holiness of the lives of individual members of the Church. Subjective holiness is to be desired; in the ideal condition of the Church it would be complete; but objective holiness can remain when subjective holiness is impaired.

The objective holiness of the Church is not destroyed by the existence of bad members within the Church. This was taught by our Lord in the parables of the tares, and the good and bad fish in the net. [17] In those parables our Lord was depicting the kingdom of heaven, that is, the Church; and He described the continuance of good and evil within it until the day of judgment. 'Let both grow together until the harvest: and in the time of the harvest I will say to the reapers, Gather up first the tares, and bind them in bundles to burn them: but gather the wheat into My barn.' [18] Yet, while He thus foretold that good and bad should be together within the kingdom, He promised also that the gates of hades should not prevail against the Church. [19] The same truth is implied in St. Paul's practice of addressing the whole Christian body in any particular place as holy persons, while at the same time recognizing the existence of sinners among Christians in that place. For instance, in the First Epistle to the Corinthians he salutes the Christian society to which he writes as saints, or those that are holy, and afterwards goes on to speak of many and grievous sins committed by some among them. [20] Similarly, writers of later times speak of the Christian society as being holy while they condemn the sins of many within it. To borrow an illustration from Bishop Alexander Forbes, a University which possesses and promotes learning may be said to be learned even if many of its members are unlearned. [21]

The Catholicity of the Church

The word Catholic, as applied to the Church, was used from, at any rate, the beginning of the second century to convey two ideas, that of universality, and that of communion with the Bishops in the true Church. In expansion of these two ideas, St. Cyril of Jerusalem described the Catholicity of the Church as consisting in five points, namely, that
1. The Church is the Church for the whole world.
2. It teaches the whole truth.
3. It is the ruler of all classes of men.
4. It treats and heals all kinds of sins of body and soul.
5. It possesses all forms of virtue. [22]
The essential Catholicity of the Church lies in the power to do and be all this. There may be parts of the world where for the time being the Church is not, or classes of men which for the time being she does not reach, or particular doctrines which for a time are left untaught; and yet the Church may remain essentially Catholic. Here, again, there is an ideal to which greater or less approximation may be made at different times; and there is a minimum below which a religious body could not sink without ceasing to be a part of the Catholic Church. It is of the ideal that the Church should include every nation and tribe, that it should reach all classes of whatever kind, that it should present the whole truth in the fullest and clearest way, and that its practical machinery should be in the most efficient condition for the promotion of every virtue and the extirpation of every vice. The minimum would be lost if there were anything which of necessity made it impossible to reach all nations, or tribes, or classes, or to promote virtues and extirpate vices among them, or if there should be any thing which of necessity was contradictory of the truth in a central and vital point. These form the ideal at which the Church has to aim, and the minimum which she must not lose. Between attaining the ideal and losing the minimum, there are all kinds of differing stages in which Catholicity really exists, and is more or less completely realized and manifested.

The Apostolicity of the Church

The meaning of the word Apostolic as applied to the Church is that the Church has mission, that is, it is authoritatively sent. Mission was given by our Lord to the Apostles. 'As My Father hath sent Me, even so send I you.' [23] The Apostles gave it to those whom they ordained. The Pastoral Epistles show a regularly organized method of handing on the apostolical succession. [24] St. Paul elsewhere represents the Church as an apostolic household. [25] The Church is Apostolic because she has a ministry validly ordained by means of an episcopal succession from the Apostles.

The necessity of mission, including the necessity of episcopal succession from the Apostles, is part of the historical teaching of the Church. It is the common doctrine of the early writers of the Church that there are distinctively Christian gifts which are to be found where there is an episcopal ministry, descended from the Apostles. It is not said that these gifts may be obtained elsewhere; and it is, in some cases, implied that they will not. This teaching is found both in simple assertions of the truth in instructing those within the Church and in statements of controversy with heretical and schismatical bodies. To give one instance, St. Ignatius at the beginning of the second century wrote, 'As many as are of God and of Jesus Christ, they are with the bishop; and as many as shall repent and enter into the unity of the Church, these also shall be of God, that they may be living after Jesus Christ. Be not deceived, my brethren. If any man followeth one that maketh a schism, he doth not inherit the kingdom of God. If any man walketh in strange doctrine, he hath no fellowship with the passion. Be ye careful, therefore, to observe one Eucharist (for there is one flesh of our Lord Jesus Christ, and one cup unto union in His blood; there is one altar, as there is one bishop, together with the presbytery and the deacons my fellow-servants), that whatsoever ye do, ye may do it after God.' [26] Moreover, the offices for ordination, which represent at any rate the general lines of the Church's methods from the earliest times, imply the existence of and the necessity for an episcopal succession from the Apostles. [27]

In the matter of Apostolicity the ideal is the complete organization of the ministry of the Church; the mini mum is episcopal ordination.

According to the Roman view of the Church, Apostolicity requires communion with Rome in addition to what has been specified already. On this subject, two opinions have been held by Roman theologians. According to the first, all jurisdiction comes to the bishops through the Pope, the successor of St. Peter and necessary channel of this gift. This opinion has at various times been taught in Roman theology. At present it is not held by the large majority of Roman theologians. According to the other opinion, which is now the most usual in Roman theology, the bishops have mission and jurisdiction which is inherent in their office and in their sees, and they receive this from our Lord; but, since the episcopate forms one body with the Pope, there is no power of exercising this mission and jurisdiction, which they possess by divine right and receive from Christ, unless they are in communion with the Pope. Either form of this theory fails to establish the crucial point, namely, that St. Peter possessed powers which were different in kind from those of the other Apostles; and the first form of it, which is illogical unless the powers of the Apostles were given to them through St. Peter, is inconsistent with passages in the Gospels, the appointment of St. Matthias, and the appointment of St. Paul. [28] The theory in general is not in accordance with the patristic view of the Church. Representative Church writers speak of communion with the episcopate handed down from the Apostles as a condition of Apostolicity. They do not so speak of communion with Rome. To a certain extent St. Leo, who was Bishop of Rome in the fifth century, is an exception, St. Leo looked upon himself as being in a special sense the successor of St. Peter. He regarded the power given to St. Peter and inherited by himself as differing from that of the other Apostles. His teaching is not entirely free from inconsistency. Besides this view of St. Peter's position, he says also that St. Peter and St. Paul were the seeds of the Church at Rome and the twin eye of the body of Christ. It is not clear that he would himself have pushed his view of the powers of St. Peter and his own inheritance of them so far as to expressly assert that to be out of communion with the Bishop of Rome is to be separated from the lawful and beneficial use of the covenanted means of union with the life of Christ. At the same time, the modern Roman position would be no more than the developed logical inference from what St. Leo does say, since he taught that St. Peter was the channel to the other Apostles of the apostolic powers, and that his successor, the Bishop of Rome, is similarly the channel to the Church. 1 But there is nothing to show that in what St. Leo thus said he was more than an individual teacher; and there is much evidence that the line he took formed an early point in a claim which was inconsistent with the ordinary and authorized teaching of the Church. This evidence includes the absence of teaching like St. Leo's in representative writers generally; the presence in such writers of teaching inconsistent with it; and the resistance to the authority of St. Leo when he tried to enforce some of his claims in Gaul.

The general stream of patristic teaching represents the test of Apostolicity as communion with the historical episcopate. This may be especially noticed in the teaching of St. Augustine. The long and elaborate series of works which he wrote against the Donatists contains the fullest ancient teaching which we possess about the nature of the Church. In these works the appeal always is, not to any one see, but to what he calls the 'orbis terrarum,' that is, the whole Church, marked out by the possession of the historical episcopate.

The inferences which may be drawn from the writings of the Fathers generally are strongly supported by historical facts. In the troubled times and external divisions of the fourth and fifth centuries there were Easterns and Gallicans who lived and died out of communion with the See of Rome who are now recognized saints of the Church. [30]

From an entirely different point of view it has been contended that the Church is an invisible body, and that therefore nothing external is necessary; or that, while the Church is a visible society, yet episcopacy is not necessary to the true life of the Church, and that a religious body is apostolic so far as it reproduces the spirit of the Apostles, not because of anything external. Behind this theory lie's what is good and true, the recognition of the obligation on individuals to correspond with the life which the Apostles learned from Christ; but it is marked by a confusion between what makes an individual a good man and what makes a religious body the Church, two questions which, though connected, are distinct from one another. This theory has nothing to support it in Holy Scripture; it is inconsistent with the uniform teaching of historical Christianity; and it explains the word Apostolic in the Creed in a different sense from that in which it was ordinarily used in the early Church. [31]

The assertion of the necessity of episcopacy raises the question of the relation to the Church of Christians who are baptized but outside the communion of any religious body which possesses an apostolic ministry, as, for example, the great majority of English dissenters. In one sense they cannot be said to be within the Church because they are separated from the apostolic ministry, while at the same time they have received the Sacrament of Baptism, which joins them to the sacred humanity of Christ and brings them within the Christian operations of the Holy Ghost. All that can be said is that the position of religious bodies which retain Holy Baptism and are without an apostolic ministry is an altogether abnormal one; and that the persons who belong to them have been placed within the Church by their Baptism, but by remaining separated from the apostolic ministry fail to receive the full and proper life of covenanted grace. A schismatic religious body which has retained Christian Baptism is separate,' says St. Augustine, from the bond of charity and peace but joined in the one Baptism. And so there is one Church which alone is called Catholic; and whatever of her own she has in communions of others separated from her unity, by virtue of this which she has in them of her own, it is she herself who in fact gives birth, not they. [32] Yet those thus born, he says in many places, need to be reconciled to the Catholic Church, that they may obtain from their real mother in their true home the profit of their sonship. [33]

[1] Acts ii. 41, 42, 46, 47.
[2] St. John xv. 16-19; xvii. 6-21; St. Matt. xvi. 18.
[3] See, *e.g.*, St. Matt. xiii. 24-50.
[4] 1 Cor. xii. 12-28; Eph. i. 23.
[5] Eph. ii. 19-22.
[6] 1 Cor., *passim*.
[7] Eph. iv. 11, 12.
[8] *E.g.*, 1 Cor. xiv. 34; xvi. 19.
[9] *E.g.*, Acts viii. 1; 1 Cor. i. 2.
[10] *E.g.*, Rom. xvi. 4.
[11] *E.g.*, I Cor. xii. 28; xv. 9. For other references for each of these senses of the word, see note 32 in the concluding Notes.
[12] St. Leo, *Serm.*, lxiii. 6. See also note 33 in the concluding Notes.
[13] Eph. iv. 4, 5; 1 Cor. x. 17; xii. 13-27.
[14] 1 Cor. xi. 3; Eph. v. 23; Col. i. 18.
[15] Forbes, *A Short Explanation of the Nicene Creed*, pp. 276, 277. Cf. Pusey, *Eirenicon,* part i. pp. 45-66.
[16] See *Church Quarterly Review,* January, 1897, pp. 289-317.
[17] St. Matt. xiii. 24-30, 37-43, 47-50.
[18] St. Matt. xiii. 30.

[19] St. Matt. xvi. 18.

[20] Cf. 1 Cor. i. 1-2 with, *e.g.*, v.-vi.

[21] Forbes, *A Short Explanation of the Nicene Creed,* pp. 278-279.

[22] St. Cyril of Jerusalem, *Cat.,* xviii. 23. See also note 34 in the concluding Notes.

[23] St. John xx. 21.

[24] 1 St. Tim. iii. 1-12; iv. 14; v. 22; 2 St. Tim. i. 6; St. Tit. i. 5.

[25] Eph. ii. 19, 20.

[26] St. Ignatius, *Ad Phil.,* 3, 4. See also note 35 in the concluding Notes.

[27] See Gore, *The Church and the Ministry,* pp. 144-152, 177-181, 363-370 (in fourth edition, pp. 131-140, 163-166, 331-337).

[28] *E.g.,* St. Matt. x. 1-5; St. John xx. 21-23; Acts i. 15-26; Gal. i. 1.

[29] For St. Leo's belief about St. Peter and the See of Rome, see *Serm.,* iv. 2; v. 5; Ep., x. 1. Contrast *Serm.,* lxxxii. 6, 7. For the further development of his idea by St. Gregory the Great, see Church, *Miscellaneous Essays,* pp. 253-257. For a passage in St. Jerome, see note 36 in the concluding Notes.

[30] See Puller, *The Primitive Saints and the See of Rome.*

[31] See note 37 in the concluding Notes.

[32] St. Augustine, *De Bapt. c. Don.,* i. 14. See also Benson, *Cyprian, his life, his times, his work,* p. 420.

[33] See, *e.g.,* *De Bapt. c. Don.,* vii. 103.

Chapter Ten - The Teaching Office of the Church

The work of the Church is twofold. It corresponds, in this respect, to the work of our Lord. 'Grace and truth,' says St. John, 'came by Jesus Christ.' [1] The Church, as His mystical body and His organ in the world, is the teacher of truth and the storehouse of grace. The subject of this chapter is the first part of this work, the office of the Church as the teacher of truth.

It was part of the promise of our Lord that the Holy Ghost would teach the Apostles all things and guide them into all the truth; that the Holy Ghost would be with the Apostles for ever, that is, He would always be with them and their successors; and that the gates of hades should not prevail against His Church. In accordance with this promise St. Paul speaks of the Church as 'the pillar and ground of the truth.' [2]

The Church teaches the truth in the following ways:

1. As the giver and keeper of Holy Scripture.

2. By means of Oecumenical Councils.

3. By necessary inferences from universal worship.

4. By the common teaching of representative writers.

The Church as the Giver and Keeper of Holy Scripture

In the earliest days of Christianity the Church taught by word of mouth what Christ had committed to the Apostles before His ascension, and what the Holy Ghost revealed to them afterwards. In this primitive teaching the books of the Old Testament were regarded and used as the word of God. This may be seen in the sermons in the Acts, which represent the teaching of the Apostles in its earliest form. [3] As the time grew longer since the life of our Lord upon earth, and as the special needs of Christians became more marked, the teaching of the Apostles about the life of our Lord and about the faith was committed to writing in the books of the New Testament, which, as well as the Old Testament, were regarded and used as the word of God. Thus, the primitive Church accepted as divine truth the Old Testament which had been received from the Jews and the New Testament which the Christian Church herself had formed. It was believed that Holy Scripture was divinely true because it was written under the guidance of God the Holy Ghost.

It has, then, to be considered what the Church meant in regarding Holy Scripture as divine truth; in other words, what is meant by Inspiration.

Inspiration

No definite detailed theory about inspiration has been laid down by the Church in any councils, or expressly formulated by teachers who, when taken together, represent the mind of the Church. This absence of a definite and detailed theory has not hindered the existence among Christians of the most intense conviction that Holy Scripture is the word of God. St. Paul's belief about the Old Testament is shown both by his habitual use of it as a divine work, and by a passage in his Second Epistle to St. Timothy. He continually refers to and uses it in a manner which can only be justified by the belief that in it God has spoken. In the passage written to St. Timothy he either asserts or implies that the Old Testament is inspired by God. [4] In his Second Epistle, St. Peter, also referring to the Old Testament, writes, 'No prophecy ever came by the will of man: but men spake from God, being moved by the Holy Ghost.' [5]

After the formation of the New Testament, Christian writers generally regard both the Old and New Testaments in the same way as St. Paul and St. Peter speak of the Old Testament, as being inspired of God, the work of 'men' who 'spake from God, being moved by the Holy Ghost.' That they do so is shown by the language in which they speak of Holy Scripture, and by the use to which they put it. Fathers of widely differing characters, writing in different places and under different circumstances, agree in describing Holy Scripture as the work of God. St. Clement of Rome calls the prophets 'the ministers of the grace of God through the Holy Ghost;' he quotes the Old Testament with the words, 'the Holy Ghost saith;' he speaks of the Apostles as 'assured by the word of God, having the fulness of the Holy Ghost.' [6] St. Ignatius refers to the prophets as those into whom the grace of Christ breathed. [7] The prophets, says St. Justin Martyr, were 'filled with the Holy Ghost.' [8] Later writers speak no less emphatically. Thinkers so different as Clement of Alexandria [9] and Origen [10] on the one side, and St. Cyprian [11] and St. Augustine [12] on the other, refer to the Scriptures as the utterances of the Holy

Ghost. St. Cyril of Jerusalem, in an instructive phrase, mentions 'the Holy Ghost who spake in the prophets and came down upon the Apostles on the day of Pentecost.' [13] In the Creed of the Universal Church it is affirmed that the Holy Ghost spake through the prophets. [14] A phrase used in Gaul at the beginning of the sixth century, which may have been derived from an expression of St. Augustine, [15] asserted that God is the 'author of the Old and New Testaments,' and passed into the ordinary language of the Church. [16]

The use made of the Holy Scriptures by the Fathers corresponded to the ways in which they spoke of them. They universally appealed to the Bible as a book with an origin and a meaning higher than human. To their minds it had a signification deeper than any on the surface. Its teaching finally decided truth and duty.

By taking into consideration Holy Scripture itself, the teaching of the writers of the Church, and the use which they made of the Bible, it is possible to form some idea of the work of God the Holy Ghost in the inspiration of Holy Scripture. He guided the writers of the different books so that they were led to undertake the task of writing. In many cases this divine guidance appears to have used circumstances of life which showed a present need. The state of affairs at Corinth made known to St. Paul the necessity for his First Epistle to Christians at that place. The false teaching of the Judaizers and the revolt against his authority in Galatia showed the same Apostle the necessity for his Epistle to the Galatians. The need of exhortation to contend earnestly for the faith led St. Jude to write an epistle on that subject rather than on the subject previously in his mind. [17] On the other hand, Isaiah, Ezekiel, and St. John were given their work by a revelation of a very different kind. [18]

There are signs that the Holy Ghost allowed the writers of the books to use the knowledge which they naturally possessed; and that, if He aided their faculties and their memory, He did not interfere with their in dividual characters. His work in them did not free them from the necessity of taking pains. They used the documents mentioned in many parts of the Old Testament. [19] It is probable that St. Matthew and St. Luke took the genealogies of our Lord [20] from historical records. St. Luke expressly refers to the testimony of eye-witnesses. [21] Jeremiah and St. John appear to have recalled what they themselves had seen and experienced. [22] And the wide differences of language and style found among the sacred writers show that their natural temperaments were used and not destroyed. [23]

Yet, the way in which the Old Testament is regarded in the New Testament, and both Old and New Testaments are spoken of and used in the Christian Church, makes it plain that God the Holy Ghost, in allowing a true human service, imparted to the writers of the books much which, apart from this divine operation, they could not have possessed. To justify the language and the practice of the New Testament and the Fathers, and the historical teaching of the Christian Church, it is necessary to assert that the Holy Ghost filled the writers of the books with knowledge of truth about God and His dealings with men which transcended merely human thought, so that their declarations of the will of God, their prophecies of future events, and their doctrinal statements were necessarily true. The method of expression, as has been said, was largely left to the individuality of different writers. It was necessarily affected by the finite character of human language. The written book appears, as a rule, to have been the writer's expression of what he himself had been taught. Since God teaches gradually, the later teaching was fuller than the earlier. But, the whole result, besides being the acceptance and use of human faculties, was the divine work of the Holy Ghost, so that the progress in it was not from what is false to what is true, but from less complete to more perfect knowledge. To what extent the sacred writers were left to their natural know ledge in recording what was known to them by their natural senses, and how far they were under the guidance of the inspiration of God in describing such matters as the length of a king's reign, or the place where an event happened, can be ascertained only as the result of knowledge of the purposes of the Bible and of the exact details of the historical facts which it records. To suppose that every word in the original writings was directly controlled by the Holy Ghost, so that the writers were in every detail the merely mechanical instruments through which the Holy Ghost worked, is nowhere asserted or implied in Holy Scripture; has never been taught by the Church; and appears to be contrary to the inferences which may naturally be drawn from the reference to research at the beginning of St. Luke's Gospel, the use of existing documents, and the very great diversities of style in the different books. On the other hand, to suppose that the Bible is full of mythical legends and distorted history is to approach a method of thought as far as possible removed from the mind of the Catholic Church, and as contrary to the historical position of Holy Scripture as it is to sober criticism.

Attention has often been drawn to the analogy between the written word of God in the Bible and the incarnate Word. Holy Scripture resembles the life of our Lord. It is human. It is divine. The two elements are so united that the teaching of the completed book is divine teaching. There is this difference between them: In our Lord the humanity is personally united to God the Word, so that there is only one Person, and that Person is divine, and by reason of the personal union every word and act spoken and done in the man hood are free from mistake. In the written word there is no such personal union; but that which is human is used by God as an instrument which remains outside His own Person. Whatever closeness of mystical union there is between the writers and Himself, this consideration suggests a possibility of the inspired writers being left to their own natural knowledge of certain details, while such a view of the working of God in them as is here supposed would be inconsistent with their recording mere myth or fiction in such a way as to represent it as fact.

It has been the general teaching of Christian theologians that Holy Scripture contains explicitly or implicitly the whole faith. Explicit teaching is that which is distinctly stated. Implicit teaching is that which may be deduced by inference from what is said or by comparison of different parts with one another. For instance, it is explicitly taught that God is One, because that truth is expressly affirmed; [24] it is implicitly taught that the Holy Ghost is a Person, because that truth may be deduced by inference from what is said about Him. [25] Some truths are taught explicitly in some parts of the Bible, and implicitly in other parts. The God head of our Lord is taught explicitly when it is said, The Word was God, The Word became flesh. [26] It is taught implicitly in references to Him and statements about Him which cannot be explained except on the fact of His Godhead. [27] The doctrine of His manhood is taught explicitly in the words of St. Paul, the man Jesus Christ; [28] implicitly in passages which imply His humanity. [29] A complete doctrine is generally taught partly explicitly, partly implicitly. For instance, some parts of the doctrine of the Holy Trinity are definitely stated; other parts of it are deduced from inferences; the whole is gained by the comparison and co-ordination of many statements and inferences.

Since Holy Scripture contains the truth, it has to be asked what is meant by Holy Scripture. On this point there is no authoritative formal decision of the whole Church; but it may be truly said that the whole Church eventually, without any doubt, accepted as the revealed word of God the New Testament, and all the proto-canonical books of the Old Testament. Some of these books were always unquestioned. Others of them, as Esther and the Revelation, were for a long time subjected to doubt. The eventual universal admission of them all is clear. The relation of the deutero-canonical books, which are sometimes called the Apocrypha, to the proto-canonical books presents a most difficult problem, the adequate consideration of which falls outside the scope of the present work. But it may be said that representative Christian writers of the early Church recognized these books as of high value; that they frequently refer to both classes of books without making any clear distinction between their authority; but that the whole Church has not certainly received them as the revealed word of God. In the early Church, St. Augustine and St. Jerome took different views on this subject. St. Jerome limited the revealed word to the proto-canonical books; St. Augustine extended it to the deuterocanonical books. At the present time, different positions have been taken up in different parts of the Church; and it does not appear that the authorized formularies of any part were drawn up after real consideration of this very complex question. [30]

The first part of the teaching office of the Church may, then, be said to be: The Church teaches the truth in giving Holy Scripture as an infallible exponent of Christian faith; and the books which unquestionably have been universally recognized as this infallible exponent are the books of the New Testament and the proto-canonical books of the Old Testament.

Oecumenical Councils

The second part of the teaching office of the Church is accomplished by means of Oecumenical Councils. The declarations of an Oecumenical Council are the declarations of the Church herself. This may be seen to follow from the definition of an Oecumenical Council and the distinction between a council which is Oecumenical and one which is merely general. A merely general council is a council which in its constitution is representative of the whole Church. An Oecumenical Council is one which is accepted by the whole Church as representing her position. A merely general council may affirm what is untrue, because it is possible for its decisions to fail to be in accordance with the real and permanent mind of the Church of which in its constitution it is representative. Such a failure may be compared with the way in which a secular representative body may in its constitution be completely representative of the country which elects it, and may at the same time in action which it takes fail to be representative of the mind and wishes of the country. To give instances, the Councils of Ariminum and Seleucia in A.D. 359 were convoked to form a general council, and, taken together, they practically were so. They adopted a compromising position on the vital question of the deity of our Lord, a position which the Church after wards rejected. What is known as the Robber Council of Ephesus in A.D. 449 was formally convoked as a general council. It affirmed the Eutyckian heresy. Thus, while it may, as an ordinary rule, be anticipated that a council which is universal in its constitution will affirm the real mind of the body which it represents and by subsequent general acceptance pass into being also an Oecumenical Council, it is by no means certain that this will be the case. Consequently, a general council may fail to be Oecumenical and may affirm what is untrue. On the other hand, a council which is not general may come to be Oecumenical because of the subsequent acceptance of its decisions. The Council of Constantinople in A.D. 381 was convoked from the East only, and no Western Bishop was present at its meetings. Its doctrinal teaching was universally received as the true expression of the belief of the Church, and the Council has been reckoned Oecumenical because of this subsequent acceptance. When the proper definition is thus kept in view, it is obvious that the teaching of an Oecumenical Council is the teaching of the Church herself. [31]

Inferences from Worship

In the third place, the Church teaches the truth by what is necessarily implied in worship which is universally commanded or allowed. What is done in the permanent worship of the whole body is the act of the body itself, as what is taught in a council permanently accepted by the whole body is the teaching of the body itself. For example, if the worship of the whole Church ascribes to our Lord adoration which on the part of those who ascribe it is recognized as being lawfully offered only to God, such worship shows that the Church herself recognizes Christ as God no less clearly than the affirmation of His Godhead in the Creed.

Common Teaching of Representative Writers

Fourthly, the Church teaches the truth by means of representative writers. The uniform teaching of different theologians, when it extends over a sufficient period of time and is not protested against, comes to be the accepted teaching of the whole body. The existence of such a consensus is often difficult to ascertain. It is always open to investigation by comparison with teaching on similar subjects at different times. When it can be definitely ascertained, it cannot be regarded as less the voice of the Church than an accepted council; for to permanently acquiesce in the universal teaching of error within her pale would seem to be such a failure on the part of the Church as our Lord said she should be protected against. The universally allowed teaching of theologians cannot have the same obligatory character as the plain statements of Holy Scripture, or the definite decisions of accepted councils, because the Church by leaving it without more formal ratification has abstained from saying that it is to be held under pain of anathema. Nevertheless, such teaching, although the acceptance of it has not been made a term of Communion, has a strong claim on the willing belief of those who wish to be faithful to the teaching of the Church.

In each of these four ways the Church is the divinely appointed teacher. It is a necessary inference that the teaching given by one method cannot be in conflict with that which is given by another method; and that, supposing one part of the teaching should appear to contradict another part, there must be some mistake or misinterpretation about one or the other. The different ways of the Church's teaching are regarded by ancient writers as the drawing out and expression of that which is contained in Holy Scripture. For instance, St. Vincent of Lerins, in a passage which is representative of much in the early Church, says, 'Often inquiring with great zeal and the greatest attention from very many men eminent for piety and doctrine in what way I could by some fixed and as it were general and regular way distinguish the reality of the Catholic faith from the falsity of heretical wickedness, I almost always received an answer of this kind from all, that if I or anybody else should want to detect the craft of rising heretics, and to avoid their snares, and to remain whole and unharmed in the sound faith, one ought, with the help of God, to fortify one's faith in two ways, first, that is, by the authority of the divine law, and, secondly, by the tradition of the Catholic Church. Here perhaps some one may ask: Since the Canon of Scripture is complete and is in itself sufficient and more than sufficient for every purpose, what need is there that the authority of the mind of the Church should be joined to it? The reason is that because of the very depth of Holy Scripture all do not understand it in one and the same way, but different persons place different interpretations upon its statements, so that almost as many opinions appear to be derived from

Scripture as there are men...And therefore, because of so great windings of such varied error, it is very necessary that the method of interpretation of the Apostles and Prophets be governed by the rule of the mind of the Catholic Church. Again, within the Catholic Church herself, the greatest care must be taken that we hold that which has been believed everywhere, always, and by all. For this is truly and properly Catholic, as the very force and effect of the word declares, which includes all things with practical universality. But this will be found precisely in this way, if we follow that which is universal, that which is ancient, that about which there is consent. Now, we shall follow that which is universal if we confess that the one true faith is that which the whole Church throughout the world confesses; we shall follow that which is ancient if we do not depart at all from those ideas which it is clearly shown our holy ancestors and fathers proclaimed; and we shall follow that about which there is consent if we hold fast to the definitions and judgments within antiquity itself of all, or at any rate almost all, priests and teachers alike.' [32]

This statement by St. Vincent of Lerins, that the truth is that which has been taught everywhere, always, and by all within the pale of the Church, raises the question whether there is any sense, and, if so, what is the sense, in which the development of true doctrine is possible.

Development of Doctrine

The word development may be used with more meanings than one. It may denote expansion of expression or expansion of belief. It is clear that there can rightly be development which merely expands the expression of truth, because of changes in the use of language and in the needs which language has to meet. For example, in the earliest days of Christianity it was sufficient to say simply that our Lord is God. At a later time, when quibbling interpretations were applied to the word God, it became necessary that the same truth should be expressed by saying, He is of one essence with the Father. This is an instance of the need for expansion of expression arising from changed circumstances. An instance of a similar need arising from change in the use of language is with regard to the word ὑπόστασις. At the first, this word meant essence: later, it meant person. Obviously, it was as necessary with the later use to say, There are three ὑποστάσεις, that is, three Persons in the Godhead, as it would have been heretical to say with the older use of the word, There are three ὑποστάσεις, that is, three Essences of the Godhead. When there is such a change in either circumstances or language itself, the change or expansion of the expression of the truth is simply the re-assertion of the same doctrine in the ways which are necessary if it is to be preserved.

In its other meaning, the word development is used to denote expansion, not only of expression but also of belief. Such a case occurs when inferences which have not always been expressed but are true deductions from what has always been held are expressly affirmed. Such affirmation is the result of the ordinary processes of thought under the guidance of the Holy Ghost. An individual, if his mind is in a healthy state, gradually gains clearer knowledge of the meaning and consequences of truth which he knows. Similarly, the healthy action of the mind of the Church gradually and increasingly apprehends the full force and bearing of truth which has been revealed once for all. A useful statement on this subject is in the treatise of St. Vincent of Lerins, from which a quotation has already been made. St. Vincent supposes that what he, in the passage already quoted, has laid down, might be questioned on the ground that progress ought not to be lacking in religion. He answers by saying, 'As in the case of individuals, so in the case of the whole Church, at the different stages of life and age, there must be great and vehement progress in understanding, in know ledge, in wisdom.' [33] In addition to this, he lays down the methods and limits of progress, saying, 'It must be truly a progress of the faith, not an alteration; since, indeed, it is progress if a thing grows in itself; but it is alteration if something be changed from one thing to another,' [34] This line of thought may be expressed by saying that there can rightly be development, if it is expansion which does not assert or imply anything contrary to the truth which has once been revealed, but harmoniously unfolds its true consequences. It was natural that in the earliest days of Christianity many theological questions did not present themselves. Some of these questions, when subsequently raised, touch what is vital in central truth; and an answer is imperatively needed. Others concern matters of belief and practice of greater or less importance: and an answer is in varying degrees desirable. When in such a case there are only two possible alternatives by way of answer, and one of them contradicts the original belief, the maintenance of the original belief requires the rejection of that which contradicts it, and consequently the affirmation of the other alternative. For example, it is probable that the question whether there was in our Lord an independent centre of human personality was never raised in the first century. At a later time, it had to be considered. It was seen that, if it was said He had an independent centre of human personality, the unity of His life and work, to which the Church had been committed from the first, would be rejected, and the scriptural methods of speech about Him could not be defended. Consequently, the assertion of the other alternative, that He had not an independent centre of human personality, was a necessity if the original faith was to be maintained. In such cases, development rightly takes the form of asserting what is true for the reason that, apart from such assertion, what is untrue must be admitted. Inferences of this kind in the progress of the exposition of revealed truth are, if ratified by the acceptance of the whole Christian body, part of that action of the Church under the guidance of God the Holy Ghost which may look for the fulfilment of the promises of our Lord. It is for the whole Church, not an individual Christian or a local Church, to decide whether any particular expansion is a true development or a corruption.

Rejection of the Authority of the Church

The belief as to the teaching office of the Church here given has been denied by some of those who assert the authority of Holy Scripture; and, according to them, the decisions of the Church, however universally and permanently accepted, have no real and binding claim. This rejection of the authority of the Church is in conflict with the history of the composition and acceptance of the Gospels and the New Testament generally, since these books were not the source of the Church, but the outcome of the Church's life; and it is opposed to the statements of our Lord about the work of the Holy Ghost and the office of the Church. It came into prominence chiefly in reaction from an excessive stress laid on the authority of the Church in the middle ages. During the last three hundred and fifty years it has been of great influence. Of late, its influence has become much less, partly because of a revival of know ledge about the history and doctrine of the Church and partly because critical investigations have made it increasingly difficult to accept the authority of the Bible without accepting also the authority of the Church.

Papal Infallibility

It is the doctrine of the Church of Rome, not only that the whole Church is divinely guided in accordance with the promises of our Lord, but also that the *ex cathedrâ* utterances of the Bishops of Rome on matters of faith and morals are in themselves infallible. This doctrine has been practically held for some centuries by a majority of theologians in communion with Rome. It was expressly asserted by the Vatican Council of 1870. The definition then given was as follows: 'The Bishop of Rome, when he speaks *ex cathedrâ,* that is, when performing the office of shepherd and teacher of all Christians in virtue of his own supreme apostolic authority, he defines the doctrine that is to be held by the whole Church in faith and morals, by means of the divine assistance which was promised to him in blessed Peter, possesses that infallibility where with the divine Redeemer willed His Church to be endowed in defining doctrine about faith and morals; and therefore such definitions of the Bishop of Rome are unchangeable truth of themselves, not from the consent of the Church.' [35]

In this definition it was evidently intended to avoid committing the council to an extreme opinion of the infallibility of all Papal utterances. The infallibility was restricted to *ex cathedrâ* declarations and to matters of faith and morals. On the other hand, it was intended to commit the council to a condemnation of the Gallican view that the decisions of the Pope are not necessarily infallible unless they are ratified by the Church. For this reason the words of themselves, not from the consent of the Church were inserted in the decree. A suggestion has been made that these words only deny the necessity of subsequent consent. If this were so, the decree would not be inconsistent with a view that the infallibility does not exist unless the Pope is ratifying that to which the whole Church is already committed. It may well be hoped that this interpretation of the decree may eventually come to be accepted by Roman theologians; but there can be little doubt from the proceedings of the council that it was not worded with the intention of expressing such a view. [36]

Taking, then, the ordinary interpretation of the decree, the doctrine which it asserts implies four things:

1. That our Lord conferred on St. Peter powers of a distinctive kind greater than any which the other Apostles possessed.

2. That these greater powers could be handed down.

3. That St. Peter was Bishop of Rome in some such sense as that in which the later diocesan bishops are bishops of their dioceses; or, at the least, that he stood in some special relation to the Church at Rome.

4. That the Bishops of Rome inherited the distinctive powers of St. Peter.

The theory breaks down in the following ways:

1. The Vatican Council quoted three passages in the New Testament which, according to the Council, show that our Lord gave to St. Peter distinctive powers, so that he possessed what the other Apostles did not possess. The three passages are, Thou art Peter, and upon this rock I will build My Church; Simon, Simon, behold, Satan asked to have you, that he might sift you as wheat; but I made supplication for thee, that thy faith fail not: and do thou, when once thou hast turned again, stablish thy brethren; 'Jesus saith to Simon Peter, Simon, son of John, lovest thou Me more than these? He saith unto Him, Yea, Lord; Thou knowest that I love Thee. He saith unto him, Feed My lambs. He saith to him again a second time, Simon, son of John, lovest thou Me? He saith unto Him, Yea, Lord; Thou knowest that I love Thee. He saith unto him, Tend My sheep. He saith unto him the third time, Simon, son of John, lovest thou Me? Peter was grieved because He said unto him the third time, Lovest thou Me? And he said unto Him, Lord, Thou knowest all things; Thou knowest that I love Thee. Jesus saith unto him, Feed My sheep.' [37]

It will be well to examine these passages at some little length.

(a) In the first passage the Vatican Council assumed that the word 'rock' denotes St. Peter in such a sense that he is the foundation of the Church, and that any external separation from him divides from it. If the passage had this momentous import, we should expect a continuous and uniform traditional interpretation of our Lord's words in this sense. [38] Such a tradition does not exist. The Fathers interpret the passage in varying ways. In some cases, the same Father interprets it differently at different times. The word 'rock' is sometimes taken of our Lord Himself, sometimes of the doctrine of His Godhead, sometimes of the confession of His Godhead, sometimes of St. Peter. To take two instances, one from the East, the other from the West, St. Cyril of Alexandria interprets the 'rock' as Christ, and as the declaration of faith which St. Peter made; [39] St. Augustine interprets it of the apostolate of St. Peter, of St. Peter himself as the symbol of the Church, and of Christ; and, writing at the end of his life, and referring to the different interpretations which he had at different times placed on the word, he left the right interpretation open. [40]

(b) As to the second passage, the Vatican Council assumed that when our Lord commanded St. Peter to stablish his brethren, He meant that the guarantee of divine truth and grace was to be in him. Here, again, if this was the right interpretation, we should expect to find a continuous and uniform tradition to that effect. There is no such tradition. The passage is frequently referred to in the first five centuries as illustrating the general dealings of God, the human need of divine grace, that Christ prays for sinners, or that the strength of God is greater than that of Satan. Even St. Leo, although he thought that the words had special reference to St. Peter, and that St. Peter was the channel through which grace came to the other Apostles, does not appear to have attached any great importance to the passage as indicating this. St. Chrysostom refers to it in connexion with the part taken by St. Peter in the election of St. Matthias; but he elsewhere regards it as showing that after sin there can be restoration through penitence and a useful life. [41]

(c) As to the third passage, the Vatican Council assumed that the command given by our Lord to St. Peter marked his specific jurisdiction. The patristic evidence does not support this interpretation. For example, in the East, St. Cyril of Alexandria says the words were especially spoken to St. Peter to show that our Lord had forgiven his denial; and in the West, St. Augustine says the charge was given to all the Apostles and St. Peter was particularly addressed because he was the first in order of the apostolic band. [42]

Further, even if these passages had the meaning which the Vatican Council assumed, there would still remain serious obstacles to the conclusion of the Council. There is no evidence what the position of St. Peter at Rome was; or what, if any, was his special relation to the Bishops of Rome; and there is the greatest obscurity as to the details of the episcopate at Rome in the first century. Even supposing it were clear that our Lord conferred on St. Peter distinctive powers, that fact would not, of itself, supply an argument as to the Bishops of Rome.

2. The theory of Papal Infallibility was never affirmed by, and is inconsistent with many facts and much teaching in, the undivided Church. For instance, no special importance was attached to the declaration of Victor I. about the keeping of Easter, [43] or the condemnation by Stephen I. of St. Cyprian's view about Baptisms administered by schismatics. [44] In controversies of great length and perplexity, such as the Arian controversy, appeal was made, not to the Bishop of Rome, but to the whole Church. The letter of St. Leo on the Incarnation, accepted by the Council of Chalcedon as supplying true definitions on the question at issue in the Eutychian controversy, was affirmed after consideration, not because it was the judgment of the Bishop of Rome, but because the Council found its teaching to be in agreement with the acknowledgment of our Lord by St. Peter. [45] Even as late as the seventh

century and afterwards, Pope Honorius was condemned for heresy by many councils and Popes; and it is difficult to deny that his teaching was *ex cathedrâ*. [46]

3. The theory of Papal Infallibility necessarily depends upon the view that communion with the See of Rome is necessary to communion with the Church. The whole position of which the infallibility of the Pope is the climax rests on the idea that separation from the Pope is necessarily schism. It has been seen already that external communion with the Bishop of Rome, however greatly to be desired, is not a necessity for the maintenance either of the unity or of the apostolic character of the Church. Since this is so, Papal Infallibility is not the outcome of, but in contradiction to, the true belief in the Catholic Church.

The Scope of the Teaching Office of the Church

The Church is the exponent of and witness to the divine truth which has been committed to her charge. She is the teacher of faith and morals. It may sometimes be her duty to warn her children that political and social theories which ignore God and the claims of righteousness must fail to meet the deepest needs of the human race; and that philosophical and scientific opinions which exclude from consideration the spiritual faculties of man and the reality of the work of God put out of sight the greatest of all facts. Her office, as the organ of our Lord Jesus Christ in the world, is not to dictate in political or social systems, and in matters of philosophy or science; but to maintain the truths of religion which have been made known by the revelation of God.

The English Church as a Teacher

It is the office of national Churches to bear witness for truth and righteousness and God to the nations in which they have been placed by the divine providence. The authority of their teaching, like the source of their life, is beyond themselves. They have their life by means of that union which, linking them inwardly with the Catholic Church as a whole, unites them also with our Lord Himself. Their authority rests on their possession of the truth which belongs to the whole mystical body of Christ indwelt by God the Holy Ghost.

In the Bible and the Creeds, and the doctrine taught and implied in the Book of Common Prayer, the Church of England possesses the truth. She inherits, together with her apostolic ministry, the historical belief of the Church of Christ. In teaching the doctrines of the Holy Trinity and the Incarnation, she declares truth which is indeed her own, but which she has by virtue of her descent from the Apostles and her present essential union with the rest of the Church and with our Lord. In everything which is simply her own there is necessarily a tentative element. That which her Christian instinct suggests has to be brought to the test of Holy Scripture. That which is new has to be tried in the light of what is old. The action of a part of the body is subject to the revision of the body itself.

It is the strength of the Church of England that she has been content to recognize the limitations of her work. One of the causes of the divisions which broke up Western Christendom in the sixteenth century was the attempt to impose canons, ordinances, and doctrines which were local and of no great antiquity, as if they had been permanent and universal, or even the dictates of the inspired word of God itself. In the chaos which ensued, the Church of England made her appeal to the Bible and the undivided Church. Amid whatever imperfections, she has never abandoned that appeal. Taking their stand on the belief and practice of the Universal Church, her children are upheld by the Catholic faith and, at the same time, possess a freedom which, if sometimes unwisely used, has often enabled them to be faithful to demands of truth which a narrower view might have excluded. Through times of much ignorance and confusion her formularies have borne continuous witness to the central doctrines of historical Christianity, while she has never altogether lost the power of assimilating what is good in the results of the revived learning which marked the close of the middle ages. Except as a part of the whole body and as conveying its voice, she does not and can not claim finality or infallibility for any of her utterances. 'She is to us only an authority, so far as, and because, she echoes the voice of what is greater than herself, the Universal Church. The defectiveness of the formularies of the sixteenth and seventeenth centuries (granting them to be not heretical) is no more to us except in the way of temporary inconvenience than the defectiveness of the formularies of any other particular moment of the Church's life. The whole Church is our mother. It is the doctrinal heritage of the whole Church that now in the days of completer knowledge, as the mists clear away, is coming out in its indissoluble coherence before the eyes of men, and being taught to the children of the Church.' [47]

In thus appealing to what is wider than herself, the Church of England has been able to maintain the hope of performing her appointed work in bringing nearer that 'distant but blessed prospect of a reunited Christendom,' at the thought of which 'the pulse quickens and the eyes fill with tears.' [48] 'The hope of being allowed, it has been lately written by one of her most distinguished sons, through faith and toil and patience, to bear a special part in forwarding, when and as God wills, His purpose of unity, is a serious and chastening hope to entertain: but it cannot be declined when the call to entertain it comes to the Church of England from a sober study of its own history, and heritage, and conditions.' [49]

[1] St. John i. 17.
[2] St. John xiv. 26; xvi. 13; xiv. 16; St. Matt. xvi. 18; 1 St. Tim. iii. 15.
[3] Acts i. 16-22; ii. 14-39.

[4] 2 St. Tim. iii. 16. A.V., 'All scripture is given by inspiration of God;' R.V., 'Every scripture inspired of God.'
[5] St. Peter i. 21.

[6] St. Clement of Rome, *Ad. Cor.* i. 8, 13, 16, 42.

[7] St. Ignatius, *Ad Magn.*, 8.

[8] St. Justin Martyr, *Dial. c. Tryp.*, 7.

[9] Clement of Alexandria, *Strom.*, vii. 16.

[10] Origen, *De Princ.*, praef., 4.

[11] St. Cyprian, *De Op. et Eleem.*, 9.

[12] St. Augustine, *De Civ. Dei*, xviii. 43. See also note 10 in the concluding Notes.

[13] St. Cyril of Jerusalem, *Cat.*, xvi. 4.

[14] Nicene Creed as enlarged in A.D. 381 or A.D. 451.

[15] St. Augustine, *C. Advers. Leg. et Proph.*, ii. 13.

[16] See note 38 in the concluding Notes.

[17] 1 Cor. i. 11; v. 1; vii. 1; Gal. i. 6, 7; St. Jude 3.

[18] Isa. vi. 1-8; Ezek. i.-iii.; Rev. i. 9-20.

[19] *E.g.*, Josh. x. 13; 2 Sam. i. 18; 2 Kings xii. 19.

[20] St. Matt. i. 1-16; St. Luke iii. 23-38.

[21] St. Luke i. 1, 2.

[22] *E.g.*, Jer. xxviii.; St. John xviii. 15, 16; xix. 27.

[23] See St. Irenaeus, *C. Haer.*, III. vii. 2.

[24] Deut. vi. 4.

[25] See Chapter One.

[26] St. John i. 1, 14.

[27] See Chapter Six.

[28] Rom. v. 15.

[29] See Chapter Six.

[30] See note 39 in the concluding Notes.

[31] On the number of the Oecumenical Councils, see note 40 in the concluding Notes.

[32] St. Vincent of Lerins, *Commonitorium*, 4-6.

[33] St. Vincent of Lerins, *Commonitorium*, 55.

[34] *ibid.*

[35] Vatican Council, Sess. iv., cap. iv.

[36] See *Acta et Decreta Sacrosancti Oecumenici Concilii Vaticani* (*Collectio Lacensis*, tom. vii.)

[37] St. Matt. xvi. 18; St. Luke xxii. 32; St. John xxi. 15-17. See Vatican Council, Sees, iv., cap. i., iv.

[38] On the official teaching of the Church of Rome as to the relation of tradition to Holy Scripture, see note 41 in the concluding Notes.

[39] St. Cyril of Alexandria, *In Isa.*, iii. 3; iv. 2; *Dial, de Trin.*, 4 (ii. 460, 593, v. (i). 507, 508, ed. Aubert).

[40] See Puller, *The Primitive Saints and the See of Rome*, pp. 97-115.

[41] See note 42 in the concluding Notes.

[42] See Puller, *The Primitive Saints and the See of Rome*, pp. 371-391.

[43] See Puller, *ibid.*, pp. 23-31.

[44] *ibid.*, pp. 72-86.

[45] Council of Chalcedon, Act. ii., v.

[46] For a view that the teaching of Honorius was not *ex cathedrâ* in the sense of the Vatican Council because he did not impose it as of obligation, see Addis, Arnold and Scannell's *Catholic Dictionary*, p. 452 (fifth edition).

[47] Gore, *Roman Catholic Claims*, p. 171.

[48] Liddon, *The Divinity of our Lord and Saviour Jesus Christ*, p. 507.

[49] Paget, *An Introduction to the Fifth Book of Hooker's Treatise on the Laws of Ecclesiastical Polity*, p. 227.

Chapter Eleven - The Sanctifying Office of the Church - Part One

Since the day of Pentecost, the day of the creation of the Christian Church, the ordinary way in which God bestows grace on the souls of men is through the glorified humanity of our Lord and the working of God the Holy Ghost. The closest means of union with the glorified humanity of Christ, and the most immediate mode of contact with God the Holy Ghost are in the mystical body of Christ, that is, the Church, and are open to man in the use of the Sacraments. Thus, the Christian Church is the channel of grace.

The sacramental principle thus affirmed is in harmony with much besides. The Old Testament contains many instances of the divine use of material means. [1] In the Incarnation what is visible and tangible was used for the purposes of divine grace. During His ministry our Lord deigned to employ external means of healing. It is an answer to the felt needs of man that he should receive grace in objective ways by means of that which can be seen and felt. The Christian Church is a visible society, a fellowship and brotherhood of men. It is reasonable that incorporation into the society and maintenance in its life should be accomplished by sacramental rites.

The Word Sacrament

The word Sacrament has had the following meanings: -

1. The sum of money which the parties in a law suit were required by Roman law to deposit in court before a suit was heard, as a pledge of good faith.

2. A military oath.

3. A solemn oath of any kind.

4. In early Christian writers the word denotes any sacred event, as, for example, the Incarnation; or action, as, for example, the celebration of the Holy Eucharist; or thing, as, for example, the blessed salt given to catechumens.

5. In mediaeval theology one result of the desire for clear terminology and classification was the restriction of the use of the word Sacrament, so that it was limited to certain definite rites in which an outward sign was used as a means of conferring grace. This limitation of the word came to be general both in the East and in the West. It was accepted by the Church of Rome at the Council of Trent, and has been followed in the Articles of Religion and the Catechism of the Church of England. [2]

The Number of the Sacraments

According to the primitive use of the word Sacrament no limit could be put on the number, because anything regarded as sacred could be so called. According to the mediaeval use of the word the number is necessarily restricted; and seven specified rites of the Church came to be distinctively called

Sacraments. The first known instance of the specification of seven Sacra-
ments is in the first half of the twelfth century in the treatise of Gregory of
Bergamo, *On the Reality of the Body of Christ*. After explaining how Christian
Sacraments differ from Jewish Sacraments, and the Sacrament of our Lord's
birth from the Sacraments of the Church, Gregory mentions three groups
Baptism, Confirmation, and the Eucharist; Ordination and Matrimony; Holy
Scripture and an oath. A little later, Roland Bandinelli, afterwards Pope Alexander III., applied the name Sacrament to the Incarnation, which he described as 'the chief Sacrament,' Baptism, Confirmation, the Body and Blood
of Christ, Penance, Unction of Oil, and Matrimony. He placed the 'conferring
of the keys of the priest' in this list between 'Unction of Oil' and 'Matrimony;
but did not apply to it the name Sacrament, possibly so as to make the number seven. In the second half of the twelfth century Peter Lombard specified
as Sacraments the seven rites of Baptism, Confirmation, the Holy Eucharist,
Penance, the Last Unction, Holy Orders, and Matrimony. From Peter Lombard this particular restriction was adopted by the schoolmen generally, and
it came to be taken for granted in all Western theology. In A.D. 1439 it received Papal sanction in the decree of Pope Eugenius IV. to the Armenians. It
was again made by the Council of Paris in 1528, and was confirmed, some
twenty years later, by the Council of Trent. By at any rate the seventeenth
century the same limitation had been made in the East and had been expressed by the Councils of Constantinople and Bethlehem in A.D. 1642 and
1672.

Thus, seven specific rites came to be singled out both in the West and in
the East as having certain features in common which made it convenient that
each of them should be called a Sacrament and that the word Sacrament
should not be applied to anything else. In this use of the word theologians
have recognized differences between them. One difference is as to their necessity. Baptism and the Eucharist have been described as generally, that is,
universally, necessary to salvation. Penance has been described as necessary
only when there has been mortal sin committed after Baptism, which in the
primitive Church was regarded as something exceptional, the hypothesis being that a baptized person would abstain from mortal sin. Putting aside Confirmation as involving a question which must be considered later on, the rest
of the seven rites are not necessary to an individual, so far as his own salvation is concerned, except for some special reason, as his obedience to the vo-
cation of God. To give an instance of another distinction which has been
made among the seven rites, Baptism and Penance have been called Sacraments of the dead because the object of them is to convey grace to persons
who are in a state of spiritual death, either because of original sin or because
of postbaptismal mortal sin. The other five have been called Sacraments of
the living because they are to be ad ministered to persons in a state of spiritual life, that is, persons who have been baptized and, if they have committed mortal sin after Baptism, have been forgiven. Distinctions of this kind

have been common among theologians who have restricted the word to the seven rites and have used it for all the seven.

In the sixteenth century the Church in England, as has been pointed out, followed the restricted use of the word Sacrament which was due to the theologians of the middle ages, not the wider use which was customary in the early Church. A further limitation to the two Sacraments which are generally necessary to salvation came to be usually made in the phraseology of English Churchpeople. Whether this further limitation was meant to be asserted in the Catechism and the Articles of Religion is open to doubt. These documents use language of great caution. The Catechism, in the answer to the question 'How many Sacraments hath Christ ordained in His Church?' adds the qualification 'as generally necessary to salvation' to the words 'Two only;' and the twenty-fifth Article of Religion does not say that 'Confirmation, Penance, Orders, Matrimony, and Extreme Unction' are not Sacraments; but that they are not to be counted for Sacraments of the Gospel, and that they 'have not like nature of Sacraments with Baptism and the Lord's Supper.' That the intention was rather to affirm the distinctive position of the two Sacraments 'generally necessary to salvation than to deny the sacramental nature of the other rites is to some extent supported by the Homilies. The Homilies are not authoritative expressions of doctrine, and they represent differing types of English teaching in the sixteenth century; but they have value as in some cases illustrating the meaning of the divines who compiled the Edwardine and Elizabethan Prayer-books; and parts of their contents received the general approval of the Articles of Religion as containing a godly and wholesome doctrine.' In them Matrimony and Orders are spoken of as Sacraments; and the limitation of the word Sacrament to Baptism and the Holy Communion is regarded rather as a repudiation of any idea that other rites were on a level with these Sacraments than as a denial that they were Sacraments at all. [3]

Before beginning the consideration of the seven rites to which the word Sacrament was applied and limited in the middle ages, it will be well to define certain terms. The 'materia,' or 'matter,' is the thing used in a Sacrament. The word 'forma,' or 'form,' denotes the sacramental words. The union of matter and form is the saying of the words by the minister in conjunction with the thing used. The 'res sacramenti,' or 'substance of the Sacrament,' is the inward part or thing signified. The phrase 'virtus sacramenti,' or 'virtue of the Sacrament,' denotes the benefits intended to be conveyed. The last three questions and answers in the Catechism of the Church of England afford a good instance of the use of three of these terms with regard to the Holy Eucharist. The outward part or sign (that is, the 'materia,' or matter,' or 'signum sacramenti,' or 'sign of the Sacrament') is defined to be bread and wine; the inward part, or thing signified (that is, the 'res sacramenti,' or 'substance of the Sacrament') is defined to be the body and blood of Christ, which are verily and indeed taken and received by the faithful in the Lord's Supper; and the 'benefits' (that is, the 'virtus sacramenti,' or 'virtue of the Sacrament') are described as 'the strengthening and refreshing of our souls by the body and blood of Christ.'

Holy Baptism

The institution of the Sacrament of Holy Baptism was prepared for by the baptism of St. John the Baptist following upon the Jewish baptisms of proselytes. The Sacrament was referred to by anticipation by our Lord in His discourse with Nicodemus. [4] It was instituted before the ascension, when our Lord gave His Apostles the command, 'Go ye therefore, and make disciples of all the nations, baptizing them into the Name of the Father and of the Son and of the Holy Ghost.' [5] After the descent of God the Holy Ghost on the day of Pentecost, it was administered by the Apostles; [6] and the administration of it has always since remained in the Church.

The matter in Baptism is water. At the time of our Lord's ministry the word Baptism suggested the use of water. Our Lord spoke of water in the discourse with Nicodemus; and passages in the New Testament in which Baptism is referred to imply that it was administered by means of water. The history of the Church, also, clearly shows that water is the matter of this Sacrament. Baptism has sometimes been administered by immersion, that is, by the person baptized being plunged in the water. It has been administered, also, by affusion, that is, by the water being poured upon the person baptized. Both methods appear to have been in use in the period to which the New Testament refers and in subsequent times. At present, it is agreed throughout Western Catholic Christendom that, so far as the application of the water is concerned, a Baptism is valid if the water is made to flow upon the head of the person baptized. The same doctrine is, practically speaking, held in the East. The Russian Church asserts that Baptism either with or without immersion is valid. The Greek Church, in words, asserts that no Baptism is valid other than that administered with threefold immersion. Practically, however, the Greek doctrine comes to be the same as that of Westerns and the Russian Church because the Greeks say that any Baptism with water may be allowed as valid Baptism after it has taken place by the economy of the Church, and now admit to their communion without administering Baptism those who have been baptized without threefold immersion.

The form of Baptism consists of the words 'In the Name of the Father and of the Son and of the Holy Ghost,' together with the mention of Baptism. These were the words commanded by our Lord when the Sacrament was instituted; and they have been used in the common practice of the Church. At the present time the Roman and English forms are identical, 'N. I baptize thee in the Name of the Father and of the Son and of the Holy Ghost.' The Eastern form differs only by avoiding the phrase which appears to ascribe the act of Baptism to the minister. It is The Servant of God *N.* is baptized in the Name of the Father and of the Son and of the Holy Ghost. In the Acts of the Apostles [7] Baptism in, or upon, or into the Name of Jesus Christ, or the Lord, or the Lord Jesus is spoken of. Probably this phraseology means that the Baptism was the means of enrolling those who were baptized into the service of our Lord Jesus Christ, not that a different form from that which has been mentioned was used. [8] The question has been raised whether Baptism administered with the form, 'In the Name of Christ' or 'In the Name of the Trinity,' would be valid. The usual opinion is that it would not be valid, that in the case of Baptism the command of our Lord, as interpreted by the Universal Church, restricts the sacramental grace to the particular phrase in which the three Persons of the Holy Trinity are severally mentioned. However this may be, it may at least be said that no devout and instructed person wishing to carry out our Lord's command would desire to use any but the recognized form, 'In the Name of the Father and of the Son and of the Holy Ghost.'

The minister in Baptism ought to be either a bishop or a priest. In the absence of a priest, a deacon may validly baptize, and for any sufficient reason ought to do so. In cases of necessity any person may validly baptize and ought to do so. It is not even necessary that a person so doing be within the communion of the Church. A heretic, or a schismatic, or even an unbaptized person, can validly administer the Sacrament, provided the right matter and form are used. The validity of Baptism administered by heretics was denied by some in the East, in the early Church. That of Baptism administered by any outside the Church was denied in North Africa, and notably by St. Cyprian, in the third century. Both denials alike were rejected by the Church, at any rate in the West. So far as words go, there is a difference on this point in different parts of the East. The Russian Church, like the West, asserts that Baptism by any person is valid. The Greek Church asserts that Baptism by a deacon, or a Catholic layman, or a schismatic, or a heretic, is not valid. Practically, this comes to the same thing as the Western doctrine, because the Greeks say that such Baptisms after they have taken place can be allowed as valid by the economy of the Church. [9]

Any unbaptized person is capable of receiving Baptism. The validity and the lawfulness of the Baptism of infants are shown by the common practice of the Church from the earliest times; and it is probable that some of the Baptisms mentioned in the Acts of the Apostles included children. The theological reason which allows the Baptism of infants is, that, if they can unconsciously inherit and possess the distortion of original sin, they are capable also of unconsciously receiving the grace of Baptism; and our Lord's action in blessing infants shows the possibility of their receiving gifts from God. The effects of Baptism are

1. It unites the person who is baptized to the sacred manhood of Christ, and makes him a member of Christ's body, so that he receives the grace to enable him to live a holy life. [10]

2. It removes the guilt of original sin and of all previously committed actual sin, and also the eternal penalties due to sin, and is thus a means of salvation. [11]

3. It confers on the soul the gift of God the Holy Ghost. [12]

4. It makes the baptized person to be a son of God. [13]

5. It gives the capacity of receiving the other Sacraments. Baptism is regarded as the beginning of the spiritual life which brings a person from death to life. [14] This is the reason for the universal rule of the Church that no other Sacrament can be administered to a person who is unbaptized.

6. It imprints on the soul what is called character, which cannot be effaced, so that a baptized person always remains baptized. [15]

These effects are all produced in an infant who is baptized or in an adult who worthily receives Baptism. The question as to the effect of Baptism in an adult who unworthily receives it has some special difficulties. The objectivity of the sacramental grace shows that he becomes a baptized person. As to the rest, it is not possible to say more than that, while, because of his sin in wrongly receiving the Sacrament, he only potentially and not actually obtains remission of sins and sanctifying grace at the time of Baptism, these become actually his, if he subsequently repent, by virtue of the objective union with the manhood of Christ which was made his when he was baptized.

Baptism is declared to be necessary to salvation by our Lord in His discourse with Nicodemus. The same truth is implied in those parts of the teaching of St. Paul in which Baptism is regarded as the means of passing from death to life. The common teaching of the Church has always regarded Baptism as a Sacrament necessary to salvation. The necessity of Baptism has been asserted partly because of the precept of our Lord ordering that all those admitted into the Church are to be baptized ('necessitas praecepti'), and partly because of the need of union with the life of Christ ('necessitas medii'). To this general law of the necessity of Baptism, two exceptions have been recognized in the ordinary teaching of the Church.

1. The Baptism of desire, that is, perfect contrition of heart and love towards God which include either explicitly or implicitly the desire to receive Baptism.

2. The Baptism of blood, that is, martyrdom for the cause of Christ, which may be taken to imply contrition and love, and a desire explicit or implicit for Baptism.

The whole of the theology on this point rests on two underlying principles which the doctrine of the Sacraments presupposes.

1. Men are bound by the means which are divinely appointed; but God Himself is not bound by His own means.

2. God in His judgment takes into consideration what is imperceptible to man, while man has to define and decide upon tangible grounds.

'The invisible sanctification,' says St. Augustine, 'is present to some, and profits them without the visible Sacraments...while the visible sanctification, which is accomplished by means of the visible Sacraments, can be present without that which is invisible and therefore fail to profit. Yet the visible Sacrament is not on this account to be despised, for he who despises it can in no way be invisibly sanctified.' [16]

On the subject of infants who die unbaptized, different opinions have been held within the Church; and the Church is not committed to any dogma. In the fourth century three opinions may be found. St. Augustine, who represents the sternest view of human nature which has not been set free from original sin, in his later teaching laid down that these infants suffer, though in the lightest possible way, the pains of hell, since it is impossible for them to enter heaven, and as a place of final existence the only alternatives are heaven and hell. [17] St. Gregory of Nazianzus taught that they would receive neither the joy of heaven nor the condemnation of the lost. [18] St. Gregory of Nyssa, while he wrote in the strongest way of the risk of eternal condemnation which those who wilfully postpone Baptism run, implied that infants who die unbaptized will eventually attain to all the bliss of heaven which they are capable of enjoying. [19]

The influence of St. Augustine throughout the West gave wide prevalence to the opinion which he held, and many of its later advocates even forgot the qualification which St. Augustine himself made, that it was in the lightest possible way that such infants suffered the pains of hell. In the middle ages the popular opinion was that every person who died unbaptized under any circumstances, whether adult or infant, was eternally condemned to hell. An opinion held by many of the theologians of the middle ages was that of St. Thomas Aquinas. According to this, infants who died unbaptized, since they were without either the grace of Baptism or any desire for it, and since they were also without any acceptance by the will of the law of God, were eternally incapable of rejoicing in the Beatific Vision; but, since they were free from actual sin, they would not suffer any punishment which would give pain, and the absence from the Beatific Vision would cause them no dissatisfaction, because as the capacity for enjoying it remained undeveloped by reason of the lack of Baptism, the want of it could not be felt. [20] In other words, it was taught that infants who die unbaptized will never attain to the Beatific Vision, but will eternally enjoy natural bliss. From the mediaeval period to the present time the opinion of St. Augustine in the form in which he taught it, and in the sterner form it after wards attained, and the opinion of St. Thomas have been widely held within the Church.

In the sixteenth century it was taught by Zwingli and others that the water in Baptism is a mere outward sign and that no special grace of any kind is conveyed to the soul because of Baptism. Between this and the truth there are many varying opinions which with greater or less distinctness connect a greater or less gift of grace to the soul with the fact of Baptism. [21]

Confirmation

The New Testament does not record the institution of Confirmation. Probably it was commanded by our Lord to the Apostles after His resurrection, when He spoke to them about 'the things concerning the kingdom of God.' It was administered by the Apostles, as is recorded in the Acts. It is mentioned in the Epistle to the Hebrews as one of the fundamentals of Christianity. [22] It has been continuously administered in the Church since the earliest Christian times.

Much discussion has taken place about the matter of Confirmation. All that is mentioned in the New Testament is the laying on of hands. The practice of the Church has not been the same always and every where. At present, there are considerable differences in the different parts of the Church. In the Church of Borne the person confirmed is anointed on the forehead with chrism in the form of a cross, and the bishop in saying the prayer for Confirmation extends his hands towards all those who are being confirmed. As to which part is the matter, different Roman theologians have held that it is the touch of the bishop's hand by itself; or that it is the anointing by itself; or that it is either the touch of the hand by itself, or the anointing by itself; or that it is the combination of the two. Of these opinions the fourth is now most usually adopted in Roman Catholic theology. [23] It is possible that the Roman offices of Confirmation contemplated that the bishop in the act of anointing would place his hand on the head of the person confirmed while anointing the forehead with the thumb; and this is ordered in the rubric in the office for the Confirmation of one person by himself. [24] It is not directed in the ordinary rubrics and is not, as a rule, done in practice. In the Church of England it is directed that the bishop's hand be laid on the head of each person confirmed severally, that is, individually. In the East those who are confirmed are anointed with chrism, there being nothing which corresponds to the laying on of hands unless the use of the hand in the act of anointing is taken as being such. There is no good ground for doubt that any one of the methods adopted in different parts of the Church contains the matter of a valid Confirmation.

No authoritative declaration has ever been made as to what is necessary in respect of the form. In the absence of any authoritative declaration, it is impossible to say more than that it consists of words used by the minister containing reference to the special gift.

In the primitive Church the ordinary minister of Confirmation, as also of Baptism, was the bishop; but it was frequently administered by a priest acting with the authority of the bishop. It is probable, though it cannot be proved, that in the latter case the priest used chrism blessed by the bishop for use in Confirmation. At present, in the Church of England, Confirmation is always administered by a bishop. In the Church of Rome, it is almost always administered by a bishop in the West, though there are exceptional cases in which it is administered by a priest using chrism which a bishop has blessed. In the Eastern Churches and in the Churches of Eastern Christians in communion with Rome, it is administered by a bishop or a priest, who uses chrism, which, in the Eastern Churches and among most of those Easterns in communion with Rome, has been blessed by a bishop for use in Confirmation. [25]

93

The proper recipient of Confirmation is a baptized person who has not been confirmed. The practice of the early Church was, in ordinary cases, to confirm every person, whether infant or adult, immediately after Baptism. This custom is still observed in the East. In the middle ages a custom of separating Confirmation from Baptism grew up in the West. This was not due to any deliberate decision on the part of the Western Church, but simply to the fact that in large numbers of cases the Western diocesan bishops neglected the work of their dioceses, and the assistant bishops were too few in number to do what the diocesan bishops left undone. Thus, in some parts of the middle ages many Christians were unconfirmed; and those who were confirmed received Confirmation at such a time after their Baptism as they had an opportunity of approaching a bishop. Until the sixteenth century it still remained the rule in the West, in spite of the very imperfect regard paid to it, that infants were to be confirmed as soon after Baptism as access to a bishop was possible. [26] Since the sixteenth century, Confirmation has been definitely separated from Baptism both in the Church of Rome [27] and in the Church of England. The separation forms in both these parts of the Church alike a wide departure from the practice of the primitive Church. It has been accentuated in the Church of England by the custom of postponing Confirmation to an age older than that contemplated in the Book of Common Prayer, and in the Church of Rome by the frequency with which Confirmation has been administered after First Communion.

The effect of Confirmation is to bestow on the soul special gifts of God the Holy Ghost. The person confirmed receives what is known as the character of Confirmation, so that he becomes, and can never cease to be, one who has been confirmed. In cases of worthy reception the gifts of the Holy Ghost convey with them grace for living well, and especially strength. In cases of unworthy reception, the objective nature of the rite necessitates that there is a real act carrying with it the gifts and character of Confirmation; but the barrier interposed by the sin of the person confirmed prevents the grace from being received otherwise than potentially, so that it can be of value to the soul only after repentance.

It is necessary to consider here the relation of Confirmation to Baptism. It has usually been thought by those who believe in baptismal regeneration that the gift of the personal indwelling of God the Holy Ghost is poured into the soul at Baptism, and that in Confirmation there is an increased working of the same gift, which is bestowed in Baptism primarily to cleanse, and in Confirmation primarily to strengthen. This distinction between Baptism and Confirmation is clearly expressed in a Gallican sermon of the fifth or sixth century: 'The Holy Ghost, who comes down upon the waters of Baptism with health-giving descent, in the font gives His fulness to produce innocence, in Confirmation affords an increase to produce grace. In Baptism we are regenerated so as to attain to life; after Baptism we are strengthened for battle. In Baptism we are washed; after Baptism we are made strong.' [28] The same opinion is expressed by Peter Lombard in the twelfth century: 'The virtue in Confirmation is the gift for strength of the Holy Ghost who was given in Baptism for remission.' [29]

Of late years an opinion has been held by many in the Church of England that Confirmation sets up in the soul an entirely new relation to the Holy Ghost, who in Baptism acts upon the soul from without, but does not impart His personal indwelling or act upon the soul from within until Confirmation. The advocates of this opinion lay great stress on those passages in the eighth and nineteenth chapters of the Acts of the Apostles in which it is said, 'When the Apostles which were at Jerusalem heard that Samaria had received the word of God, they sent unto them Peter and John: who, when they were come down, prayed for them, that they might receive the Holy Ghost: for as yet He was fallen upon none of them: only they had been baptized into the Name of the Lord Jesus. Then laid they their hands on them, and they received the Holy Ghost'; 'They were baptized into the Name of the Lord Jesus. And when Paul had laid his hands upon them, the Holy Ghost came on them.' [30] These passages, it is contended, represent the personal indwelling of the Holy Ghost as a gift received after Baptism at Confirmation, and as a gift of a new kind, not merely the new activity of a presence already possessed. The same doctrine, it is pleaded, was taught by the Fathers. In the chief passages cited to support this view, Cornelius, Bishop of Rome in the third century, described one who had not been confirmed as not having 'obtained the Holy Ghost;' Tertullian distinguished the cleansing in the water and the preparation therein for the Holy Ghost from the subsequent obtaining of the Holy Ghost; and St. Cyprian similarly referred to Baptism as preparing and fitting the baptized for the reception of the Spirit. [31] It is, further, urged that in the human life of our Lord there was the operation of the Holy Ghost on His manhood from without between His conception and His baptism; that at His baptism the personal indwelling of the Holy Ghost was bestowed on His manhood; and that similarly at our Baptism we are made temples fit for the habitation of God by the operation of the Holy Ghost from without, while in our Confirmation, and not till then, the Holy Ghost takes up His abode within our soul as the temple which He thus comes to inhabit. The first of these arguments, then, is based upon Holy Scripture. It takes the statements in the Acts of the Apostles that in Confirmation the Holy Ghost dwelt in the souls of the confirmed as implying that they had not previously received His personal indwelling, and specially emphasizes the words 'as yet He was fallen upon none of them: only they had been baptized.' With reference to this argument, it is important to notice two points. In the first place, there are other passages in the Acts which appear to connect a gift of the Holy Ghost which can hardly be less than the personal indwelling with the reception of Baptism. After his sermon on the day of Pentecost, St. Peter told those who asked what they were to do, 'Repent ye and be baptized every one of you in the Name of Jesus Christ unto the remission of your sins, and ye shall receive the gift of the Holy Ghost'; and Ananias, when sent to St. Paul, evidently connected the promise that St. Paul should 'be filled with the Holy Ghost' with his coming Baptism. [32] In the second place, the other passages in themselves by no means clearly show that the words 'as yet He was fallen upon none of them' mean more than that they had not as yet received the special Confirmation gifts of the Holy Ghost, while the words 'the Holy Ghost came upon them' obviously do not preclude their having already received the personal indwelling, any more than the words spoken at the ordination of a priest and the consecration of a bishop, 'Receive the Holy Ghost,' imply that the person ordained or consecrated is not already a temple inhabited by God the Holy Ghost. If the Scriptural argument stood alone, it would by no means be free from difficulty; but a complete view of all the passages in the Acts bearing on the subject shows that, at the least, they do not deny the gift of the personal indwelling at Baptism. Further, St. Paul, writing to the Romans about the indwelling of the Holy Ghost, says, 'If any man hath not the Spirit of Christ, he is none of His;' [33] and it is impossible to suppose that he could have spoken of a person who had been baptized but was not confirmed as 'none of' Christ's.

But the Scriptural argument does not stand alone. On turning to the teaching of the Fathers, we reach a very complicated question. In the patristic period Baptism and Confirmation were in ordinary cases administered at the same time, and it is often difficult to ascertain whether in any particular passage the reference is to the whole ceremony of Baptism and Confirmation or to one of the two separately. The Fathers repeatedly say that the personal indwelling of the Holy Ghost is received in Baptism. To quote one instance, St. Chrysostom affirms that 'in Baptism' 'we received remission of sins, sanctification, participation of the Spirit, adoption, eternal life.' [34] If it were clear that in such statements as this the Baptism itself and not the Confirmation which was administered immediately after was meant, it would follow that the personal in dwelling of the Holy Ghost was expressly declared to be a result of Baptism. But, it has been suggested that these passages do not refer to the Baptism itself, but to the whole rite of which Baptism and Confirmation formed the two parts, and therefore connect the personal indwelling of the Holy Ghost with Confirmation rather than with Baptism. Thus, those who take this view put aside these general references to the gift of the Holy Ghost in Baptism, and fall back on the passages previously mentioned in which the personal indwelling is thought to be restricted to Confirmation. Such a course, and the inferences drawn from it, ignore three considerations of great weight. In the first place, it is possible that the statements quoted from Cornelius, Tertullian, and St. Cyprian, only mean that the special Confirmation gifts are not received in Baptism. Secondly, St. Cyprian elsewhere expressly speaks of a baptized person possessing the personal indwelling in a case in which Baptism had been administered on a sick bed and consequently without Confirmation. [35] Thirdly, St. Basil, [36] St. Athanasius, [37] and Origen, [38] all connect the personal indwelling of the Holy Ghost either with the water or with the act of regeneration, that is, with Baptism even apart from Confirmation. Consequently, when the different aspects of the teaching of the Fathers are considered, the usual doctrine of the early Church appears to have been that the gift of the personal in dwelling of the Holy Ghost is to be referred to Baptism, though there are special gifts of His presence which He bestows when He is received in Confirmation.

Mention has been made of another argument based upon the gift of the Holy Ghost to the manhood of our Lord. The consideration of this gift really tends in an opposite direction from that thus suggested. The personal indwelling of the Holy Ghost was bestowed upon the sacred manhood of our Lord on three occasions. At His conception He received it for the existence of His human life. At his baptism He received it with the gifts to His manhood for His ministry. At His ascension He received it to bestow the joy and glory of His ascended life. [39] There are three gifts to Christians parallel to these three gifts to our Lord. At Baptism there is the gift of Christian life. At Confirmation there is the gift of strength. In the resurrection there is to be the gift of the joy and glory of the future life. If this parallel is to be used at all on this subject and it seems to have a very reasonable bearing the tendency of it is to support the belief that the gift of the personal indwelling of the Holy Ghost to the soul takes place in Baptism as being parallel to the truth that He who was always personally God possessed this close union with the Holy Ghost in His sacred manhood, not merely from the time of His baptism in Jordan, but also from the first beginning of His human life. Thus, a comparison of Holy Scripture with the teaching of the Fathers and the inferences from the gifts to the sacred manhood of our Lord supports the belief that at Baptism the personal indwelling of the Holy Ghost is vouchsafed to the soul.

In addition, the following points are deserving of attention: -

1. Regeneration in Baptism constitutes a Christian.

The personal indwelling of the Holy Ghost appears to be one of the distinguishing marks of a Christian; and it is most in harmony with Christian doctrine generally to say that the Holy Ghost acts upon the soul from within in the case of all who are made Christians.

2. Baptism makes the baptized person a member of Christ, that is, it unites him to the glorified manhood of Christ. In the manhood of Christ the Holy Ghost dwells with His personal presence. It is difficult to suppose that one who is thus made a member of Christ does not receive that which permanently abides in the sacred humanity, the personal indwelling of the Holy Ghost.

3. It is in harmony with much we know of the gifts of God that the indwelling presence of the Holy Ghost should be bestowed at Baptism and that at Confirmation there should be His new activity; and that the method of His working in the two rites should be less sharply distinguished than some have supposed.

Some modern Eastern teaching, especially that of the Russian Bishop Macarius, has been cited to support the view which restricts the personal indwelling to the confirmed. There is no doubt that Macarius, who on most matters is representative of the Russian Church, teaches this view. [40] At the same time, it is not in the formularies of either the Russian or the Greek Church. The Greek Church in its Baptismal Office connects the 'gift of the Holy Ghost' with the water; [41] and the Council of Bethlehem, which was accepted by the Greek Church in 1672 and by the Russian Church in the present century, describes the baptized as the 'shrines of God,' [42] words which, deliberately used in a formal document, can only be properly explained by asserting the personal indwelling in the baptized.

The question does not appear to have been discussed by writers in the Church of Rome. The general Roman teaching takes it for granted that the Holy Ghost dwells in the baptized.

The formularies of the Church of England very distinctly affirm such a gift of the Holy Ghost in Baptism as appears to imply the personal indwelling. Thus the Baptismal Office speaks of 'all things belonging to the Spirit' living and growing in the baptized, and uses the prayer 'Give Thy Holy Spirit to this infant' (or 'these persons'); and the exhortation in the Office for adults definitely asserts that God will 'bestow' 'the Holy Ghost' upon those then to be baptized. There is no trace of any idea that this bestowing the Holy Ghost is merely an operation on the soul from without which does not imply the personal indwelling. [43]

The Holy Eucharist

The institution of the Holy Eucharist by our Lord is recorded by St. Matthew, St. Mark, and St. Luke as having taken place on the night before the crucifixion. [44] It had been anticipated in our Lord's teaching at Capernaum, recorded in the sixth chapter of St. John's Gospel; [45] and it should be noticed, with regard both to this Sacrament and to Baptism, that the institution itself is mentioned by the first three evangelists only, while the discourses during our Lord's ministry which looked on to and were explained by the Sacraments are given only by St. John. From the time of the descent of the Holy Ghost on the day of Pentecost the Eucharist has been continuously administered in the Church. [46]

The matter in the Eucharist consists of bread, either leavened or unleavened, and wine, which ought to have water mixed with it, but is a valid element if unmixed. The matter is known from the account of the institution by our Lord and the common practice of the Church. It is practically certain that the bread used at the institution of the Sacrament, as being a passover cake, was unleavened. There is little evidence what kind of bread was generally used in the early Church. For many centuries the ordinary Western practice has been to use unleavened bread, and the ordinary Eastern practice, except in some of the separated Churches, has been to use leavened bread. As to the wine, it is practically certain that the cup used at the institution was of wine mixed with water. So far as there is evidence, it was ordinarily mixed in the early Church. At the present time it is mixed in the Church of Home and in the East, except in some separated Churches. As to the Church of England, there is no express direction whether the chalice is or is not to be mixed; but it was stated by Archbishop Benson of Canterbury that, 'without order,' 'no person had a right to change the matter in the chalice,' and that 'wine alone may have been adopted by general habit but not by law.' [47]

The form in the Eucharist consists of words of consecration. There has been much discussion as to the essential words. The ordinary Western view is that since our Lord is the real officiant and speaks through the priest who is His minister, consecration is effected by the mere recitation of the words which our Lord Himself used, 'This is My body,' 'This is My blood,' in connexion with the act of consecrating. The Church of England appears to be committed to this ordinary Western view by the rubric which directs that, in the case of a second consecration in either kind, simply the portion of the prayer of consecration referring to the kind required is to be used. The ordinary Eastern view is that the whole form of prayer which culminates in the Eastern Liturgies in the invocation of the Holy Ghost is consecrating, and that, since the change in the elements is due to the operation of God the Holy Ghost, He ought to be invoked in express terms, so that a consecration cannot rightly be without this invocation. As to the history of the form, every existing Eastern Liturgy contains an invocation of the Holy Ghost, and liturgiologists think there are traces of its formerly having existed in the Western rites. With unimportant exceptions, the words of institution are in all Eastern and Western Liturgies now existing. As to the minimum that is necessary for a valid consecration, it can hardly be doubted that the words our Lord used are sufficient, and that the absence of the invocation of the Holy Ghost in the Western rites for many centuries does not invalidate them. On the other hand, liturgical history shows the propriety of the use of the invocation, which is also subjectively valuable as emphasizing the operation of the Holy Ghost in this Sacrament. [48]

The universal practice of the Church requires a bishop or a priest as the minister of this Sacrament. This has been questioned on insufficient grounds. Thus, a passage in Tertullian [49] has been quoted in which he speaks of a layman celebrating the Eucharist as well as baptizing. This passage does not support the position in defence of which it has been quoted, because Tertullian was a Montanist when he wrote this treatise, and is stating the Montanist position. In another work, written before he became a Montanist, he distinguishes between the powers of priests and laymen, and mentions as a mark of heretical bodies that they give the laity the offices of the priests. [50] The Council of Aries in A.D. 314 forbade deacons to offer; and the Council of Nicaea in A.D. 325, in forbidding a local practice of the deacons administering to priests the Holy Eucharist which a bishop or priest had consecrated, referred to deacons, in distinction from priests, as those who had not authority to offer. [51] There is no instance in the history of the undivided Church of the consecration of the Eucharist by others than bishops or priests being authorized under any circumstances.

The recipient of the Eucharist must have been baptized. In the early Church, as now in the East, infants received it. Confirmation ought to precede Communion; but a person baptized and not confirmed may under some circumstances rightly communicate.

The Eucharist differs from other Sacraments as regards the effect produced in the matter itself. In the case of Baptism the matter, that is, the water, is used as an instrument whereby a result is effected in the person who is baptized; but the water itself remains water only. In the case of the Eucharist the matter, that is, the bread and wine, not only is used as the instrument whereby the person who receives the Sacrament is benefited, but also becomes the body and blood of our Lord. In considering the effects of the act of consecration it is necessary to consider three points, the effect of consecration in the elements; the nature and effects of the Eucharist as a sacrifice; the nature and effects of the Eucharist as Communion.

The effect of consecration in the elements is that the bread and wine become the body and blood of our Lord by virtue of the act of consecration. This is the most natural interpretation of our Lord's words. In the discourse at Capernaum He spoke of eating His flesh and drinking His blood. In the institution of the Sacrament He said, 'This is My body,' 'This is My blood.' [52] Language so strange and unusual as that recorded by St. John must be interpreted in connexion with the only other recorded place in which our Lord used similar language. Both sets of passages most naturally mean that that which is received is itself the body and blood of our Lord. In the First Epistle to the Corinthians St. Paul speaks of the cup and the bread as the communion of the blood and body of Christ in connexion, not with the reception by the communicant, but with the act of the minister. 'The cup of blessing which we bless, is it not a communion of the blood of Christ? The bread which we break, is it not a communion of the body of Christ?' [53] Even if these passages were taken by themselves, their most natural meaning would be that the bread and wine, apart from their reception by the communicants, are the body and blood of Christ. That this natural meaning is their true meaning may be seen by considering the uniform teaching of the early Church.

Typical passages from representative teachers of different parts of the Church distinctly connect the body and blood of Christ with the elements. St. Ignatius, who represents Asia Minor, speaks of the Eucharist as 'the flesh of our Saviour Jesus Christ.' [54] St. Irenaeus, who represents Gaul, says that in the consecrated Eucharist there are two parts, an earthly and a heavenly;' and that our Lord 'acknowledged the bread as His body, and established the mixed cup as His blood.' [55] St. Athanasius, who represents the Eastern section of the African Church, affirms that at the prayer of consecration 'the bread becomes the body, and the cup the blood, of our Lord;' and that 'the

Word descends upon the bread and the cup, and His body comes to be.' [56] St. Ambrose, who represents Italy, says that the Sacraments 'by means of the mystery of the holy prayer are transformed so as to be flesh and blood.' [57] St. Augustine, who represents the Western section of the African Church, uses the strong phrase that our Lord in saying 'This is My body' 'was carried in His own hands,' and was 'giving His own body itself.' [58] St. Chrysostom, who represents the East generally, speaks of touching the flesh of Christ with the tongue. [59] These selected passages rightly represent the general teaching of the writers from whom they are taken. The teachers themselves are of acknowledged authority; they are from different parts of the Church; and, when taken together, they are representative of the whole Christian Society. Their teaching requires that the presence of our Lord's body and blood is in the elements themselves, not merely connected with the reception of them. [60]

This doctrine is further supported by the natural inference from the practice of Christians. It is known that as early as the first half of the second century the consecrated elements were taken from the Church to absent persons. [61] This custom shows that at this early date the gift was connected with the elements themselves; and in the fifth century St. Cyril of Alexandria expressly declares, in opposition to an error which was springing up in his time, that the Sacrament when reserved is the body of Christ. 'I hear that they say,' he writes, 'that the mystic blessing is of no avail for consecration, if it be reserved to another day. In so saying, they are senseless. For Christ undergoes no alteration, neither is His holy body changed; but the efficacy of the blessing and the life-giving grace abide in it.' [62] In the middle of the fourth century the care taken of the consecrated elements points in the same direction. St. Cyril of Jerusalem instructs the newly baptized, 'Ye hear the chanter inviting you with a sacred melody to the communion of the Holy Mysteries and saying, "O taste and see that the Lord is good." Trust not the judgment to thy bodily palate; no, but to faith unfaltering. For they who taste are bidden to taste, not bread and wine, but the body and blood of Christ of which the bread and wine are types. In approaching, therefore, come not with thy wrists extended, or thy fingers spread; but make thy left hand a throne for thy right hand, which is to receive a King; and, having hollowed thy palm, receive the body of Christ, saying over it, Amen. So then, after having carefully sanctified thine eyes by the touch of the holy body, partake of it, giving heed lest thou lose any portion thereof; for whatever thou losest is evidently a loss to thee, as if it were from one of thine own members. For tell me, if any one gave thee grains of gold, wouldest thou not hold them with all carefulness, being on thy guard against losing any of them and suffering loss? "Wilt thou not then much more carefully keep watch, that not a crumb fall from thee of what is more precious than gold and precious stones? Then, after thou hast been partaker of the body of Christ, draw near also to the cup of His blood, not stretching forth thy hands, but, bending and in an attitude of worship and reverence saying, Amen, sanctify thyself by receiving also the blood of Christ.' [63] Similarly, the practice of the adoration of our Lord present in the consecrated Eucharist, referred to by St. Ambrose when he says, 'The flesh of Christ which to this day we adore in the mysteries,' [64] and by St. Augustine in his words, 'No one eats that flesh unless he has first adored it,' [65] denotes the same connexion of the body and blood of Christ with the consecrated elements. Thus, there is every reason for confidence that the belief which was afterwards universal throughout the Church, that the consecrated elements become, because of the act of consecration, the body and blood of Christ, was the belief handed down from the Apostles and embodied the true interpretation of the Scriptural language about the Eucharist. To use the exact language of the later systematized theology, in the act of consecration our Lord Jesus Christ becomes present in the Sacrament with the sacred humanity of His glorified, spiritual, risen, and ascended life. This presence is real, that is, it is the true presence of the essential being of Christ. It is corporal, that is, the body of Christ is present. It is spiritual, that is, He is present by virtue of the spiritual character of His risen body. To put it otherwise, the presence is that of Christ Himself, of Christ in His human nature, of Christ in that human nature in its glorified condition. In saying as much as this we are on solid ground because these definite statements are simply the clear expression of the ordinary teaching of the whole Church. Beyond this there have been almost endless speculations as to the method and manner of the presence.

The most important of the attempts at such further definition is that known as Transubstantiation. The word Transubstantiation has been used in two senses. The first of these is that at the act of consecration the bread and wine are annihilated; that only the appearance of them remains; that this appearance causes a delusion to those who trust to sense; and that the place of the bread and wine is taken by the body and blood of Christ. According to this view, the consecrated host is not in any way bread, and the consecrated contents of the chalice are not in any way wine. This form of Tran substantiation is probably held by very many ignorant persons who believe in the real presence of the body and blood of Christ in the Sacrament. In its other meaning, the word Transubstantiation has been used to denote the doctrine which was elaborated with great care by the schoolmen and affirmed by the Council of Trent, and is commonly taught by Roman theologians. The elaboration of it was one part of a great work which the schoolmen undertook, namely, to endeavour to present the Christian religion in such an aspect as would make it to be in harmony with the philosophy of their time. The dominant system of philosophy was Aristotelianism; and it was the aim of the schoolmen to serve the cause of faith by stating the Christian religion according to the methods of this philosophy. What they did about the Eucharist was one part of what they did in theology generally. According to the Aristotelian philosophy as presented in the middle ages, in every material object there are (1) the 'accidents,' that is, everything which can be discerned by the senses and nourishes the body; [66] and (2) the 'res,' or essential being, which gives to everything its nature, which cannot be discerned by the senses, but truly exists as an underlying substance. The philosophy further asserted that every object has at one time one 'res' and one 'res' only. Taking this ground, the technical doctrine of Transubstantiation asserted that before consecration the elements have the res and the 'accidents' of bread and wine, but after consecration, while they still have the accidents of bread and wine (that is, have everything in bread and wine which can be seen or felt or tasted or nourishes the body), they no longer have the 'res' of bread and wine, since the underlying substance has ceased to be that of bread and wine and become that of the body and blood of Christ. The first form of Transubstantiation is certainly contrary to passages in the Fathers in which two parts of the Sacrament are spoken of after consecration, and the elements are said to remain what they were before, as well as being something different, so that the co-existence of the elements and the body and blood of Christ may be compared with the co-existence of the human and divine natures of our Lord. [67]

The consideration of Transubstantiation in the second sense raises a philosophical rather than a theological question. The assertion of it has the disadvantage of identifying a truth of religion with a particular philosophical theory, an identification always dangerous; and there is difficulty in harmonizing the assertion of the absence of the 'res' of the bread and wine with the comparison which the Fathers use of the bread and wine with the humanity of Christ, because it is certain that whatever the 'res' may be, the 'res' of the humanity was in the incarnate life. The Council of Bethlehem of A.D. 1672 asserted what is practically the doctrine of Transubstantiation, and its decrees have been accepted by the Greek Church. They were not, however, accepted by the Russian Church without important alterations which affect this subject, the intention of which appears to have been to avoid committing the Russian Church to the doctrine taught by the Church of Rome. [68]

The term Consubstantiation was invented by the Zwinglians, who denied any presence of Christ in the Sacrament, as a term of reproach against the teaching of Luther. This led to the word being ordinarily used to describe the Lutheran doctrine. The teaching of Luther has been taken to mean that there was a union in the Eucharist of the body and blood of Christ with the bread and wine after the manner of the union of earthly and material substances; and that this was complicated both by his theory of the ubiquity of the manhood of Christ and by a notion of confusion, as well as union, of the body and blood with the bread and wine, in the same way that the divine and hu^ n natures of our Lord were confused in some forms of Monophysitism. Except so far as the theory of the ubiquity of the manhood of Christ is concerned, it may be doubted whether Luther so taught. The truth probably is that his teaching involved many inconsistencies, and varied at different times; but it is fair to notice that his positive doctrine about the Eucharist does not imply either the material and carnal union or the confusion between the body and blood and the bread and wine with which he is commonly charged; and also that the few modern Lutherans who have continued to believe in the real presence do not appear to regard the union as material and carnal, although their sacramental teaching is complicated by their failure to recognize the permanence of the presence and by the error of ascribing to the divine nature the humiliation of the human nature, and to the human nature attributes of the divine nature. [69]

On this whole subject it is best to be content with the positive statements for which there is ample justification, that the body and blood of our Lord are present in the Sacrament, and that what we ordinarily understand by bread and wine is there also, and not to attempt to formulate any more definite theory on the philosophical point which the technical form of Transubstantiation raises.

The term concomitance is used to denote the fact that the whole humanity of Christ, including both His body and His blood, is present in each of the consecrated species, and in the smallest fragment or drop of either. This fact follows from the truths that it is Christ Himself who is in the Sacrament and that He cannot be divided. If the Eucharistic presence was the carnal presence of a natural body, there might be a division in it, and there might be blood separately from flesh, though hardly flesh entirely without blood; but, since the Eucharistic presence is the presence of the spiritual, glorified, living humanity of Christ, it follows that wherever it is, it must wholly be. To assert that there is a division and that His blood is not in the consecrated bread, and that His body is not in the consecrated contents of the chalice would imply a presence of a merely natural kind, if not that of a dead body.

The next point to be considered is that of the nature and effects of the Eucharist as a sacrifice. The main idea of sacrifice is that of dedication to God; and what is essential in sacrifice may be described as that it is offered to God in a religious rite with a religious end. The fact of sin brought into sacrifice the idea of death; but sacrifice in itself does not necessarily include death. It may be a gift of life, as well as a gift of death; and even where death has become a necessary part of sacrifice, as in the Atonement, because of sin, what is most fundamental of all is still the oblation of the will, so that, in St. Bernard's phrase, it was not the death itself but rather the will of him who freely died which was pleasing to God the Father, though 'salvation was in the blood.' [70] The true idea of sacrifice is thus the dedication of life, although in the Atonement it necessarily took the form of dedication through death.

There are indications in Holy Scripture that the Eucharist is a sacrifice. St. Luke records that our Lord used the words, 'Do this for My memorial' (τοῦτο ποιεῖτε εἰς τὴν ἐμὴν ἀνάμνησιν). [71] The word 'do' (ποιεῖτε) may or may not have a sacrificial meaning. If it stood by itself, the sacrificial meaning would not be inappropriate because it is employed in a sacrificial sense in the Greek version of the Old Testament used by the Hellenistic Jews, and because the passover meal would naturally suggest sacrificial ideas; but it could not be pressed. The word 'memorial' (ἀνάμνησις) is the key word of the sentence. In the Greek version of the Old Testament it usually means a memorial before God. [72] In the New Testament, it is used in this passage in St. Luke's Gospel; in 1 Cor. xi. 24, 25, where also it refers to the Eucharist; and in Hebrews x. 3, in connexion with the remembrance before God made in the Jewish sacrifices. It is therefore rightly regarded as a sacrificial word; and it naturally implies that the memorial or remembrance of which our Lord speaks is a memorial before God. The whole view of the high priesthood of Christ which is worked out at length in the Epistle to the Hebrews implies that His priestly work includes the continual pleading of an abiding sacrifice; and a connexion between the intercession of Christ in heaven and the Eucharist is obviously appropriate. Moreover, the New Testament in several places implies that the worship of Christians is a sacrificial worship. [73] If the New Testament evidence stood by itself, it would be a fair statement about it to say that, while by no means great in amount and somewhat involved in difficulty, it certainly points in the direction of the Eucharist being sacrificial.

The teaching of the Church establishes the interpretation of the New Testament which regards the Eucharist as sacrificial. From the earliest times, and in all parts of the Church, representative writers call the Eucharist a sacrifice. In the book entitled *The Teaching of the Twelve Apostles* it is described as your sacrifice; and the prophecy of Malachi that 'a pure offering' should be offered in every place is applied to it. [74] St. Ignatius uses the word altar in connexion with the Eucharist. [75] St. Irenaeus calls the Eucharist the sacrifice of the New Testament, and says it is offered to God. [76] St. Cyprian calls it a 'true and full sacrifice,' [77] The Council of Nicaea speaks of it as being offered. [78] St. Athanasius calls it 'the bloodless propitiatory sacrifice,' [79] St. Augustine describes it as the sacrifice of our redemption,' and 'the sacrifice of the Mediator,' [80] The newly-discovered book of liturgical prayers used by Bishop Serapion not later than the middle of the fourth century calls it this living sacrifice,' 'this bloodless offering,' [81] These passages represent the general patristic teaching on the subject. When this assertion of the sacrificial character of the Eucharist is joined with the patristic teaching about the presence of the humanity of Christ in the elements, it may be seen in what way the Eucharist is a sacrifice. A distinction is made between the bloody sacrifice and the unbloody sacrifice. The bloody sacrifice is the offering of the as yet unglorified humanity in agony and death on the cross. The unbloody sacrifice is the offering of the now glorified humanity without pain or death on the altar. The sacrifice is the same sacrifice, because in each case that which is offered is the body and blood of Christ, and because the priest is the same, that is, our Lord acting by Himself on the cross, acting through His ministers at the altar. The mode in which the sacrifice is offered is different, because on the cross the humanity was offered in its natural condition, and therefore in humiliation, pain, and death, while at the altar it is offered in the glorified condition in which it lives in the risen life of our Lord. The sacrifice on the cross is the Atonement for all the sins of all men. The sacrifice of the Eucharist is the pleading of that Atonement by the presentation of the same offering to the Father. When the Eucharistic sacrifice is properly regarded, it does not imply any incompleteness of Christ's work on the cross. On the contrary, it necessitates the completeness and perfection of the sacrifice on the cross, because, unless the sacrifice on the cross was perfect and complete, the pleading of it in the Eucharist would miss its force. In addition to the intimate connexion between the sacrifice of the Eucharist and the sacrifice on the cross, it is necessary to notice also the intimate connexion between the Eucharist and our Lord's offering of His sacrifice in heaven. On the cross the sacrifice of our Lord's manhood was perfectly offered. In heaven our Lord continually pleads that sacrifice, offering to the Father His living and glorified manhood made to be a sacrificial offering by having passed through death. On the altar the Christian Church presents to the Father the same offering which our Lord is continually pleading in heaven. Alike on the cross, in heaven, and on the altar, the offering which is made is that of the sacred manhood of our Lord Himself. [82]

It has already been seen that the presence of the body and blood of Christ in the consecrated elements is an objective reality which depends upon the fulfilment of certain external conditions, so as to be independent of anything in those who receive the Sacrament. It follows that all who receive the Sacrament receive the same gift so far as the Sacrament is concerned; that is, they receive the body and blood of Christ. Nothing less than this can be implied in the truth that the presence of Christ in the Sacrament is connected, not with the faith of the receiver, but with the act of consecration of proper elements with the proper form by a priest. Therefore, the 'sacramentum,' or consecrated bread and wine, and the 'res sacramenti,' or inward part of the body and blood of Christ, are received by all communicants. The 'virtus sacramenti,' or benefit of reception, is received by some only. As might be expected, there is no detailed teaching on this point in Holy Scripture; but what has been said is what would be most naturally understood from the few passages in Holy Scripture which bear on the subject. Thus, the accounts of the institution of the Sacrament and the words of St. Paul associating the presence with the acts of the priest do not suggest any connexion between the presence of Christ in the Sacrament and the faith of the receiver, while a comparison of St. John vi. 54 and 1 Cor. xi. 27-29 shows that the results of the reception of the Sacrament are different in different persons. That all communicants receive the body and blood of Christ, but only some receive to profit, has been the ordinary teaching in the Church. [83]

Taking it, then, that all communicants receive the 'res sacramenti,' but that only those who partake worthily receive the 'virtus sacramenti,' the 'virtus sacramenti,' has been generally explained as including the continuance and strengthening of the union with the life of Christ which was given in Baptism, the purifying of the soul by means of that union, strength to avoid sin and overcome temptation and do good by virtue of the same union, being well pleasing to God because of this participation in the life of Christ, the spiritual joy of communion with Christ, and the reception of the gift of eternal life of happiness with God.

The necessity of receiving the Eucharist is expressed in our Lord's words, 'Except ye eat the flesh of the Son of Man and drink His blood, ye have not life in yourselves;' [84] and has been part of the common teaching of the Church. It is to be understood in the same way as the necessity of any Sacrament is to be understood; that the Sacrament is the appointed means of God which we are bound not to neglect, though we cannot tell to what extent God will bind Himself by His own means.

The following errors about the Holy Eucharist may be here mentioned: -

1. Symbolism is the teaching that the bread and wine after the prayer of consecration, as well as before, are only symbols of the body and blood of Christ; and that no communicants receive anything in or with the elements except bread and wine as such symbols.

2. Virtualism is the view that the bread and wine remain only bread and wine after consecration; but that, together with them, the faithful communicant receives the benefit or virtue of Christ's body and blood, though not the body and blood itself.

3. Receptionism is the view that the bread and wine remain only bread and wine after consecration; but that, together with them, the faithful communicant really receives the body and blood of Christ.

4. These different errors about the presence of Christ involve the denial of the doctrine of the Eucharistic sacrifice, which depends upon the bread and wine being the body and blood of Christ. Accordingly, any who have not recognized the presence of Christ in the elements have denied the true doctrine of the sacrifice, although there have been some who, while denying the presence of Christ in the elements, held that there was in the Eucharist a material sacrifice of bread and wine.

5. Any way of stating the doctrine of the presence which makes it to be the presence of the body and blood of Christ in their natural state as before the resurrection, instead of the spiritual body and blood of Christ with which He rose from the dead.

6. Any way of stating the doctrine of the sacrifice which dissociates it from the sacrifice of Calvary, and makes it a new or repeated sacrifice.

Against these errors the true doctrine asserts -

1. Against Symbolism. There is a presence of Christ's body and blood in the elements.

2. Against Virtualism. This presence is a real presence, that is, the true presence of Christ Himself.

3. Against Receptionism. This real presence is objective, that is, independent of the faith of the recipient.

4. Against denials of the sacrifice. Christ's body and blood thus present in the Sacrament are offered in sacrifice.

5. Against a carnal presence. It is the spiritual body and blood of the risen and ascended Christ which are present in the Sacrament.

6. Against any repetition of the sacrifice. The Eucharistic sacrifice is the presentation of the same offering as the sacrifice of Calvary and the sacrifice in heaven.

In the Eucharist the baptismal union between God and man is maintained through participation in the life of our Lord. It is a means, also, by which Christian souls are united to one another. 'We, who are many,' wrote St. Paul, 'are one bread, one body: for we all partake of the one bread.' [85]

[1] See the volume on *Holy Baptism in the Oxford Library of Practical Theology,* pp. 1-6.

[2] See note 43 in the concluding Notes.

[3] See note 44 in the concluding Notes.

[4] St. John iii. 5.

[5] St. Matt, xxviii. 19.

[6] Acts ii. 38, 41.

[7] Acts ii. 38; viii. 16; x. 48; xix. 5.

[8] See note 45 in the concluding Notes.

[9] On the unworthiness of the minister and on intention, see notes 58 and 59 in the concluding Notes.

[10] 1 Cor. vi. 11-15; Gal. iii. 27; Eph. v. 25-30; Col. ii. 12.

[11] St. Mark xvi. 16; Acts ii. 38, 41, 47; xvi. 30, 33; xxii. 16; St. Titus iii. 5-7; 1 St. Peter i. 3, 4; iii. 21.

[12] Acts ii. 38; ix. 17, 18; St. Titus iii. 5.

[13] Rom. viii. 14-19; Gal. iii. 26-27.

[14] Rom. vi. 1-4.

[15] See note 46 in the concluding Notes.

[16] St. Augustine, *Quaest. in Lev.,* 84; Cf. St. Ambrose, *De Obit. Val.,* 51-53; St. Thomas Aquinas, *Summa Theol.,* III. lxviii, 2; Andrewes, *Sermons (Library of Anglo-Catholic Theology,* v. 94).

[17] St. Augustine, *Ep.,* clxxxvi. 27; ccxvii. 22; *C. Jul. Pelag.,* v. 44; *Serm.,* ccxciv. 3. In *De Lib. Arbit.,* iii. 66-67, an earlier work, he referred to the possi-

bility of a future middle state for those who die without having done either good or evil.

[18] St. Gregory of Nazianzus, *Orat.,* xl. 23.

[19] St. Gregory of Nyssa, *Cat. Orat.,* 35, *De Infant, qui praemat. abripiuntur, passim.*

[20] St. Thomas Aquinas, *Sent.,* II. xxxiii. 2; *Summa Theol.,* III. i. 4, ad 2; App. i. Cf. Councils of Lyons (A.D. 1274) and Florence (A.D. 1438) (Hardouin, Cone., vii. 696; ix. 424).

[21] For fuller details on the history of Holy Baptism, the Baptism of infants, the matter, form, minister, and necessity of the Sacrament, with references and quotations, see the volume *Holy Baptism in the Oxford Library of Practical Theology.*

[22] Acts viii. 14-17; xix. 6; Heb. vi. 1, 2.

[23] See, *e.g.,* Schouppe, *Elementa Theologiae Dogmaticae,* xii. 22.

[24] *Pontificale Romanum,* Confirmatio uni tantum conferenda.

[25] See note 47 in the concluding Notes.

[26] See, *e.g.* Maskell, *Monumenta Ritualia Ecclesiae Anglicanae,* i. 25, 31. Cf. Councils of Worcester (A.D. 1240), cap. 6, and Exeter (A.D. 1287), cap. 3. Councils of Cologne (A.D. 1280, cap. 5; A.D. 1536, p. vii. cap. 9) recognized the postponement of Confirmation till seven years old or older.

[27] *Catechism of the Council of Trent,* II. iii. 17. Cf. Council of Milan (A.D. 1565), p. ii., cap. 3. The Roman Rubrics, however, still contemplate the Confirmation of infants: see *Pontificale Romanum.*

[28] The passage quoted was assigned to Pope Melchiades in the forged decretals, and is quoted as his by, *e.g.,* St. Thomas Aquinas, *Summa Theol,* III. lxxii. 1, and the *Catechism of the Council of Trent,* II. iii. 5.

[29] Peter Lombard, *Sent.,* iv. 7.

[30] Acts viii. 14-17; xix. 5,6.

[31] Cornelius, ap. Eusebius, *H. E.,* vi. 43; Tertullian, *De Bapt.,* 6; St. Cyprian, *Ep.,* lxxiv. 5, 7.

[32] Acts ii. 38; ix. 17-19.

[33] Rom. viii. 9.

[34] St. Chrysostom, *In Act. Ap. Rom.,* xl. 2.

[35] St. Cyprian, *Ep.,* lxix. 13-15.

[36] St. Basil, *Adv. Eunom.,* v. (t. i. p. 303 A, edit. Benedic.).

[37] St. Athanasius, *Ep. ad Serap,,* i. 4.

[38] Origen, *In Ezech. Hom.,* vi. 5.

[39] St. Luke i. 35; iii. 22; Acts ii. 33.

[40] *Théologie Dogmatique Orthodoxe,* par Macaire, traduite par un Russe, Paris, 1860, 210 (t. ii. p. 425).

[41] See Goar, *Euchologion,* p. 289.

[42] Council of Bethlehem, cap. 16.

[43] For a fuller treatment of this point, with references and quotations, see the volume on *Holy Baptism,* pp. 67-85, 242-251, in the *Oxford Library of Practical Theology.*

[44] St. Matt. xxvi. 26-28; St. Mark xiv. 22-24; St. Luke xxii. 19, 20.

[45] St. John vi. 26-58.

[46] Acts ii. 42, 46; xx. 7, 11; 1 Cor. x. 16; xi. 23-29, are New Testament instances.

[47] *Read and others* v. *the Lord Bishop of Lincoln Judgment,* p. 13.

[48] There is a remarkable variation in the liturgical prayers of Serapion of Thmuis, 1, where the invocation is for the descent of the Word upon the elements, without any invocation of the Holy Ghost.

[49] Tertullian, *De Exhort. Cast.,* 7.

[50] Tertullian, *De Praes. Haeret.,* 41.

[51] See note 48 in the concluding Notes.

[52] St. John vi. 51-56; St. Matt. xxvi. 26-28; St. Mark xiv. 22-24; St. Luke xxii. 19, 20.

[53] 1 Cor. x. 16.

[54] St. Ignatius, *Ad Smyr.,* 6.

[55] St. Irenaeus, *C. Haer.,* IV. xviii. 5; xxxiii. 2.

[56] St. Athanasius, *Serm. ad Bapt.*

[57] St. Ambrose, *De Fid.,* iv. 124.

[58] St. Augustine, *In Ps. xxxiii. Serm.,* i. 10.

[59] St. Chrysostom, *In 1 Cor, Hom.,* xxvii. 5.

[60] For a very large collection of passages, see Pusey, *The Doctrine of the Real Presence.* The student should work through the quotations in the original languages, noting which of them require the presence of our Lord's body and blood in the elements, as well as the reception of them by the communicant.

[61] See St. Justin Martyr, *Apol.,* i. 67.

[62] St. Cyril of Alexandria, *Ep. ad Calosyrium* (t. vi. p. 565, Aubert).

[63] St. Cyril of Jerusalem, *Cat. Myst.,* v. 20-22.

[64] St. Ambrose, *De Spir. Sanc.,* iii. 79.

[65] St. Augustine, *Enar. in Ps. xcviii.,* 9.

[66] See, *e.g.,* St. Thomas Aquinas, *Summa Theol.,* III. lxxvii. 6; De Lugo, *De Sacr, Euch.,* Disp. x.; *Catechism of the Council of Trent,* II. iv. 38.

[67] See note 49 in the concluding Notes.

[68] The facts are stated in a correspondence and an article in the *Guardian,* March 17, 24, 31, 1897.

[69] See note 50 in the concluding Notes.

[70] St. Bernard, *Tract, de Err. Abael.,* 21, 22.

[71] St. Luke xxii. 19.

[72] See note 51 in the concluding Notes.

[73] See Rom. xv. 16; Heb. xiii. 10, 15; 1 St. Peter ii. 5. Cf. Moberly, *Ministerial Priesthood,* pp. 267-272.

[74] *Teaching of the Twelve Apostles,* 14.

[75] St. Ignatius, *Ad Eph.,* 5; Ad Phil, 4.

[76] St. Irenaeus, *C. Haer.,* IV. xvii. 5; xviii. 1. Cf. fragment 36 (as to the genuineness or otherwise of this fragment, see Harvey's *Irenaeus,* i. clxx.-clxxiii.; Lightfoot, *St. Paul's Epistle to the Philippians,* p. 204).

[77] St. Cyprian, Ep., lxiii. 14.

[78] Council of Nicaea, canon 18, quoted in note 48 on page 321.

[79] St. Athanasius, *Orat. de Defunc.*

[80] St. Augustine, *Conf.,* ix. 32; *Enchir.,* 110.

[81] Serapion of Thmuis, 1.

[82] Cf. Bishop Jeremy Taylor, *The Rule and Exercises of Holy Living,* IV. x. 1-5.

[83] There are valuable materials and a careful discussion of the relation of some of the English formularies to this doctrine, in Hodges, *Bishop Guest, Articles Twenty-eight and Twenty-nine.* See, also, note 52 in the concluding Notes.

[84] St. John vi. 53.

[85] 1 Cor. x. 17.

Chapter Twelve - The Sanctifying Office of the Church - Part Two Penance

During our Lord's ministry He promised to give the keys of the kingdom of heaven to St. Peter, and spoke of the future use of these keys by the Apostles. 'I will give unto thee the keys of the kingdom of heaven: and whatsoever thou shalt bind on earth shall be bound in heaven: and whatsoever thou shalt loose on earth shall be loosed in heaven.' 'What things soever ye shall bind on earth shall be bound in heaven: and what things soever ye shall loose on earth shall be loosed in heaven.' [1] These words appear to apply to the powers of government and decision granted by our Lord to His Apostles as the rulers of His Church. A particular part of this work of government and decision, by which the authority to forgive and retain sins was conferred on the Apostles, was conveyed to them by our Lord on the day of His resurrection: 'Jesus therefore said to them again, Peace be unto you: as the Father hath sent Me, even so send I you. And when He had said this, He breathed on them, and saith unto them, Receive ye the Holy Ghost: whose soever sins ye forgive, they are forgiven unto them; whose soever sins ye retain, they are retained.' [2] It is probable that the power thus conveyed was referred to by anticipation in the mystical washing of the disciples' feet before the institution of the Holy Eucharist. This washing was placed before Communion. Our Lord said of it, 'He that is bathed (XeXoujulvoe) needeth not save to wash (vtyavQai) his feet,' [3] apparently meaning, He who has been bathed in Baptism needs before Communion only the cleansing of Absolution. The authori-

110

ty conveyed by our Lord to the Apostles after His resurrection was made effective by the descent of God the Holy Ghost on the day of Pentecost.

Instances of the exercise of this authority are found in the writings of St. Paul. 'I verily, being absent in body but present in spirit, have already, as though I were present, judged him that hath so wrought this thing, in the name of our Lord Jesus, ye being gathered together, and My spirit, with the power of our Lord Jesus, to deliver such a one unto Satan for the destruction of the flesh, that the spirit may be saved in the day of the Lord Jesus;' 'If I have forgiven any thing, for your sakes have I forgiven it in the person of Christ;' 'Hymenaeus and Alexander, whom I delivered unto Satan.' [4]

In some form this authority to remit and retain sins has always been exercised in the Church. Belief in the existence of so great a boon is found throughout the Fathers. St. Ignatius wrote to the Church at Philadelphia, The Lord forgives all those who are penitent, if in their penitence they have recourse to the unity of God and the council of the bishop. [5] Tertullian, before he became a Montanist, spoke of the work of repentance as including the act of the penitent in 'throwing himself on the ground before the presbyters.' [6] St. Cyprian says, 'The remission accomplished by means of the priests is pleasing in the sight of the Lord,' [7] Origen, in spite of idiosyncrasies and changes in belief, acknowledged that the Christian priest can forgive sins. [8] St. Ambrose speaks of repentance and confession restoring to grace the baptized who have sinned, of the exercise of the forgiveness of sins by the power of the Holy Ghost, and of the act of the priest conveying the pardon of God. [9] St. Chrysostom asserts that the powers of the clergy are greater than those of kings, since the acts of kings have value only on earth, while the forgiveness which the priest conveys extends also to heaven. [10] St. Augustine, [11] St. Jerome, [12] St. Leo, [13] and later writers generally associate forgiveness with the ministrations of the Church.

In addition to such assertions of belief, there is testimony to the actual administration of Penance. Reconciliation may possibly be referred to by St. Clement of Rome, [14] and in the second-century document wrongly ascribed to him, [15] The *Shepherd* of Hennas appears to imply the practice of excommunication, [16] The history of Montanism would lose much of its meaning if it were not for the penitential discipline of the Church. [17] The witnesses to the existence of an organized system of Penance include St. Irenaeus, [18] Tertullian, [19] Origen, [20] St. Cyprian, [21] the Apostolical Constitutions, [22] and the Councils of the fourth century. [23]

The earliest method of the administration of Penance was in the majority of cases public and very rarely private. [24] At a later time, the private administration became more common; and it eventually superseded the public administration in all cases except those of notorious sins.

This change took place in the fifth century. In the time of St. Leo it was becoming customary for the confession to be made and the absolution received in private, instead of this privacy being, as before, exceptional. This brought up the question whether there was any difference between the objective value of the old method and that of the new method. Some Christians appear to have been afraid that this private reception of Absolution might not be equally effectual with the public reception of it. In his Epistles St. Leo deals with this mistake. 'The manifold mercy of God,' he writes in one place, 'has so come to the help of human falls that not only through the grace of Baptism, but also through the medicine of Penance the hope of eternal life is restored, so that they who have done violence to the gifts of regeneration, condemning themselves by their own judgment, may attain to the remission of their offences, the protection of the divine goodness having been ordered in such a way that the indulgence of God can only be obtained by means of the ministrations of the priests. For the mediator between God and men, the man Christ Jesus, has bestowed upon the rulers of the Church this authority, that they should grant the performance of Penance to those who make confession, and, when these are cleansed by healthful satisfaction, should admit them to communion in the Sacraments by the gate of reconciliation.' In another Epistle, when he has laid down that it is better for several reasons that penitents should not make their confessions in public, as had hitherto been the case, he says, 'For that confession is sufficient which is in the first instance offered to God and then also to the priest who comes as one who prays for the faults of the penitent.' [25]

The matter in Penance consists of the contrition, confession, and satisfaction of one who has sinned. [26] These have always been required in some shape, though the method of both confession and satisfaction has varied. The confession was at first usually open, and afterwards usually secret. The penitential acts of satisfaction were at first usually performed before receiving Absolution and afterwards usually performed after receiving Absolution.

The form in Penance consists of words of Absolution. Probably for centuries the words were precatory everywhere: May God absolve thee. The earliest known instance of an indicative absolution is in a tenth-century copy of an eighth-century Office Book, the Pontifical of Archbishop Egbert. [27] From at any rate the middle of the thirteenth century the indicative form, 'I absolve thee,' has been universal in the West. It is now used also in the Russian Church. The precatory form is still in use elsewhere in the Churches of the East and among some of the Eastern Christians united to Rome.

The uniform teaching and practice of the Church imply that the minister must be a bishop or a priest. The object of the mediaeval custom of a dying person making confession to a layman in the absence of a priest was that he might show an outward sign of contrition as a means of imploring God for pardon, not with a view to Absolution. [28] Probably any priest can give a valid absolution to any person, though it is gravely irregular for an unlicensed priest to absolve except in case of necessity. [29]

The subject in Penance is a baptized person who has committed sin.

The effects of Absolution are that through it there is forgiveness of sins, restoration to the favour of God, and re-admission to the profitable use of other Sacraments.

The early Church held that reconciliation was necessary in the case of the most grievous sins, while lighter sins needed only the prayer of those who had sinned. This came to be stereotyped into the later distinction that Absolution is necessary for the forgiveness of mortal sin, but not necessary for the forgiveness of venial sin. Any full discussion of mortal and venial sin belongs to moral theology, but it may be said here that the ordinary definitions of mortal sin require knowledge, deliberation, an act of the will, and grave matter. This distinction became general in the West; and the idea contained in it may be found in the East. It is obvious that the gravity of offences differs according to the knowledge of the persons committing them, and according to the deliberateness and malice and persistency with which they are committed. In recognizing this fact, it must be remembered that, while no theologian in any part of the Church would regard sacramental reconciliation as in itself required for the forgiveness of venial sins, yet venial sins are real and serious both in themselves and because, if acquiesced in, they lead to graver sins.

As to the method of administration of Penance, both in the Roman and Eastern Churches, a necessary element, and therefore a necessary condition of receiving sacramental Absolution, is that, in all ordinary cases, there should be a detailed confession of sins to a priest. Both Rome and the East limit sacramental Absolutions to the Absolutions given after such confessions, and agree that the prayers for Absolution used by a priest in the offices, or in the confession at the beginning of the Eucharist, or in the confession before the Communion of the people, are not sacramental Absolutions. In connexion with this, a question has been raised as to the relative value of the three Absolutions which are contained in the English Prayer-book. It has been thought by some that the three Absolutions used in the Morning and Evening Prayer, the Order of Holy Communion, and the Order for the Visitation of the Sick are objectively equal, each one of the three being the exercise of the power of the keys. It has been thought by others that the Absolutions in the Order of Holy Communion and the Order for the Visitation of the Sick are objectively equal, each one of these two being the exercise of the power of the keys; but that the Absolution in the Morning and Evening Prayer is simply a declaration with a prayer added, and has no sacramental force. Others, again, have thought that only the Absolution used to an individual, as in the Order for the Visitation of the Sick, is the exercise of the power of the keys and sacramental, the Absolution in the Order of Holy Communion being a prayer, and that in the Morning and Evening Prayer a declaration with a prayer added, neither of the last two having sacramental force.

The first and second of these opinions have been held upon the grounds that it is within the power of a properly constituted local Church to modify the method in which the Sacraments are administered; that this power was exercised by the Church in England in the sixteenth century, when it was intended that the Absolution in the Order of Holy Communion (or those in the Order of Holy Communion and the Morning and Evening Prayer) should be objectively equivalent to the Absolution which always previously had been given only after detailed confession; and that consequently this action of the local Church in England avails to make these methods of giving Absolution sacramentally efficacious.

On the other hand, it has been urged that there are the following reasons against this identification of the objective value of the three methods of giving Absolution: -

1. It is true that within certain limits a local Church can modify the method of administering the Sacraments. For instance, a local Church would be acting within its powers in any regulation as to the method in which the water of Baptism should be applied to the bodies of the baptized, and might well in a cold climate order that water should be poured upon infants, and in a warm climate order that they should be immersed. But this power is one which can only be exercised within limits; and the limits would always be passed if there was anything which came to be inconsistent with the institution of our Lord. In the institution of Penance, our Lord gave two parallel powers, the power to forgive sins, and the power to retain sins. The existence of the power to retain sins depends on the act of reconciliation being individual, and on the priest knowing what the sins are. If the sacramental Absolution can be received in the course of a service without any individual recourse to a priest, and consequently without any submission of the case to him, the power to retain sins disappears. If this is so, our Lord's words in the institution of Penance make the knowledge of the sins by the priest an essential condition for the existence of a sacramental Absolution. It is in the same line of thought that the Church has always regarded the priest in the work of reconciliation as being a judge; and he cannot be a judge unless the case is submitted to him.

2. If these considerations are of weight, it will follow that whatever the intention of the Church in England in the sixteenth century was, the Absolutions in the Morning and Evening Prayer and in the Order of Holy Communion cannot be sacramental Absolutions. Moreover, it is by no means clear that the intention of the Church in England was to make the three Absolutions or two of them equivalent. English theologians have distinguished between them. [30] The most obvious interpretation of the warning before Communion directed to be read on the Sunday or Holy Day preceding every Celebration is that 'the benefit of Absolution' cannot be obtained unless there has been confession to a priest. It is unlikely that the Church in England would have retained public Absolutions resembling the medieval public Absolutions, which were not regarded as sacramental, and also the private Absolution resembling the mediaeval private Absolution, which was regarded as sacramental, unless the difference between them was also retained.

There are reasons, then, for questioning the identification of the different Absolutions, partly because it is not clear that the Church of England meant to identify them; and partly because such an identification may be regarded as an act outside the limits of the power of a local Church.

The rite of Penance is the merciful provision of the loving God who knows the needs of His children. It is altogether misunderstood if it is regarded as a stern provision which imposes hard conditions of receiving benefit. Every right view of sin has indeed its stern side; for sin, and especially the sin of a Christian, is an awful thing. But that which is prominent in Penance is the personal forgiveness granted by the merciful God. In Dr. Pusey's application of the words of the Psalmist, [31] it is 'a gracious rain' sent by God 'upon His inheritance,' which 'refreshed it when it was weary.' [32] It is the application by our Lord Himself to the individual soul, which is turning from sin to Him who is its true end, of that precious blood which, in His exceeding love, He shed on Calvary for the sins of the world.

Unction of the Sick

There is no mention in Holy Scripture of the institution of the Unction of the sick. Possibly, it was anticipated in the command of our Lord which presumably preceded the anointing with oil practised by the Apostles during His ministry; [33] and the Unction itself may be referred to in the Epistle of St. James. [34] Passages in Origen [35] and St. Chrysostom [36] sometimes interpreted as referring to it, which mention forgiveness of sins in connexion with the words of St. James, probably denote Penance, not Unction. The blessing of oil as a liturgical action is alluded to in the *Canons of Hippolytus*, [37] as in use at Rome at the end of the second or the beginning of the third century. Prayers for the consecration of oil for use in sickness are found in the *Testament of our Lord,* [38] a Syrian or Cilician document probably written about the middle of the third century; the liturgical prayers of Serapion, Bishop of Thmuis in Egypt, [39] who died about A.D. 365; and the *Apostolical Constitutions,* [40] which show the Syrian usages of the fourth century. *The Testament of Our Lord* and the *Apostolical Constitutions* mention the use of water as well as oil, and the prayers of Serapion refer to oil, bread, and water. Both bodily and spiritual healing are evidently in view as the purpose of the rite. Early in the fifth century this Unction is referred to by Pope Innocent I. in a letter to Decentius; [41] and in the sixth century it is mentioned in the writings of Caesarius of Aries. [42] Instances of healing by means of oil are recorded in Egypt and Syria in the fourth century. [43]

The passages in the *Testament,* the prayers of Serapion, and the *Apostolical Constitutions* contemplate the oil being blessed by a bishop or priest and do not show by whom it was to be administered to the sick person. Those in Innocent I. and Caesarius contemplate the oil being blessed by a bishop and applied either by the sick person himself or by others, whether priests or laymen. By the eighth century it had come to be the ordinary custom that the oil was applied by a priest.

The earliest known instance of the name 'Unctio extrema' is in the writings of Peter Lombard [44] in the twelfth century. It means 'the last of the Unctions,' and distinguishes this anointing from others, as those in Baptism or Confirmation. When the word Sacrament was restricted in meaning, and the number of Sacraments came to be regarded as seven, this Unction was counted as one of the seven. At the present time it is retained by the Church of Rome; by the Greek and Russian Churches: and, with various modifications, in the Eastern Churches which are separated from the Orthodox Church. [45] It was retained in the Church of England in the Prayer-book of 1549. The provision for it was omitted in 1552 and has not been restored in any subsequent Prayer-book.

The matter of Unction consists of olive oil, which has been blessed, applied to the body of the sick person. The Church of Rome as a rule limits the blessing of the oil to a bishop in the West; but allows a priest to bless it among the Eastern Christians in communion with Rome. The Eastern Churches allow the blessing to be by either a bishop or a priest.

The form consists of words of prayer, which have differed greatly in different parts of the Church. The Roman form is, By this holy anointing and His most sacred pity, the Lord forgive thee whatever thou hast sinned, repeated seven times, with the addition at the seven anointings of 'by sight,' 'by hearing,' 'by smelling,' 'by taste and speech,' 'by touch,' 'by walking,' 'by sensual delight,' respectively. In practice the seventh is generally omitted. The Eastern form, and the form used by Easterns in communion with Rome, consists of a long prayer beginning, 'Holy Father, healer of souls and bodies,' the crucial words in which are 'heal this thy servant from that weakness of body and soul which holds him down.' The English Prayer-book of 1549 had a long prayer specifying inward anointing with the Holy Ghost, health of body and mind, pardon of sin, strength against temptation.

The earliest notices of Unction which say anything about the minister show, as already mentioned, that it might be administered by any one, including the person who was ill, whether priest or layman. Probably the oil in the early Church was usually blessed by a bishop, though sometimes by a priest. At present, in the East the Unction is administered, if possible, by seven priests, the ordinary method being for the oil to be blessed by them at the time of administration. If seven priests cannot be had, it may be blessed and administered by three, or, in cases of necessity, by two or one. In the Roman Church, anointing is administered by a priest; and the oil must be blessed by a bishop or a priest who has explicit or implicit leave from the Pope, all priests of Eastern Christians in communion with Rome being included in those who have implicit leave.

The recipient of Unction was originally any Christian seriously ill. In the middle ages it became common for the laity to refuse this Unction except at the point of death, with the result that in the West especially, but also to a large extent in the East, it became practically a Sacrament for the dying. Now, its use is almost entirely so limited. In the East the faithful are allowed to ask for it in any sickness; and this is very occasionally done when there is no immediate danger of death. In the Roman Church there is nothing formal to prevent any person dangerously ill from being anointed; but the practical use is that of a Sacrament for the dying.

As to the effects of Unction, the usual statement is that it conveys forgiveness of venial sins, purification of soul, spiritual strength, and sometimes bodily health.

'One must at once confess and deplore,' writes Bishop Alexander Forbes, 'that a distinctly Scriptural practice has ceased to be commanded in the Church of England. Excuses may be made of "corrupt following of the Apostles," in that it was used, contrary to the mind of St. James, when all hope of the restoration of bodily health was gone; but it cannot be denied that there has been practically lost an apostolic practice, whereby, in case of grievous sickness, the faithful were anointed and prayed over, for the forgiveness of their sins, and to restore them, if God so willed, or to give them spiritual support in their maladies.' [46] 'Since...the Visitation of the Sick is a private office, and uniformity is required only in the public offices, there is nothing to hinder the revival of the apostolic and Scriptural custom of anointing the sick, whensoever any devout person may desire it. It is, indeed, difficult to say on what principle it could be refused.' [47]

Holy Orders

During His ministry our Lord chose and appointed His Apostles. [48] They were ordained by Him after His resurrection, and received the fulness of the ordination gifts on the day of Pentecost. [49] In the Apostles thus appointed and ordained were all the powers of the Christian Ministry. The account of the process by which the different powers were differentiated into the different Orders is an historical question outside the scope of the present work; but as a result of the process the Orders of bishop, priest, deacon, sub-deacon, acolyte, exorcist, reader, and doorkeeper had come to be recognized by, at any rate, the middle of the third century.

It is agreed that only the sacred Orders, and not the minor Orders, are sacramental. There is a difference of opinion as to the division between the sacred and the minor Orders. Easterns count bishop, priest and deacon as comprising all the sacred Orders. Roman theologians count the episcopate and the priesthood as one Order and reckon this Order, with those of deacon and sub-deacon, as the sacred Orders. Thus, there is a difference between the Eastern and the Roman theologians as to whether the office of sub-deacon is a sacred Order. Roman theologians, while all agreeing that the office of sub-deacon is a sacred Order, differ as to whether it is sacramental.

The matter in Orders is the laying on of hands. For a long time it was held by many in the West that the matter was the delivery of the Book of the Gospels to the deacon, and of the paten and chalice to the priest, known as the 'delivery of the instruments,' in the case of those two Orders. The investigations of Morinus embodied in his book *De Sacris Ordinationibus,* published in 1686, showed that this ritual act had never been the custom in the East, and was not earlier than the eleventh century in the West. Practically all theologians in the East and West now say that the laying on of hands is by itself valid matter.

The form of Orders consists of words of prayer referring to the special gift. There do not appear to be any exact words which are necessary to the validity of the rite. Forms which all theologians agree are sufficient vary greatly. It is generally agreed that the office must contain what will show the object of the laying on of hands.

The common practice of the Church shows that the minister must be a bishop. Some supposed exceptions to this which have been controversially cited will not bear investigation. [50]

The recipient must be a baptized person.

All who are validly ordained receive the character of the office to which they are ordained, and the authority needed for the particular grade of the ministry to which they are ordained. Those who worthily receive ordination receive also sanctifying grace.

English Orders

The validity of English Orders has been questioned or denied by Roman theologians on the following grounds:

1. As to matters of fact, it has been alleged (*a*) that Matthew Parker, who became Archbishop of Canterbury in 1559, to whom the subsequent succession is due, was never consecrated; and (*b*) that Barlow, who has been represented as the consecrator of Parker, had never himself been consecrated bishop.

2. As to the offices of ordination, it has been alleged (*a*) that they are insufficient in point of ritual because of the absence of the delivery of the instruments; and (b) that they are insufficient because they do not specify or distinctly refer to the sacrificing power of the priest hood.

3. As to the intention [51] of the Church, it has been alleged (*a*) that it is requisite that the Church should intend to continue the offices derived from the Apostles; and (*b*) that the Church of England in the sixteenth century intended to create a new ministry, not to continue the historical ministry.

4. As to the intention of the minister, it has been alleged (*a*) that it is requisite that the ordaining prelate intend to make deacons, or priests, or bishops, as it may be; and (*b*) that the English officiants in the sixteenth century did not so intend in the historical sense of the words.

As regards these four points it is to be noticed

1. (*a*) There is the strongest historical proof of Parker's consecration. All documents relating to it still exist. There is abundant historical evidence that it took place. The contention that he was not consecrated has now been abandoned by all Roman theologians who have studied the question.

(*b*) It is true that the documents relating to the actual consecration of Barlow are not known to exist. This is the case also with other bishops of the same period whose consecration has never been doubted. The existing documents for the consecrations of that period are fragmentary. There is documentary proof of the steps which would naturally lead up to his consecration, and of his having habitually acted as bishop; and there is no reasonable doubt that he was consecrated bishop in 1536. The denial of his consecration has not of late years been used by Roman theologians who have studied the question. Even if Barlow had not been consecrated, there would still remain the action of the others who consecrated Parker, who unquestionably were bishops. It is most probable that in the consecration of a bishop each of the bishops joining in the laying on of hands is a consecrator and not simply a witness; and, however this may be in some other cases, there is a strong probability it was so in Parker's consecration, because, in that case, each of the bishops, not Barlow only, said aloud the words of consecrating.

2. The English Offices show clearly the Orders to which Ordination is being made. If they are invalidated by the absence of the 'delivery of the instruments,' and of any reference to the sacrificing power of the priest hood, it is probable that there are no valid Orders in Christendom, because the earliest forms of Ordination Offices, including those of the Church of Rome, were without this ceremony and this reference. The requirement that the Office must show to what Order Ordination is made is fully satisfied in the English Offices.

3. The preface to the English Ordinal states in express terms that the object of the Ordinal, and therefore the intention of the Church, was to continue the Orders which had been in the Church since the time of the Apostles.

4. The argument as to the intention of the minister would make a kind of intention necessary in Orders which is not necessary in the case of any other Sacrament. It appears to have been merely a controversial point, and has not been used by recent Roman Catholic writers of position.

Matrimony

Matrimony was instituted by God after the creation of man. [52] At Cana of Galilee, our Lord by His presence gave His divine sanction to marriage; [53] at a later point in His ministry he reaffirmed the sacred character of the marriage bond; [54] and it is possible that Matrimony was one of 'the things concerning the kingdom of God' of which He spoke to His Apostles during the forty days between His resurrection and His ascension. [55]

As to what is essential to make a valid marriage, there is some difference in Eastern and Western theology. According to the ordinary teaching of Western theology, what is essential is the formal consent of persons who are free to contract marriage with one another, and this is independent of any religious ceremony, so that to constitute a valid marriage two points are necessary:

1. There must be no impediment of such a kind as to make the marriage invalid, technically called 'impedimentum dirimens,' such as relationship within particular degrees; the existing marriage of either person; or what is called 'disparitas cultus,' that is, when one person is baptized and the other is not.

2. The consent of the two persons contracting the marriage, of which it is generally said that it must be (a) mutual; (b) deliberate and voluntary; (c) externally shown; (d) not a promise only, but a consent taking effect at once.

According to Western theology, any such marriage of two unbaptized persons is valid, but not sacramental; and every valid marriage of baptized persons is sacramental, whether it is contracted before a priest or not. [56]

According to Eastern theology, there can be no Sacrament of Matrimony, and no ecclesiastically valid marriage unless, in addition to the two points mentioned, there is the administration of a bishop or a priest.

The usual Western opinion has been that the persons contracting the marriage are themselves the ministers; and this harmonizes with the ordinary Western belief that the essential point in matrimony is the consent of the parties. Thus, in a marriage contracted before a priest, the ordinary Western teaching is that the priest is the witness to that which the contracting parties do, and bestows the blessing of God on what they have done.

According to Eastern theology, the minister in Matrimony is a bishop or a priest.

The matter in Matrimony is the contract made by the persons married.

The form consists of the words by which the contract is expressed.

The effects are generally defined as being that the marriage places the persons who contract it in the indissoluble marriage relation; and that, if it is contracted worthily, it confers grace for right living in the married state. [57]

According to the original ordinance of God, marriage was indissoluble. [58] Under the Mosaic law, a wife who committed adultery was put to death, so that by her death the husband was set free to contract a new marriage. [59]

Under the Mosaic law also, a husband was not prohibited from putting away his wife for a cause less than adultery described as 'some unseemly thing;' and, under such circumstances, a fresh marriage, though it is spoken of as defiling by a word which is elsewhere used in connexion with adultery, was not expressly forbidden. [60] The concession of Moses, which thus spoke slightingly of re-marriage, but did not forbid it, was described by our Lord as an allowance because of the hardness of the Jews' hearts, and was recalled by Him. [61]

Our Lord's teaching on the subject of the indissolubility of marriage is contained in four passages in the Gospels. [62] In two of these [63] He declares that the re-marriage of husband or wife after separation is adultery. He does not say whether in this declaration He is including cases where the separation has taken place because of adultery; but there is no indication of any exception to the law which He lays down, that the marriage of a divorced person is adultery. In another passage [64] He forbids separation for any cause except fornication; and declares that to put away a wife for any other cause is to lead her to commit adultery; and that the marriage of any divorced woman is adultery. It is clear from this passage that our Lord declares that if a divorced woman re-marry, she commits adultery. The passage says nothing either way as to the possibility of the re-marriage of a husband who has divorced his wife for the one allowed cause of separation. In the remaining passage [65] our Lord says that the re-marriage of any divorced woman is adultery. The meaning as to the husband who puts away an adulterous wife and re-marries has been disputed; and there is some doubt as to the right reading of the Greek text. Taken as it stands in the received text, it reads, 'Whosoever shall put away his wife, except it be for fornication, and shall marry another, committeth adultery.' If the received text is correct, the right interpretation probably is that the clause 'except for fornication' simply refers to the separation, and the re-marriage of the husband is declared to be adultery, whatever the cause of separation has been, the words 'and shall marry another' being introduced to show how the adultery comes to be. If it is so interpreted, this passage is in harmony with the others; and the re-marriage of either husband or wife is declared to be adultery whatever the cause of separation may have been. [66]

The teaching of St. Paul on the same subject is contained in three passages in his Epistles. [67] One of these passages [68] is parallel to our Lord's teaching that husband and wife become one flesh. It simply asserts the doctrine, and does not enter into detail. In another passage [69] St. Paul declares that the re-marriage of a wife to another man, while her husband is living, is adultery. He does not enter into the question of the possibility of any exception. The third passage [70] is also general; but it says that if a wife is separated from her husband, she is either to remain unmarried or to be reconciled to him.

The teaching of our Lord and that of St. Paul, taken together, comprise all there is on the subject in the New Testament. Every part of this teaching prohibits the re-marriage of any divorced wife. Unless one passage [71] allows an exception after divorce for adultery, the whole of it prohibits also the re-marriage of a husband who has divorced his wife for any cause.

During the first six centuries there are a few writers who allow re-marriage after divorce under certain circumstances. Lactantius [72] appears to teach that, when adultery has been committed, either husband or wife may marry again. Asterius [73] and the writer known as Ambrosiaster [74] allow the innocent husband of a guilty wife to re-marry if the guilt has been that of adultery; but prohibit the innocent wife of a guilty husband, or either guilty party, from doing so. St. Epiphanius allows re-marriage after divorce, where there has been adultery, and also for other reasons; but he appears to say that this is really wrong, only it may be tolerated by the Church out of mercy to individuals. [75] St. Basil speaks somewhat similarly, saying that the Christian law forbids re-marriage; but that it is well in view of many existing evils to deal gently with offenders. [76] It should be noticed that all these writers base their allowance of re-marriage on general principles, not on anything in our Lord's teaching. With these exceptions, the Fathers either say in general terms that marriage is indissoluble without considering special cases; or, if they consider special cases, they say that in all cases of separation, even for adultery, neither husband nor wife, neither innocent nor guilty person, can contract a new marriage without committing adultery. The ordinary decisions of the Councils of the Church similarly prohibit re-marriage after divorce. [77]

The usual teaching of the Fathers and the Councils has remained as the law of the "Western Church. The Roman Church declares that neither person can remarry in the lifetime of the other without committing adultery. [78] As to the Church of England, the Form of Solemnization of Matrimony does not contemplate that either person will marry again in the lifetime of the other; and canons 106 and 107 of 1603, in recognizing annulling of pretended matrimony,' and 'divorce and separation *a thoro et mensa*,' require that the sentence of divorce in the latter case is not to be pronounced until those who are to be separated have given security that neither of them will, 'during each other's life, contract matrimony with any other person.'

In the Eastern Church the case is different. Easterns allow that re-marriage may take place after divorce for any of the causes specified in the Civil Code of Justinian. These causes include many besides adultery. [79] In practice it rests partly with the bishop to decide whether dissolution of marriage and re-marriage shall be allowed in any particular case. [80] The letter of the law of the Greek Church still prohibits re-marriage generally; [81] but a note is added in the official collection of the Greek canons that the contrary custom has been introduced from the civil law. [82] In the Russian Church there is more uniformity than in the Greek Church, and it is usual to allow re-marriage after adultery, desertion, or banishment. [83] The Eastern Christians in communion with Rome are allowed to follow their own custom in this matter. [84]

As to heathen marriages, there is a difficult passage in the First Epistle to the Corinthians. [85] In the preceding verses, which have been already referred to, St. Paul has been speaking of the indissolubility of marriage; and has declared that in what he has said on that subject it was not he who gave charge, but the Lord, that is, he was not speaking by virtue of his general apostolic authority and inspiration, but was repeating the teaching which our

Lord Himself had given in His personal ministry. He then goes on to speak about some special cases of the relations of Christians to heathen; and on this subject declares that there is no teaching given by our Lord in His personal ministry; but that he is speaking by virtue of his apostolic authority and inspiration. He next says that, supposing two persons have been married when heathen, and that either husband or wife becomes a Christian, and the person who remains a heathen is willing to continue to live with the one who has become a Christian, they are to continue to live together. So far the passage is perfectly clear. St. Paul then proceeds to consider the further case in which the person who remains a heathen refuses to live with the one who has become a Christian because of his or her Christianity. This necessarily brings up the question as to whether in such a case the Christian is at liberty to contract a fresh marriage. On this subject St. Paul says that the Christian οὐ δεδούλωται which may be translated 'is not under bondage' or 'is not bound by the bond.' The ordinary interpretation of this passage, in favour of which there appears to be a consensus of Christian teachers since the fourth century, is that in this particular case supposing, that is, that the marriage was a heathen marriage and not a Christian marriage; that the act of desertion is due to the person who remains a heathen, not to the one who becomes a Christian; and that the cause of the desertion is the Christianity of the latter the Christian may validly and lawfully contract another marriage. As a result of this interpretation, the common teaching in both East and West has been that, in this particular case, a second marriage is possible while the other party in the first marriage is still alive. It has been suggested that the words οὐ δεδούλωται simply mean that the desertion of the heathen sets the Christian free from the obligation of living with the heathen, and have nothing to do with the marriage bond itself. If this were so, the Christian in the contemplated case would remain incapable of contracting a fresh marriage so long as the other party should live. It is contended that the acceptance of the former interpretation, for which, as has been said, there appears to be a consensus of Christian teachers, is not hindered by the fact of the indissolubility of Christian marriage, since the marriage in view in this particular case is a marriage contracted by unbaptized persons. [86]

In Matrimony, as in the whole system of the rites of the Church, the love of God has provided that His laws may be means of promoting the good of man. His love is not least exhibited in the restraints which His laws impose. 'Beyond all things else marriage derives its essential and specific character from restraint: restraint from the choice of more than a single wife; restraint from choosing her among near relatives by blood or affinity; restraint from the carnal use of woman in any relation inferior to marriage; restraint from forming any temporary or any other than a lifelong contract. By the prohibition of polygamy it concentrates the affections which its first tendency is to diffuse; by the prohibition of incest it secures the union of families as well as individuals, and keeps the scenes of dawning life and early intimacy free from the smallest taint of appetite; by the prohibition of concubinage it guards the dignity of woman and chastens whatever might be dangerous as a temptation in marriage through the weight of domestic cares and responsibilities; by the prohibition of divorce, above all, it makes the conjugal union not a mere indulgence of taste and provision for enjoyment, but a powerful instrument of discipline and self-subjugation, worthy to take rank in that subtle and wonderful system of appointed means by which the life of man on earth becomes his school for heaven.' [87]

[1] St. Matt. xvi. 19; xviii. 18.

[2] St. John xx. 21-23.

[3] St. John xiii. 10.

[4] 1 Cor. v. 3-5; 2 Cor. ii. 10; 1 St. Tim. i. 20.

[5] St. Ignatius, *Ad Philad.*, 8. The reference is to those who have sinned by separating themselves from the Church.

[6] Tertullian, *De Poen.*, 9. This passage by itself would show little

[7] St. Cyprian, *De Laps.*, 29.

[8] Origen, *e.g.*, In Lev. Rom., v. 12; *De Orat.*, 28. Cf. Bigg, *The Christian Platonists of Alexandria*, pp. 214-218.

[9] St. Ambrose, *De Poen.*, ii. 19; *De Spir. Sanc.*, iii. 137; *In Ps. cxviii. Expos.*, x. 17.

[10] St. Chrysostom, *De Sac.*, iii. 5. Cf. *In Ill. vidi Dom. Hom . v 1 In Joan. Hom.*, lxxxvi. 4.

[11] St. Augustine, *e.g.*, *Serm. ad Cat.*, 14, 15; *Enchir.*, 65.

[12] St. Jerome, *e.g.*, *Ep.*, xiv. 8; C. *Pelag.*, ii. 7.

[13] St. Leo, *Ep.*, cviii. 2; clxviii. 2.

[14] St. Clement of Rome, *Ad Cor.*, i. 57.

[15] Pseudo-Clement of Rome, *Ad Cor.*, ii. 8.

[16] Hennas, *Pastor, Vis.*, iii. 5; *Sim.*, vii.

[17] See Thorndike, *Laws of the Church*, III. x. 2. Cf. Tertullian, *De Pud.*, 1, 21.

[18] St. Irenaeus, *C. Haer.*, I. xiii. 5.

[19] Tertullian, *e.g.*, *De Poen., passim.*

[20] Origen, *e.g.*, *Hom. i. in Ps. xxxvi.*, 5; *Hom. ii. in Ps. xxxvii.*, 6.

[21] St. Cyprian, *e.g.*, *De Lapsis, passim.*

[22] *Const. Ap.*, viii. 8, 9.

[23] *E.g.*, Council of Elvira, A.D. 305.

[24] See St. Basil, *Ep.*, cxcix. canon 34. Cf. Sozomen, *H. E.*, vii. 16.

[25] St. Leo, *Ep.*, cviii. 2; clxviii. 2. See clxvii. 19, for cases needing public Penance.

[26] On the difference between the Thomist and Scotist theologians as to the matter of Penance, see, *e.g.*, Addis, Arnold and Scannell's *Catholic Dictionary*, p. 698 (fifth edition).

[27] In *Surtees Soc.*, xxvii. 124.

[28] See St. Thomas Aquinas, *Sent.*, IV. xvii. 3 (2); *Summa Theol.*, Suppl. viii. 2.

[29] See note 53 in the concluding Notes.

[30] See note 54 in the concluding Notes.

[31] Psalm lxviii. 9.

[32] Pusey, *The Church of England leaves her Children free to whom to open their Griefs*, p. 4.

[33] St. Mark vi. 13.

[34] St. James v. 14, 15.

[35] Origen, *In Lev. Hom.*, ii. 4, 5.

[36] St. Chrysostom, *De Sac.*, iii. 6. But cf. *In Mat. Hom.*, xxxii. 6; *Hom. in mart.*

[37] *Canons of Hippolytus*, canon iii. 28.

[38] *Testamentum Domini*, i. 24, 25.

[39] Serapion of Thmuis, 5, 17.

[40] *Apostolical Constitutions*, viii. 29.

[41] Innocent I., *Ep.*, i. 8.

[42] Caesarius of Arles, inter opera St. Aug., v. 437C, 465FG, App.

[43] See Brightman in *Journal of Theological Studies*, January, 1900, pp. 260, 261.

[44] Peter Lombard, *Sent.*, IV. ii. 1.

[45] *E.g.*, the Armenians use the prayers without the anointing in the case of the people, and anoint priests only. See, *e.g.*, Dulaurier, *Histoire Dogmes, Traditions, et Liturgie de l Église Arménienne Orientale*, p. 177.

[46] Forbes, *An Explanation of the Thirty-nine Articles*, pp. 465, 466.

[47] *ibid.*, p. 474.

[48] See (1) St. John i. 35-40; (2) St. Matt. iv. 18-22; ix. 9-13; St. Mark i. 16-20; St. Luke v. 1-11; (3) St. Matt. x. 1; St. Mark iii. 13-15; St. Luke ix. 1.

[49] St. John xx. 21-23; Acts ii. 1-4.

[50] See Gore, *The Church and the Ministry*, for the whole subject. Some of the most usually cited instances of supposed exceptions are dealt with in that book, pp. 137-144, 357-363, 374-377 (in fourth edition, pp. 122-130, 325-330, 340-343); and in Bright, *Early English Church History*, pp. 133-136.

[51] On the unworthiness of the minister, and intention, see notes 58 and 59 in the concluding Notes.

[52] Gen. ii. 18-21.

[53] St. John ii. 1-11.

[54] St. Matt. xix. 4-6.

[55] Acts i. 3.

[56] See note 55 in the concluding Notes.

[57] For the Western opinions, see, *e.g.*, Schouppe, *Elem. Theol. Dogm.*, xvii. 53-59; Lehmkuhl, *Theol. Mor.*, ii. 680-692. For the Eastern opinions, see, *e.g.*, *Theol. Dogm. Orth.*, par Macaire, §§ 233-237 (t. ii. pp. 565-583).

[58] Gen. ii. 24; cf. St. Matt. xix. 4-8.

[59] Lev. xx. 10; Dent. xxii. 22.

[60] Deut. xxiv. 1-4. For the right translation of this passage, see note 56 in the concluding Notes.

[61] St. Matt. xix. 4-8.

[62] St. Matt. v. 31, 32; xix. 2-9; St. Mark x. 2-12; St. Luke xvi. 18.

[63] St. Mark x. 2-12; St. Luke xvi. 18.

[64] St. Matt. v. 31, 32.

[65] St. Matt. xix. 9.

[66] See note 57 in the concluding Notes.

[67] Rom. vii. 1-4; 1 Cor. vii. 10, 11; Eph. v. 22-32.

[68] Eph. v. 22-32.

[69] Rom. vii. 1-4.

[70] 1 Cor. vii. 10, 11.

[71] St. Matt. xix. 2-9.

[72] Lactantius, *Div. Inst.*, vi. 23.

[73] Asterius, *Hom. v.*

[74] Ambrosiaster, *Comm. in Ep. ad Cor. Prim.*, vii. 10, 11.

[75] St. Epiphanius, *Haer.*, lix. 4.

[76] St. Basil, *Moralia, Reg.*, lxxiii., Ep., clxxxviii., cxcix., ccxvii., canons 9, 21, 77.

[77] See Watkins, *Holy Matrimony*, pp. 198-346; *Church Quarterly Review*, April, 1895, pp. 20-34; January, 1896, pp. 429-432.

[78] Council of Trent, Sess. xxiv., canon 7.

[79] A list may be seen in Covel, *Some Account of the Present Greek Church*, pp. 218-227; Watkins, *Holy Matrimony*, pp. 352-362.

[80] See, *e.g.*, a statement by the Archbishop of Athens in *Divorce, Report as received by the Lower House of the Convocation of York*, second edition, pp. 36, 37.

[81] *Can. Ap.*, 48.

[82] Πηδάλιον, s. *Can. Ap.*, 48.

[83] To take the year 1891 as an instance, the official returns for that year show, besides 'divorces 'which were 'declarations of nullity,' divorces *a vinculo* allowing re-marriage in 213 cases for adultery, 317 cases for disappearance, and 389 cases for banishment. On the other hand, divorce and re-marriage are stated to be lawful only when there has been adultery by Macarius in *Theol. Dogm. Orth.*, 237 (t. ii. pp. 581-583).

[84] See, *e.g.*, Schouppe, *Elem. Theol. Dogm.*, xvii. 90.

[85] 1 Cor. vii. 12-16.

[86] There is a very valuable statement of the evidence on this point by Father Puller in No. 8 in the first series of the *Occasional Papers on Missionary Subjects* edited by members of the Oxford Mission, Calcutta.

[87] *Quarterly Review,* July, 1857, pp. 285, 286.

Chapter Thirteen - The Doctrine of Grace

The teaching about grace in Holy Scripture is not definitely formulated; but the following statements are based on Holy Scripture: -

1. Adam before the Fall was positively righteous in the sight of God; was free to obey or disobey God; and in this state of freedom was under probation. [1]

2. Adam after the Fall was sinful in the sight of God. [2]

3. Mankind as a whole is involved in the consequences of the sin of Adam. [3]

4. The salvation of mankind as a whole is desired by God. [4]

5. The death of Christ and the consequent redemption are applicable to mankind as a whole. [5]

6. Man is free to choose good or evil; [6] and is consequently responsible for his choice. [7]

7. Man is unable to do what is good without the grace of God. [8]

8. Nations and individuals are predestined simply because of the will of God. [9]

9. God's treatment of nations and individuals, and the eternal state of men, are dependent upon their actions. [10]

10. Actions are foreseen by God. [11]

If we put together these various statements on the subject of Grace, the teaching of Holy Scripture may thus be stated in a summary form. Man since the Fall is born in a state of sin by reason of his condition being necessarily affected by Adam's transgression. He can do nothing good by himself. The grace of God is given to him in sufficient force to enable him to do what is good, but not in such a way as to overpower him and compel him to do it. The will of man cannot choose that which is good without grace, yet it is free either to co-operate with grace or to resist and reject it. Men are predestined to privileges given in time, especially those conveyed in the rites of the Church, simply because of the will of God without any regard to their own merits. They are conditionally predestined to eternal glory, if they rightly use these privileges. Holy Scripture thus asserts without any attempt at system or reconciliation that all the springs of action are given to man by God and yet that man is free. The statements of Holy Scripture may be seen to be in harmony with natural religion and with the facts of human life. Any worthy idea of God includes His supremacy, so that man can do nothing independently of Him. Yet man is conscious in himself of freedom. He is conscious that he can do or leave undone that which he knows to be right. He is troubled when he has done wrong; and this trouble implies his consciousness that it was possible for him to have done otherwise, and that the wrongdoing is his own action. Thus, Holy Scripture and natural religion leave us with the two unreconciled statements that man can do nothing without God; and yet he is free to choose his own course.

There is no complete system of doctrine on the subject of grace laid down by any authoritative utterance of the whole Church or by an entire consensus of representative teachers. The general method of expression in the Church, the authorized language of devotion, the universal practical ways of working, have implied the belief that God is supreme, that apart from Him man can do nothing, but that individual men are free to accept or reject salvation as they will.   Before going into the history of the doctrine of grace within the Church, it will be convenient to notice the belief in the processes of grace which practically came to be the Church's teaching.

Repentance. A person baptized in infancy who had always perfectly responded to the grace of God would not need repentance. Taking facts as they generally are, repentance is the necessary first step at some period in the lives of both baptized and unbaptized. In repentance the grace of God stirs contrition in the heart; man yields to the working of grace; he allows contrition to be produced in him by God, and by adding to it confession of sin and purpose of amendment he completes the act of repentance. All that is thus done is the work of God. At the same time, the co-operation of the human will is necessary.

Faith. The full meaning of the word faith includes belief in God and His revelation [12] and complete surrender of self to God in action. [13] In the work of faith the grace of God calls man to belief by disposing the conscience and will to accept what is revealed and moves man to the self-surrendering attitude of soul. Man, on his part, allows himself to believe the truth to which God's grace prompts him, and surrenders himself to God. The grace of God may produce elementary faith in the unbaptized; the capacity for true Christian faith is given in Baptism.

Conversion. Repentance and faith combine in conversion, in which the will of man, making response to the grace of God, moved by repentance and acting in faith, turns away from past sin to righteousness. Conversion may precede or follow regeneration. In the case of those who are baptized in infancy, either they do not need to be converted because their will has never been separated from God by sin, or their conversion, if it is necessary, follows the regeneration which they have already received in Baptism. In the case of those who are not baptized in infancy but afterwards worthily receive Baptism, conversion precedes regeneration, because they are not fit for Baptism until they are turning to God in conversion. An adult who should unworthily receive Baptism would be regenerate by his Baptism, but would be without the benefits of regeneration until his subsequent conversion. Conversion differs from regeneration in conversion being a change of will, while regeneration is a change in nature.

Justification denotes the condition of the soul where by, being repentant, actuated by faith, converted and regenerate, it is under the approval of God, who accounts it as righteous. The objective cause of justification is everywhere represented in Holy Scripture as the death of Christ, the merits of which, together with the power of His life, are communicated to Christians through the mystery of His risen life. [14] The subjective cause of the justification of an individual, whereby he is enabled to lay hold of the merits of Christ, is variously described in Holy Scripture as his words, [15] his works, [16] and his faith. [17] These three verbally conflicting statements are different ways of expressing the same truth. The value of words consists in their being representative of an inward condition. The value of works is in the spirit which prompts them. Faith is the inward condition which the words represent and the spirit which prompts the works. Man is justified by surrendering himself to the action of the grace of God, the inward movement being faith, the outward results being words and works. Thus, in the Epistle to the Romans, St. Paul says, 'With the heart man believeth unto righteousness; and with the mouth confession is made unto salvation.' [18] It was faith,' he says also, which was reckoned to Abraham for righteousness. [19] 'Was not Abraham our father justified by works?' asked St. James, [20] referring to the same passage in the Book of Genesis, [21] and drawing the conclusion, 'By works a man is justified, and not only by faith.' [22] There is no contradiction between the inspired writers. The faith which St. James says cannot justify is a mere intellectual quality. The faith of which St. Paul writes is the moral act and attitude of the whole man.

Sanctification. Justification necessarily implies sanctification in either a complete or an elementary form, because it would be inconsistent with the truth of God to suppose that He accounts as righteous any who are not beginning to become so; and also because justification results from the surrender of the soul to the grace of God, and this grace must be producing in a soul which is surrendered to it its due effect, that is, holiness; that is, the righteousness of Christ is being imparted to the soul. This is accomplished in ordinary cases through the instrumentality of the Sacraments, which unite the soul to the humanity of Christ and bestow on it the possession of the Holy Ghost. [23] Western theologians in general have distinguished between the 'habitual grace' which is granted in the Sacraments, and the 'actual grace' whereby, apart from the Sacraments, God moves and aids the soul.

In all this process of the working of grace, what has been said represents the general point of view which has gradually been worked out in the Catholic Church. There are two sides to notice throughout the whole, the action of God calling for a response from the soul, and the action of the soul, without which, in cases where the will can be exercised, the action of God does not profit.

In the earliest period of Christian theology outside the New Testament the doctrine of grace is treated in much the same way as in Holy Scripture. There is strong emphasis on the sovereignty and irresistible power of God and on the need of God's grace to produce any good desire or act in man. At the same time, man is regarded as free. As a rule, no attempt is made to bring the two sides into relation with one another. [24] A passage in St. Irenaeus contains an attempt to bring the two lines of thought together. It is there said, 'To make is a property of the loving kindness of God, but to become is a property of the nature of man. If then you give to God that which is your own, that is, belief in Him and surrender to Him, you will receive His workmanship and you will be a perfect work of God. But if you shall not believe Him and shall avoid His hands, the cause of your imperfection will be in you who have not obeyed, not in Him who called. For He sent messengers to bid to the marriage feast; and it was they who did not obey Him who deprived themselves of the royal feast. Therefore the workmanship of God fails not, for He is able out of the stones to raise up sons unto Abraham. But he who does not attain unto this workmanship is the cause to himself of his own imperfection. For the light does not fail because of those who have blinded themselves; but, while the light remains just as it is, they who are blinded by their own fault stand in darkness. Neither will the light, with a great compulsion, compel any one to be subject to it, nor will God use compulsion to him who is unwilling to receive His workmanship. They, then, who have gone away from the light of the Father and have transgressed the law of freedom, have departed through their own fault, being created in the possession of free-will and with the power to make their own choice.' [25]

The earliest writers thus assert the two co-relative truths of the sovereignty of God and the freedom of man. They employ the word elect to denote the baptized, following in this the ordinary use of Holy Scripture. They regard predestination as being primarily to privilege in this life, and only conditionally to future glory, since they say that the ultimate salvation of the elect is dependent upon their faithfulness in this life. For instance, in very striking passages in the *Shepherd*, Hermas states emphatically that, if the elect choose sin and remain impenitent, they will eventually be among the lost. [26] Thus, the position conferred by election is viewed as affording the possibilities of a holy life and eternal happiness. Whether the eternal happiness will be attained or not, depends on the use made of the privileges which the position of the elect confers. The method of teaching thus found in the earliest Christian writers has remained much the same until the present time in the East, where there has been little controversy about the doctrine of grace. In the West, with but few intervals, there has been continuous controversy since the end of the fourth century. About that time, divergencies began to appear, some laying stress on the freedom of man to the extent of ignoring the necessity of grace, and others emphasizing the supremacy of God to the extent of denying the freedom of man. Pelagius and his follower Coelestius taught that Adam before the Fall was not positively righteous, but was in a neutral condition, neither bad nor good, capable of becoming either; and that the sin of Adam affected himself only, so that his descendants were not born in sin and were not under the wrath of God, but were born in a neutral condition like that asserted of Adam before the Fall. The denial of original sin, it was said, was a necessary inference from the justice of God, since it was contrary to justice that one person should be punished for the sin of another. Pelagius and his followers taught that man is absolutely free to choose right or wrong and able of himself without the grace of God to choose and do that which is right. The marked feature in Pelagian teaching is the eagerness to assert free-will together with forgetfulness that free-will may exist and yet may be limited; and that man may be able to choose, and, at the same time, may not be able to choose what is right without the help of God. It was partly in development of his own thought and partly in answer to Pelagian errors that St. Augustine worked out the elaborate system of the doctrine of grace which is contained in his Anti-Pelagian treatises.

St. Augustine's ultimate teaching on the doctrine of grace may be summarized thus. Adam before the Fall was positively righteous and possessed free-will. His sin affected all mankind, so that by reason of it every human being is born in sin, is at birth under the wrath of God, and deserves eternal condemnation. By God's mercy certain individuals, who are selected by Him because of His own will, not because of any foreseen character of theirs, are absolutely predestined to privileges conferred in time; and some of these individuals, who are similarly selected, are absolutely predestined to eternal glory. The grace of God is given to these predestined souls and is irresistible. St. Augustine does not teach anywhere that there is an irresistible decree of perdition; but it is difficult to see that his teaching that all mankind, except those exempted by the gift of the predestined and irresistible grace of God, lie under condemnation, when it is taken in connexion with the rest of his doctrinal system, differs in any marked way from the assertion of such a decree. He had to meet the Pelagian argument that it is unjust for part of mankind to be condemned because of Adam's sin. He replied by saying that in the consideration of a mystery it is impossible to argue rightly from human ideas of justice; and that, since strict justice requires the condemnation of all, and it is of the mercy of God that any are spared, it cannot be unjust that some only should be spared. As to free-will, it follows from St. Augustine's teaching of the irresistible character of the grace of God that there is no really self-determining will in man. Man possesses free-will, St. Augustine says, because his will makes its choice freely without compulsion; but the will itself is so constituted by the decree of God that it is a will which is determined to evil, or determined to good, according as it has been left by God under the dominion of original sin, or has been freed from that dominion and maintained in good by a gift of grace. Thus, all grace which impels towards good and makes it possible, all choice of good, all perseverance in good which leads to eternal joy, are the gift of God because of His absolute predestination and independently of any self-determining action in the individual predestined. Many passages in the writings of St. Augustine point in a different direction. There is much that implies free-will of a real kind. His practical teaching always regards and appeals to man, not only as a being responsible for his actions, but as one who is able to make an effort to embrace good and needs to struggle to keep good; and in the earlier part of his Christian life he did not hold all which has thus been ascribed to him. Still, the final judgment of his later theological works is as has been stated. Probably there was a contradiction in his mind; and, while a supposed logical necessity drove him to the dogmatic assertions which characterize his teaching, a spiritual instinct, which did not cease to affect his thought, pointed at the same time to a real freedom in man. [27] The marked feature in St. Augustine's theology on the doctrine of grace is his eagerness to assert the absolute power of God and to emphasize as strongly as possible that side of St. Paul's teaching. This is mixed with forgetfulness that the almighty power of God is not at all depreciated when it is said that God cannot do what is inconsistent with His own attributes, or that, in creating man, God has by the exercise of His own almighty power placed limitations upon Himself, so that, if man is free, his freedom exists by a gift from the omnipotence of God.

However much St. Augustine exaggerated, it was, humanly speaking, due to him that opinions which would have been fatal to Christianity and religion generally were overthrown. Of Pelagianism it is not too much to say -

1. It denied the fundamental ideas of all religion, the supremacy of God, and man's dependence upon God.

2. It misrepresented the whole primitive condition of man and the character of the Fall by describing Adam as in a neutral state before the Fall.

3. It imperilled the doctrine of the Incarnation by its tendency to regard the sinlessness of our Lord as not different from that of many individuals, each being a self-chosen sinlessness out of possibilities of good and evil.

4. It made the Atonement and the work of the Spirit, however useful, unnecessary, by teaching that man is not born in sin, and that he can of himself live a wholly sinless life. [28]

Pelagianism was condemned at the Council of Carthage in A.D. 412, by many local councils, and by the Council of Ephesus in A.D. 431.

Semi-Pelagianism was an attempt to avoid both extremes. In making this attempt, while it escaped from the chief evils of Pelagianism, it was not altogether free from error. It held to the truths that man is born in original sin, is free, and can do what is good only by the help of God's grace. It was touched by Pelagian error in denying the necessity of divine grace to enable man to wish for and choose that which is good. [29] Semi-Pelagianism was condemned by the Second Council of Orange in A.D. 529. This Council definitely asserted the necessity of divine grace both to lead man to choose what is good and to enable him to carry out his choice. The canons of the Council were directed against Semi-Pelagianism, but, in order to avoid exaggerations in the other direction, the following statement was added to them: 'When grace has been received through Baptism, all the baptized, by the help and co-operation of Christ, are able and ought to fulfil those things which pertain to the salvation of the soul, if they are willing to labour faithfully. That any are predestined to evil by the power of God, we not only do not believe, but also, if there are any who wish to believe so great an evil, we say anathema to them with all abhorrence. This also we healthfully confess and believe, that in every good work it is not we who begin and afterwards are aided by the mercy of God, but God Himself in the first instance inspires into us, without any good deserts of our own preceding, belief in Him and love for Him, so that we both faithfully seek for the Sacrament of Baptism and after Baptism are able with His help to fulfil those things which are pleasing to Him.' [30] This council was only a local council, but its decisions were accepted as expressing the general mind of the Church, and for a time the controversies about grace came to an end.

In the ninth century these controversies were renewed, largely because of the teaching of Gottschalc, a Benedictine monk in Gaul, which may be summarized as follows: -

1. Before creation God at His own will predestined some to glory and others to destruction.

2. Those who are predestined to destruction cannot be saved; those who are predestined to glory cannot be lost.

3. God does not wish all men to be saved.

4. Christ did not die for all men.

5. Since the Fall, man cannot use his free-will for good, but only for evil.

These opinions were condemned by councils held at Mentz in A.D. 848 and at Quiercy in the following year. Gottschalc was degraded from the priesthood and imprisoned. [31]

In the scholastic period predestination was one of the chief subjects of controversy. Speaking roughly, St. Thomas Aquinas followed St. Augustine, and Duns Scotus came perilously near Pelagianism. St. Thomas Aquinas, like St. Augustine, is eager to guard the supremacy of God, and the truth that God is the source of everything; and he does not appear to allow sufficiently for the balancing truths that the omnipotence of God must be considered in relation to all His attributes, and that God Himself in creation made disobedience to His will possible. Thus, in maintaining the fundamental truth that all things are of God, St. Thomas Aquinas and his followers fell into exaggerations on one side such as those in the writings of St. Augustine. St. Thomas Aquinas was greatly influenced by that Father, and by the passages in St. Paul's epistles, especially the Epistle to the Romans, which St. Augustine had thought must mean predestination in the sense affirmed by him. Consequently in his writings there is a tendency to interpret the Scriptural passages which refer

132

to predestination to privilege and grace in time as if they referred also in the same sense to predestination to eternal glory. At the same time, the other side is expressed with some clearness by St. Thomas Aquinas. For instance, in his commentary on the Epistle to the Romans, in the midst of some of the passages about predestination, he speaks, in distinguishing foreknowledge and predestination, of predestination being to the benefits which God was to give to His saints, and as being about the good things that bring salvation. And he says a great deal in different parts of the *Summa Theologica* about the reality of free-will. [32] It would probably be near the truth to say that St. Thomas Aquinas represents very much the position of St. Augustine, though with some clearer distinction between predestination to grace and predestination to glory, with a somewhat fuller conception of free-will, and with an habitual relaxation of the Augustinian teaching which must have been either intentional or the result of a spiritual conviction, practically speaking, of man's freedom side by side with the supposed logical necessity of the absolute character of predestination.

The Thomists held that certain individuals were inevitably predestined by the sole will of God both to privileges in time and to eternal glory; but they do not appear to have asserted that any were inevitably predestined to condemnation, or that Christ died only for some. The Scotists followed Scotus in strong assertions of the freedom of the will. [33]

These two schools of thought continued side by side in the West. At the Council of Trent one of the most difficult tasks before the Council was to deal adequately with the doctrine of grace without alienating one or the other of them. The subject was discussed at great length, and thirty-three canons were enacted, forming a series of careful statements of co-ordinate truths, in which the need of grace and the freedom of man were alike strongly affirmed. [34]

At the time of the Council of Trent the Church in England was becoming separated from the Church of Rome; and in England controversies about grace went on with great bitterness through the sixteenth and seventeenth centuries. This controversy in England was probably rather the result of the writings of foreign Protestants than an inheritance of the older controversies. In the formation of the English Articles of Religion, an attempt was made to formulate statements which would not alienate any but the extreme wings of the different parties on the subject of grace. The Articles themselves have sometimes been described as Calvinistic; but, while there are passages in them which favour the opinions of the less extreme party of which Calvin supplied the extreme section, there are also passages which are inconsistent with Calvinism; and the attempt made to introduce the Lambeth Articles in 1595 [35] showed that the Thirty-nine Articles did not satisfy the Calvinistic school. The policy embodied in the Articles on this subject was substantially the same as that of the Council of Trent, namely, while condemning certain extremes on both sides, to find a means of holding together all the less extreme members of the two schools of thought.

As in England, so among the foreign reformers, there was much controversy about the doctrine of grace. Luther in his earlier writings denied the existence of free-will in man after the Fall. At a later time possibly he, and certainly Melancthon, taught that Christ died for all men, that God wishes all men to be saved, that individuals are predestined to privileges which it is left to them to use rightly or to misuse. [36] It is doubtful whether Calvin himself held that Adam was free or that Adam was inevitably doomed to fall by the decree of God. [37] His followers were divided into two sections; those known as Supra-lapsarians held that Adam was inevitably doomed to fall; those known as Sub-lapsarians held that Adam was free. Calvin himself and both sections of his followers held that since the Fall every individual is absolutely predestined by the mere will of God by an irreversible decree to eternal glory or to eternal punishment. The Arminians were the followers of Jacob Von Harniin of Amsterdam, who died in the year 1609. In 1610 the Arminians addressed a remonstrance to the States of Holland in consequence of the persecutions to which they were subjected by the Calvinists, who were now predominant among the Dutch Protestants. This remonstrance consists of five articles which assert the need of divine grace to enable man to think, will, or do what is good, but also that man is free to yield to or reject this grace.

In 1588 Molina, a Jesuit Professor in Portugal, published a book on free-will. He taught that man is free, and yet is predestined to glory or condemnation by an irresistible decree, the explanation being that this predestination is determined by God according to the foreseen use of free-will. This book was charged with Pelagianism by the Dominicans. A bitter dispute ensued. It led to the appointment of the *Congregationes de auxiliis,* which more than once censured Molina's book, but did not bring about any decisive result. If it is the case that Pope Clement VIII. prepared a Bull condemning Molina, it was, at any rate, never published. After the death of Clement VIII. in 1605, the Congregations continued to sit until the question was shelved by Pope Paul V. in 1607.

The dispute about Molina did much to pave the way for the Jansenist controversy and to produce the strong party feelings which gave that controversy the particular form which it took. In 1640 a book called Augustinus was published. It was the work of Jansen the Bishop of Ypres, who had died three years before. This book asserted the irresistible power of grace; that some individuals are predestined to glory; and that Christ died for these only. Five propositions said to be contained in it were condemned in 1653 by Pope Innocent X. The propositions thus condemned were the following: -

1. Some commands of God are impossible to righteous men who wish and endeavour according to the present strength which they have. Moreover, grace is lacking to them whereby they may became possible.

2. In a state of fallen nature, resistance is never made to inner grace.

3. For merit and demerit in a state of fallen nature there is not required in man freedom from necessity, but freedom from compulsion is sufficient.

4. The Semi-Pelagians admitted the necessity of prevenient inner grace for individual actions, even for the beginning of faith; and they were heretics because they wished this grace to be of such a kind that the will of man could resist or correspond to it.

5. It is Semi-Pelagianism to say that Christ died or shed His blood for all men. [38]

It has always been a matter of discussion how far the propositions thus drawn up and condemned at Rome accurately represented the teaching of Jansen. The truth probably is that the propositions were given a form of somewhat sharper aspect than that in Jansen's more lengthy treatment, but that they did not substantially misrepresent his book. Among the disputes which followed this condemnation was the controversy between Pascal and the Jesuits, in which Pascal united extreme brilliance with great unfairness, and the Jesuits, amid much which calls for strong condemnation, did a work in protecting moral responsibility from dangerous Jansenist errors. [39]

There is a valuable statement on the doctrine of grace written by a German Roman Catholic in the first half of the present century. 'God can be represented,' it is there said, 'in such relations to man as to make the latter entirely disappear; or man, again, may be conceived in such a position, relatively to God, as to subvert the notion of the Almighty as the dispenser of grace. According to the first view, God appears acting with a cruel caprice, which cannot be conceived by man; according to the second, so ruled by the caprice of man that He ceases to be who He is and through whom all goodness springs. Accordingly, the Catholic Church alike rejects an overruling of God on the part of man, to impart sanctifying and saving grace; and an overruling of man on the part of God, to compel the former to become this or that. On the contrary, she teaches, in the former case, as is well known, that the grace of God is unmerited; in the latter case, that it is offered to all men, their condemnation depending on the free rejection of redeeming aid.' [40]

[1] Gen. i. 31; ii. 16, 17.

[2] Gen iii. 8-24.

[3] Rom. v. 12, 14; 1 Cor. xv. 22.

[4] St. Matt, xviii. 14; 1 St. Tim. ii. 4.

[5] Rom. v. 18, 19; 1 St. Tim. ii. 6; Heb. ii. 9.

[6] Deut. xxx. 15-20; Ezek. xxxiii. 11; St. Matt, xxiii. 37

[7] Ezek. xviii.; St. John xii. 44-50.

[8] St. John vi. 44, 65; xv. 4, 5; 1 Cor. xv. 10; Phil. ii. 13.

[9] Deut. x. 15; Jer. i. 5; Rom. ix. 11-26; Gal. i. 15, 16; Eph. i. 5; 1 St. Peter i. 2.

[10] Deut. xxviii.; Jer. xviii. 8-10, 15-17; St. Matt. xxv. 31-46; 2 St. Peter i. 10.

[11] Gen. xv. 13, 14; Ezek. iii. 7.

[12] Heb. xi. 6.

[13] Rom. iv. 9-12; Gal. iii. 6, 7. Cf. Heb. xi. 8, 17 and St. James ii. 21-24 with Gen. xii. 1-4 and xxii. 1-12.

[14] Rom. iv. 24, 25; v. 6-11.

[15] St. Matt. xii. 37.

[16] St. James ii. 24.

[17] Rom. iii. 28; Gal. iii. 24, etc.

[18] Rom. x. 10.

[19] Rom. iv. 9.

[20] St. James ii. 21.

[21] Gen. xv. 6, quoted in Rom. iv. 3; Gal. iii. 6; St. James ii. 23.

[22] St. James ii. 24.

[23] Some writers use the phrase first justification as justification has here been used, and second justification as sanctification has here been used.

[24] See, *e.g.*, the passages in St. Justin Martyr mentioned in Ch. Five, Note 10.

[25] Irenaeus, C. Haer. IV. xxxix. 2, 3.

[26] *Hermas, Pastor, Vis.* ii. 2; iv. 2.

[27] See Mozley, *A Treatise on the Augustinian Doctrine of Predestination.*

[28] There are some valuable statements on Pelagianism in Bright *Lessons from the Lives of Three Great Fathers,* pp. 157-168, 289-292.

[29] On Semi-Pelagianism, see Bright, *ibid.,* pp. 292-303.

[30] Second Council of Orange (Hardouin, *Concilia,* ii. 1101, 1102).

[31] The facts about Gottschalc, and some references to the controversies about his opinions, may be seen in Robertson, *History of the Christian Church,* iii. 350-369. Cf. Ussher, *Gotteschalei et Praedestinationae Controversiae ab eo motae Historia,* pp. 27, 28 (Dublin, 1631).

[32] St. Thomas Aquinas, *Sent.,* I. xl. 4. 2; xli. 1. 3; *Summa Theol.,*I. xix.-xxiv; lxxxiii.; II. 1 lxxiv. 4; cxi; cxiii. 3; *In Rom.,* viii.

[33] See note 60 in the concluding Notes.

[34] Council of Trent, Sess. vi. Cf. Addis, Arnold, and Scaunell's Catholic Dictionary, p. 415 (fifth edition).

[35] See Perry, *History of the English Church,* ii. 352.

[36] See Laurence, *An Attempt to illustrate those Articles of the Church of England which the Calvinists improperly consider as Calvinistical,* pp. 218-251.

[37] On one side, see *Inst.,* III. i. 4; on the other side, see *Inst.,* III., xxiii. 8.

[38] *Innocentii Papae X. Constitutio de Quinque Propositionibus ex Jansenii Libro Excerptis.*

[39] On this, and other controversies about Grace, see Bright, *Lessons from the Lives of Three Great Fathers,* pp. 303-312.

[40] Mohler, *Symbolism,* Book I. part i. 12. For some technical terms used in connexion with the doctrine of grace, see note 61 in the concluding Notes.

Chapter Fourteen - Eschatology

The facts of Christian doctrine which have been dealt with in the preceding chapters of this book may be thus shortly stated. The Eternal God, who is three Persons in one God, created man in order that man, in obeying his Maker, might be blessed. Sin, coming into the world through the malice of the fallen angel Satan, distorted man's nature and placed him under the wrath of God instead of in the favour of God. The Incarnation and Atonement accomplished the potential restoration of all men. Man, to whom truth has been revealed through the Church, is offered the gift of actual individual restoration, which involves pardon for sin and reception of holiness, principally in the Sacraments. It rests with him to decide whether he will accept or reject the gift of God, it being impossible for man to be righteous without the grace of God, or for the grace of God to produce its due effect without the co-operation of the will of man.

It remains to consider what is the time during which this choice on the part

136

of man is to be made; what is the present condition of departed souls; and what is the future condition of those who make the right and the wrong choice.

The Time of Probation

The present life is represented as a life of probation in Holy Scripture and Christian teaching. As being a life of probation, it affords a test of character; and, since character is thus tested in it, actions in this life are represented as affording the ground upon which God's decisions about man are made. [1]

Since, then, the present life is a probation, it must be asked whether there is any other time of probation. There is no indication of any other in Holy Scripture, or in what has been taught generally within the Church; and the absence of another probation in, at any rate, ordinary cases appears to be implied in the importance attached to the decisions of this life in Holy Scripture and in the Fathers; passages in Holy Scripture which appear to imply that the eternal destiny of the soul is fixed at death; [2] and the practice of the Church in limiting those departed persons who can receive benefit from the prayers of the living. This limitation is expressly made in the liturgies of the early Church. It is referred to by the Fathers. To mention one passage which represents very fairly the general mind of the Church, St. Augustine speaks of the sacrifices of Christians being offered 'for all baptized persons deceased,' as being 'thanksgivings for the very good,' 'propitiations for the not very bad,' and as affording no help to 'the very bad.' [3] There is a remarkable exception to the ordinary patristic teaching in Origen, who thought that between death and the time of perfecting, souls could reverse their choice made in this life, whether for good or for evil. [4] This opinion is out of harmony with the previous tradition of the Church; and it was deliberately set aside by the Church after Origen had taught it. Thus, it may be concluded that the present life alone is the appointed time upon the use of which God's judgment upon individual souls is passed.

In connexion with this subject it is necessary to remember that the real state of the soul as God sees it may be very different from what man thinks it to be. The truth contained in our Lord's teaching, when He told the chief priests and the elders of the people that 'the publicans and the harlots go into the kingdom of God before' [5] them runs through human life.

On all questions of this kind, of which the destiny of the heathen is one, there is little ground for saying more than that it is certain God will do what is right in all cases. It has been argued that, while no person has more than one probation, and while in ordinary cases of baptized persons this probation is in this life and this life only, yet the heathen and some in Christian countries cannot be said to have any probation at all in this life, since they have no opportunities; and that, consequently, since all men have one probation, these will undergo theirs in the inter mediate state. [6] The truth on this subject is probably rather that God can estimate what is just from any set of circumstances; and therefore circumstances which appear to us to afford no opportunity and no probation may nevertheless afford a real test in His sight. At any rate, we are right in saying that this life is the only revealed and covenanted time of probation; and it must be left to the mercy and justice of God whether in any exceptional cases there be exceptional treatment of which the revelation and the covenant do not speak. That it is His will to estimate fully and fairly the opportunities of human life, and the use which is made of them, may be seen from the saying of our Lord Himself that it will be more tolerable for the land of Sodom in the day of judgment than for Capernaum. [7]

The Present State of the Departed

There is very little in Holy Scripture about the present state of the departed. In the Old Testament they are generally spoken of as if in a state of deep gloom. 'In death,' says the Psalmist, 'there is no remembrance of Thee: in Sheol who shall give Thee thanks?' 'What profit is there in my blood, when I go down to the pit? Shall the dust praise Thee? Shall it declare Thy truth?' 'Cast off among the dead, like the slain that lie in the grave, whom Thou rememberest no more; and they are cut off from Thy hand.' 'Sheol,' wrote Hezekiah, 'cannot praise Thee, death cannot celebrate Thee: they that go down into the pit cannot hope for Thy truth. The living, the living, he shall praise Thee, as I do this day. There is not, indeed, in the Old Testament, an entire absence of a brighter side; but that brighter side is in the hope of deliverance from what is the ordinary and present state of the departed. 'God,' says the Psalmist, 'will redeem my soul from the power of Sheol; for He shall receive me.' [8]

In the New Testament there is more about the departed. Our Lord, in the language of St. Paul, 'brought life and immortality to light.' But the greater part of what even the New Testament teaches is about the future rather than about the present. As to the present, a number of passages state or imply that the departed are alive and conscious. Our Lord definitely teaches that Abraham, Isaac and Jacob are living; the parable of the rich man and Lazarus, and our Lord's words to the penitent robber imply both life and consciousness among the departed; the work of our Lord between His death and His resurrection included preaching to the spirits in prison, and thereby shows the consciousness both of His human soul after death and of those to whom he preached; the souls of the martyrs which St. John saw 'underneath the altar' were living and able to pray. [9]

This teaching contained in the New Testament that the departed live and are conscious and can pray has been echoed through the whole course of Christian history. To take three instances, St. Jerome describes in glowing terms the prayers of departed saints. 'If,' he says, 'the Apostles and martyrs, while still in the body, are able to pray for others when they still ought to be full of care for themselves, how much more can they do so after they have been crowned in victory and triumph. One man, Moses, obtains pardon from God for six hundred thousand armed men, and Stephen, the imitator of his

Lord and the first martyr in Christ, begs forgiveness for his persecutors; and shall their power be less after they have begun to be with Christ?' [10] At the Council of Chalcedon of A.D. 451 the bishops and clergy of Constantinople cried out, 'Flavian is alive after death; the martyr is praying for us.' [11] In a very different quarter, the Saxon confession of 1551, in repudiating the practice of invoking saints, declared it to be undoubted that 'the blessed pray for the Church.' [12]

Taking it, then, for granted that there is life and consciousness and prayer among the departed, it is necessary to ask what distinctions, if any, are to be made as to differing conditions of those who are alike in this, that they have passed through death. Three passages in the New Testament appear to imply a distinction in the present condition of different souls. In our Lord's parable of the rich man and Lazarus, the rich man is described as being in torment, in a state irretrievably determined, permanently separated from those in a happier condition. In the same passage it is said of Lazarus that he is being comforted in the bosom of Abraham. In the Epistle to the Philippians St. Paul speaks of death as bringing him into the nearer presence of Christ, and so putting Mm in a condition which is better than that of earthly life. [13] If these passages may rightly be taken as having a general bearing, it may be inferred from them that

1. The souls of the lost, of whom the rich man is a representative, pass at once to pains, either identical with or like those of hell.

2. The souls of at any rate some of the faithful, of whom Lazarus is a representative, pass at once to a condition in which they receive comfort, but with regard to which nothing is said about the immediate presence of God.

3. The souls of at any rate some of the faithful, of whom St. Paul expected to be one, pass at once to a condition which is in the nearer presence of Christ than life on earth can be.

The first of these groups is obviously different from both the second and the third. So far as Holy Scripture is concerned, there is nothing to show whether the second and the third are two ways of viewing the same group or are to be distinguished from one another.

Besides these, there are two passages in the Epistle to the Hebrews. In the first passage, the writer of the Epistle speaks of the 'cloud of witnesses' (νέφος μαρτύρων) of the heroes of faith mentioned in the eleventh chapter as a ground of encouragement to those who are contending in the race of the Christian life. [14] There is nothing in the actual words to denote that the struggles of Christians upon earth are known to these faithful souls who have borne witness to God. At the same time the general imagery of the passage suggests the idea of those who are looking on the struggles and are giving the help of encouragement. 'It is impossible,' comments the Bishop of Durham, 'to exclude the thought of the spectators in the amphitheatre.' [15] In the second passage it is said, 'Ye are come unto Mount Zion, and unto the city of the living God, the heavenly Jerusalem, and to innumerable hosts of Angels, to the general assembly and church of the firstborn who are enrolled in heaven, and to God the Judge of all, and to the spirits of just men made perfect, and to Jesus the mediator of a new covenant, and to the blood of sprinkling that speaketh better than that of Abel,' [16] The writer of the Epistle is describing the great privileges of Christians in contrast to the Jews. In so doing he speaks of the access which Christians have to (1) the sacred city which is the home of God, (2) the angelic hosts, (3) the fellowship of Christians, (4) God Himself, (5) the spirits of just men made perfect, (6) our Lord, (7) the Blood of Christ. It is difficult to see what the phrase spirits of just men made perfect can mean other than holy souls which have departed from this world. [17]

The earliest evidence from the practice and teaching of the Church is somewhat less vague than that contained in the New Testament. The inscriptions in the catacombs represent the faithful departed as in a peaceful condition which is capable of an increase of peace through the prayers of the faithful upon earth; but say no more. The earliest writers speak of death in the case of at any rate some of the faithful as leading to the nearer presence of God. Thus St. Clement of Rome writes of St. Peter going into the due place of glory, and of St. Paul going into the holy place. [18] St. Ignatius describes his approaching martyrdom as attaining to God and going to the Father. [19] St. Polycarp speaks of the martyrs as being in their due place with the Lord. [20] *The Epistle of the Churches of Lyons and Vienne,* written after the persecution of A.D. 177, describes the Gallican martyrs as going away to God, as departing with peace to God. [21] Two treatises of Tertullian, [22] written after he became a Montanist, and the *Passion of St. Perpetua* [23] speak of the martyrs, as distinct from the faithful departed generally, as having attained to the vision of God. Dionysius of Alexandria in a letter written about A.D. 251 refers to the martyrs as 'now sitting with Christ and sharers in His Kingdom.' [24] Writers of the same period also regard the condition of at any rate some of the faithful departed as one of imperfection, not yet that of the special presence of God which is the privilege of the Beatific Vision. Thus, St. Justin Martyr describes the souls of the holy remaining some where in a better place and those that are unjust and wicked in a worse place, waiting for the time of the judgment; [25] and St. Irenaeus speaks of the souls waiting for the resurrection and after it coming unto the vision of God. [26] While, therefore, there is not an entire absence of doubt whether the writers of this period regard the saved as being after death in two groups, or speak from different points of view of one group, a comparison of their statements shows a probability that they believed there were two groups, those who had attained to some clear vision of God, and those who, in a somewhat lower state, were still waiting to do so. The Eastern Liturgies may be taken as representing in the main the thought of the fourth century. There is much that is obscure in the references to the departed which they contain. But it is clear that the departed are commemorated in the following ways: -

1. A merely general commemoration of the Saints, and an association of them with the prayers of the Church. [27]

2. Commemoration of the Saints in order that the living may be benefited by their prayers. [28]

3. Prayers for the departed generally. [29]

4. Commemoration of the Saints, including prayers for them. [30]

These different commemorations show that the faithful departed were regarded as being in two groups, the pre-eminent Saints, who were commemorated with a view to their praying to God for the Church on earth, and the rest of the faithful departed, who were prayed for with a view to their being benefited, prayers in some cases being also offered for the first group. In the middle of the fourth century there is a very clear statement about the Liturgy of the Church at Jerusalem in the explanation of it given by St. Cyril of Jerusalem in his *Catechetical Lectures on the Mysteries,* which were probably delivered in A.D. 348. He there says, 'Then we make mention also of those who have fallen asleep before us, firstly of patriarchs, prophets, apostles, martyrs, in order that God may accept our supplication through their prayers and intercessions; afterwards also for the holy fathers and bishops who have fallen asleep before us, and for all those generally who among us have fallen asleep before us, believing that there will be the greatest benefit to those souls on whose behalf the supplication is offered to God in the presence of the holy and most awful sacrifice.' [31] The same clear distinction is found a little later in the writings of St. Augustine, who, in a passage already referred to, divides the faithful departed into two groups, for the first of which the Sacrifice is offered in thanksgiving, and for the second of which it is offered in propitiation. [32]

The division thus distinctly made in the fourth and fifth centuries gradually became stereotyped in the West into the formal distinction that the great saints have attained to the vision of God, while the rest of the faithful departed are in a waiting state. [33]

As the division of the faithful departed into two groups is more clearly made, what is said about the state of the souls is fuller and clearer than in the earliest times. As to the second group, that of ordinary Christians, all writers appear to have regarded the souls as being at rest. Some writers speak also of suffering. One of the Montanistic treatises of Tertullian already referred to [34] and the *Passion of St. Perpetua* [35] imply a belief in some punishment after death. Clement of Alexandria, [36] Origen, [37] St. Ambrose, [38] and St. Gregory of Nazianzus, [39] writers who on many matters represent different schools of thought, write of the purifying fire through which the departed must pass. By some, at any rate, this fire was associated with the day of judgment. As to suffering, St. Augustine in different writings speaks with differing degrees of definiteness. For instance, in his treatise on Psalm xxxvii. [40] and elsewhere he definitely refers to a purgatorial fire which will cleanse the soul from sin, while in one passage in his book *On the City of God*

[41] he says he is not going to deny the existence of such a purgatorial fire because perhaps it is true. From the time of St. Augustine the idea of suffering came to be generally connected in the West with the state of the departed. In the middle ages the ordinary western belief was that the souls of the faithful suffer in purgatory pains which exceed any pains of this life and differ from the pains of hell in duration but not in severity. A milder view existed in the West, but was less common. There is an instance of it in the latter part of the fifteenth century, in the treatise of St. Catherine of Genoa, in which it is taught that the joy of the souls in purgatory is a joy which exceeds any that is possible on earth, and that the suffering which co-exists, with the joy is the bitterness of regret for their want of more complete conformity to the will of God in the past, and the sense of their being as yet, absent from the Beatific Vision. [42]

Keeping still to the West, the controversies of the sixteenth century brought into prominence the question of the state of the departed. It was considered at the Council of Trent. The decrees of the council affirmed that the saints are 'reigning with Christ' and, as to the faithful departed generally, that there is purgatory and the souls detained there are aided by the intercessions of the faithful and most of all by the acceptable sacrifice of the altar. [43] So far as the decrees of the council were concerned, therefore, any question as to the nature of purgatory was left open. In the catechism of the council somewhat more was said. After speaking of hell as the place of lost souls it went on to say: 'Besides, there is the fire of purgatory in which the souls of the holy, being disciplined for a fixed time, receive expiation, so that the way may be made open for them into the eternal country into which nothing that is defiled entereth.' [44] Since the time of the Council of Trent, the predominant idea about purgatory in the Church of Rome has been that of suffering and the most usual belief has been that the suffering is that of literal fire. As to what is of faith in the Church of Rome, it may be sufficient to quote the words of the Jesuit writer Schouppe. 'The pain of purgatory,' he says, 'is twofold, the pain of loss and the pain of sense, both lasting only for a time. The pain of loss is the delay in attaining to the Beatific Vision, as a penalty for sins. As to what pertains to the pain of sense, the opinion of the Latins has been continually affirmed, and is to be retained, that there is in purgatory material fire like to that of hell, and it is for this reason that the Church prays for the souls of the faithful a place, not only of light and peace, but also of refreshment, that is, against the heat of fire. Nevertheless, this is not of faith, since the Greeks argued at the Council of Florence that there is no true fire in purgatory, but only toils, and griefs to constitute the pain of sense; and this teaching was not condemned either by the Council of Florence, or by the Council of Trent.' [45]

In the English Church and in the Protestant bodies outside the Church any distinct idea of the intermediate state was greatly impaired by the reaction against mediaeval views of purgatory. One of the Articles of Religion of the

Church of England condemns in strong terms a 'doctrine about purgatory' which it defines as 'Romish,' probably meaning a doctrine of a purgatory of material fire, mechanically proportioned to the amount of sin for which there had not been satisfaction during life, and mechanically lessened by Masses, almsgiving, and prayers. The belief in a waiting state as a time of discipline and growth has never died out in the Church of England; and it is to be found in some off the more orthodox of the separated bodies. It may be worthwhile to quote part of what is said on this subject by the Lutheran writer Martensen in his *Christian Dogmatics.* 'As no soul,' he says, 'leaves this present existence, in a fully complete and prepared state, we must suppose that there is an intermediate state, a realm of progressive development in which souls are prepared and matured for the final judgment. Though the Romish doctrine of purgatory is repudiated because it is mixed up with so many crude and false positions, it nevertheless contains the truth that the intermediate state must in a purely spiritual sense be a purgatory designed for the purifying of the soul.' [46]

The Churches of the East believe that all the departed, righteous and wicked, are divided at death into two groups. The righteous go at once to felicity, though not the full reward to which they eventually attain. The wicked go at once to punishment, though not the full retribution which they are eventually to receive. But this second group is again divided into two divisions. Those who die impenitent are beyond hope of recovery. Those, on the other hand, who have died in a state of penitence may be delivered from punishment. One of the clearest enunciations of this belief is in the decrees of the Council of Bethlehem of A.D. 1672. It is there said: 'We believe the souls of the departed are either in rest or in torment according to the deeds of each, because immediately they have left their bodies they are carried to the place of joy, or to that of pain and lamentation, though they do not yet receive the fulness either of their happiness or of their condemnation. For after the general resurrection, when the soul shall again be united to its own body in which it behaved itself well or ill, then shall every one assuredly receive the fulness of happiness or of condemnation. But such as have not despaired because of the deadly sins with which they have denied themselves, and have begun their repentance for them in this life, but have not here brought forth works meet for repentance, that is to say, poured out tears of sorrow for sin, watched and prayed upon their knees, afflicted themselves, relieved the poor, showed their love to God and their neighbour by their works, which the Catholic Church has from the beginning rightly called satisfaction, these, and such as these, we believe are carried to hades, and there sustain the just punishment due to their sins, but know that they shall by the goodness of God be delivered from them through the prayers of the priests and the good deeds of their relatives, and to this nothing contributes so much as the unbloody sacrifice which each person severally offers for his departed relatives, and which the Catholic and Apostolic Church daily offers for all. But we know not the time of this deliverance, only we know and believe that they shall be freed from their pains before the general resurrection and judgment, but when that shall be we know not.' [47]

This article of the Council of Bethlehem was altered in some details before it was accepted by the Russian Church in 1838. The alterations were evidently designed to avoid committing the Russian Church to some features in the article which were thought to resemble too closely the teaching about purgatory found to a large extent in the West. They leave untouched the assertions that at death all souls go into one of two places, and that, of the souls which go to the place of punishment, those which have died in penitence will be delivered from punishment. [48]

To give one other instance of the teaching of the East, in the *Longer Catechism of the Russian Church* it is said -

'*Q.* In what state are the souls of the dead till the general resurrection?

'*A.* The souls of the righteous are in light and rest, with a foretaste of eternal happiness; but the souls of the wicked are in a state the reverse of this.

'*Q.* Why may we not ascribe to the souls of the righteous perfect happiness immediately after death?

'*A.* Because it is ordained that the perfect retribution according to works shall be received by the perfect man after the resurrection of the body and God's last judgment... 2 St. Tim. iv. 8 ... 2 Cor. v. 10.

'*Q.* Why do we ascribe to the souls of the righteous a foretaste of bliss before the last judgment?

'*A.* On the testimony of Jesus Christ Himself, who says in the parable that the righteous Lazarus was immediately after death carried into Abraham's bosom. St. Luke xvi. 22.

'*Q.* Is this foretaste of bliss joined with a sight of Christ's own countenance?

'*A.* It is so more especially with the Saints, as we are given to understand by the Apostle Paul, who had a desire to depart and to be with Christ. Phil. i. 23.

'*Q.* What is to be remarked of such souls as have departed with faith, but without having had time to bring forth fruits worthy of repentance?

'*A.* This; that they may be aided towards the attainment of a blessed resurrection by prayers offered in their behalf, especially such as are offered in union with the oblation of the Bloodless Sacrifice of the Body and Blood of Christ, and by works of mercy done in faith for their memory.

'*Q.* On what is the doctrine grounded?

'*A.* On the constant tradition of the Catholic Church; the sources of which may be seen even in the Church of the Old Testament. Judas Maccabaeus offered sacrifice for his men that had fallen. 2 Macc. xii. 43. Prayer for the departed has ever formed a fixed part of the Divine Liturgy from the first Liturgy of the Apostle James. St. Cyril of Jerusalem says "Very great will be the benefit to those souls for which prayer is offered at the moment when the holy and tremendous sacrifice is lying in view." *Lect. Myst.* v. 9. St. Basil the Great in his prayers for Pentecost says that the Lord vouchsafes to receive from us propitiatory prayers and sacrifices for those who are kept in hades, and allows us the hope of obtaining for them peace, relief, and freedom.' [49]

There is a consensus of Catholic theology that at any rate many of the departed may be benefited by the prayers of the living. There are those, indeed, who, being eternally lost, cannot be helped by prayer. It is only a very few exceptional writers here and there, not weighty as they stand by themselves separated from the main stream of the Christian tradition, who use language inconsistent with this fact. There may be those who have already attained so fully to perfection and glory that prayers offered on earth no longer help them. For at least all who are between these two groups, it is right and useful to pray. This simple truth is not affected by differences of belief or statement at different times and in different places. On the supposition of the state of waiting spoken of by St. Irenaeus, or the purgatory of the mediaeval West or the modern Church of Rome, or the deliverance from condemnation of the Council of Bethlehem, or the help towards the attainment of a blessed resurrection of the Russian Catechism, or even the realm of progressive development affirmed by Martensen, prayer for the departed is both a lawful practice and a useful duty. The thought of prayer for those who are known as the great saints is not altogether to be put aside. The Liturgies contain supplications even for the holy Mother of God herself. Whatever it be to which they have attained, it cannot be said there is no possibility of progress. It is the belief of some in the East that, even when there has been attainment, prayer is still of value because in far back ages it was foreseen by God. However all this may be, the truth is clear in Christian history, that for those who are ordinarily described as the faithful departed it is a duty to pray.

Reference has already been made to the Christian belief that the power of prayer is not destroyed by death. Outside the New Testament, there is nothing on this subject in the earliest writers. As soon as there is evidence, it appears to have been universally believed that at any rate the pre-eminent saints continue after death to pray for Christians upon earth; and there is no trace of any doubt of the lawfulness or expediency of Christians upon earth praying to God that the living might be aided by the prayers of departed saints.

A different but connected practice is that of the Invocation of Saints, that is, the practice of directly addressing the saints to ask them for the help of their prayers to God. There is nothing either for or against this practice in Holy Scripture or in Christian writings outside Holy Scripture in the first and second centuries. In the third century there is only one passage on the subject. In his treatise *On Prayer*, Origen, commenting on St. Paul's words, 'I exhort therefore first of all that supplications, prayers, intercessions, and giving of thanks be made for all men,' [50] limits the use of 'prayer' to words addressed to God, and says of 'supplications,' 'intercessions,' and 'giving of thanks,' 'it is not improper to address these to saints, and two of them, I mean intercession and thanksgiving, not only to saints but also to men, but supplication only to saints, as for instance to some Paul or Peter, that they may aid us, making us worthy to obtain the power granted unto them for the forgiveness of sins.' [51] The 'saints' referred to in this passage have been understood by some writers to be saints still living. [52] It is more likely that the word includes also the departed saints, and that, obscure as the passage is, its tendency is in favour of the Invocation of Saints. [53] Still, the third century supplies little more evidence than the first two. In the fourth century there is a good deal of evidence. The practice of Invocation is either used or referred to with approval by St. Ambrose and St. Augustine in the West, and St. Ephraim the Syrian, St. Basil, St. Gregory of Nazianzus, St. Gregory of Nyssa, and St. Chrysostom in the East. There is no writer of the fourth century whose works have come down to us who says anything in disapproval of the practice. Consequently, it is reasonable to infer that the writers mentioned are representative of the general Christian feeling on this subject in the fourth century. Inscriptions in the catacombs contain addresses to the departed, which include some requests for prayers. There are no Invocations in the Liturgies. This would be the case under any circumstances because of the rule that the Eucharistic prayers were to be addressed only to God the Father. From the fourth century on, the Invocation of Saints was an ordinary form of Christian devotion throughout the East and West. During the middle ages, Invocations of Saints were very largely used, in many cases with greatly exaggerated and distorted ideas. This was one of the questions which had to be faced in the West in the sixteenth century. There is a good deal on the subject in the English official publications. In the Ten Articles of 1536 it was carefully explained that the gifts of grace were bestowed by God alone, through the mediation of our Saviour Christ; that superstitions, as that the saints are more merciful than God, were to be put aside; and that the prayers addressed to the saints were that they might join with us in prayer to God. In *The Institution of a Christian Man,* of 1537, commonly known as the Bishops Book,' the same position was taken up, and it was taught that no one was to think that gifts came from any but God; and that the prayers addressed to the saints were for the help of their prayers with God. The same teaching was given in the *Necessary Doctrine and Erudition for any Christian Man,* of 1543, commonly known as the 'King's Book.' In the Forty-two Articles of 1552, the 'doctrine of school authors concerning' 'Invocation of Saints' was condemned. In the Articles of 1563, the phrase doctrine of school authors was altered to 'Romish doctrine' ('Doctrina Romanensium'). The history of the English documents, as well as the Latin phrase thus used, gives a high probability that what is condemned in this Article is what is condemned in the Ten Articles, the 'Bishops Book,' and the 'King's Book;' and that Invocation of Saints in the sense in which it is approved in those three documents is left an open question by the present Article. [54]

At the Council of Trent a very guarded position was taken up. In the decree of the Council it was simply stated that it is good and useful to invoke the saints; that all benefits come from God through the mediation of Jesus Christ; and that all superstition was to be put down. [55] The Catechism of the Council declared that no more might be rightly addressed to a saint than 'Pray for us;' and that such a form as 'Have mercy on us' addressed to a saint could only be justified if used in the sense of 'Have mercy by praying for us.' [56] Thus the position taken up by the Council of Trent on this point is the same as that in the English Ten Articles, the 'Bishops Book,' and the 'King's Book,' with which the present Thirty-nine Articles probably correspond. Both sets of documents affirm the lawfulness of asking the saints for the help of their prayers; both condemn seeking from the saints what can be given by God alone. In practice Invocations of Saints have been little used in the Church of England since the sixteenth century, and have been carried to great excess in some parts of the Church of Rome. In the East, the sixteenth century was a time of little importance, and the Invocation of Saints has gone on without any break. In many parts of the East the practice is marked by extravagance and excess.

It is an opinion held by very many at the present time that the possibility of the Invocation of Saints depends upon the belief that they have already attained to the Beatific Vision. A very careful and accurate writer, while stating that on the view which he prefers, he 'can come to no other conclusion than that Invocation is right,' has said, 'The lawfulness of the practice,' that is, of the Invocation of Saints, 'must depend on whether spirits departed, even the most pure, do "share God's knowledge." If they are already of the Church triumphant, if the Church's triumph has begun already, and if, even now, according to the later Roman teaching, they reign with Christ, then we may suppose that they also enter into His mind for the Church militant here on earth. But there is another school of thought, also Catholic, which maintains that Paradise is rather a state of expectation, and the kingdom reserved until after the final resurrection and judgment.' [57] It is certainly the case that in Western theology Invocation has very frequently and by writers of very great authority been associated with the saints vision of God. St. Gregory the Great, for instance, connects their knowledge of our prayers with their beholding the glory of Almighty God. [58] Peter Lombard says that our petitions are made known to the saints in the Word of God whom they contemplate. [59] St. Thomas Aquinas teaches, 'It is manifest that they know in the Word the vows and devotions and prayers of men who seek their aid.' [60] There can be little doubt that a true view of Christian history and doctrine leads to the belief that the great saints have already attained to some clear vision of God. But it is not to be thought that, failing this belief, it would necessarily follow that Invocation is wrong. St. Thomas Aquinas, in addition to the passage just quoted, writes, 'God alone knows of Himself the thoughts of the hearts, but none the less others know them insofar as revelation is made to them either by the vision of the Word or in some other way.' [61] 'The petitions,' he says again, 'which we direct to' the saints 'they know by the manifestation of God,'

[62] Who is to say that, even supposing the great saints are still in some waiting state without what we know as the vision of God, it cannot be that the Almighty, knowing the value of their prayers, reveals to them the prayers of Christians on earth?

The opinion that it is possible for the saints, whatever their present state, to have knowledge of the prayers of Christians living on earth is strongly supported by two facts. The first of these two facts is the existence of a school of thought in the West which does not deny the lawfulness of invoking even the souls in purgatory. Such a practice was indeed put aside by St. Thomas Aquinas both because the souls in purgatory do not yet enjoy the vision of the Word [63] and because they are not in a condition which allows of their praying at all. [64] In spite of his great authority, a different opinion has not died out in the West. Bellarmine, while considering the Invocation of the souls in purgatory as unnecessary under ordinary circumstances, does not condemn it as unlawful, and teaches what he thinks to be a certainty that the souls in purgatory pray for themselves and a probability that they pray for those on earth. [65] And, at the present time in the Church of Rome, while no Invocations of the souls in purgatory are publicly made, it is regarded as lawful to invoke them in private prayer. [66] When we consider the Western love of clear-cut distinctions and the great effect it has had on Western teaching about the departed, this absence of condemnation of Invocations of the souls in purgatory appears to be very significant, and, for what it is worth, to support an opinion that the possibility of Invocation does not depend upon those who are invoked having already attained to the Beatific Vision.

The second of the two facts is the Eastern practice of invoking the faithful departed generally. To the Eastern, the reason why a departed Christian may be invoked appears to be that he is in union with the Church. 'If any one believes,' wrote Khomiakoff, 'he is in the communion of faith; if he loves, he is in the communion of love; if he prays, he is in the communion of prayer. Wherefore no one can rest his hope on his own prayers, and every one who prays asks the whole Church for intercession, not as if he had doubts of the intercession of Christ, the one Advocate, but in the assurance that the whole Church ever prays for all her members. All the angels pray for us, the apostles, martyrs, and patriarchs, and above them all, the Mother of our Lord, and this Holy Unity is the true life of the Church. But if the Church, visible and invisible, prays without ceasing, why do we ask her for her prayers? Do we entreat mercy of God and Christ, although His mercy preventeth our prayer? The very reason that we ask the Church for her prayers is that we know that she gives the assistance of her intercession even to him that does not ask for it, and to him that asks she gives it in far greater measure than he asks: for in her is the fulness of the Spirit of God.' [67] Here, as in Eastern teaching generally, the possibility of the practice of Invocation is associated less with the person invoked beholding God than on his being a member of the mystical Body of Christ and indwelt by God the Holy Ghost. Similarly, while Macarius says that the saints placed immediately before the throne of God see the events of earth in the light of the person of God, he also compares the knowledge which the saints have of prayers offered upon earth with the supernatural know ledge which St. Peter had of the plans of Ananias, which Elisha had of the acts of Gehazi and the secret designs of the King of Syria. [68] That is, they have knowledge which is not the outcome of their own powers, which is granted to them by the gift of God, a gift which, it would seem, is not of necessity dependent upon attainment to the Beatific Vision.

It is possible then to sum up certain conclusions as to prayer for the dead and the Invocation of Saints based upon the consideration of the present state of the departed.

1. While there have been differences of teaching in the Church as to many details about the state of the departed, it came to be the general sense of Christendom that some of those who will eventually be among the saved are in a higher state, others in a lower state, and that at any rate those in the lower state are capable of development and progress which may be assisted by the prayers of Christians upon earth.

2. On the supposition that the great saints have attained to the Vision of God, there is a reasonable ground for the belief that in the Vision of God they behold all things which He wills to make known to them and that they are thus cognizant of the requests for their prayers made by Christians on earth.

3. On the contrary supposition that even the great saints are still in a waiting state without the Vision of God, there is no reasonable ground for denying that God may reveal to them the requests for their prayers made by Christians upon earth. Similarly, such requests may also be revealed by God to the faithful departed generally.

At the end of the time appointed for the probation of man in this life and for the waiting of the souls in the intermediate state, our Lord will return from heaven to this world. [69] At His coming, the bodies of men will be raised. It is probable that all the dead will be raised at the same time. St. Paul's words in his First Epistle to the Thessalonians [70] do not mean that the dead in Christ will rise before the dead who are not in Christ; but that they will rise before the transformation of those who are alive at the time of our Lord's coming. A passage in the Revelation [71] which makes mention of 'the first resurrection,' probably refers to the spiritual victory of the saints, not to a distinction between different times of rising from the dead. The bodies which are raised will be essentially the same as the bodies of the present life. They will be in a greatly changed condition, incorruptible, glorious, powerful, spiritual. [72]   After the resurrection there will be the general judgment. [73] The grounds of the judgment will be the deeds of this life. [74] At the judgment past lives will be revealed. [75] In the twelfth century a question was raised whether all sins would be revealed to all. Different answers were given. Peter Lombard taught that sins which had been blotted out by penance would not be revealed to others. St. Thomas Aquinas inclined to the view that all sins would be known to all, so as to manifest the righteousness of the judgments of God, and also because unless the sin was known, the penance which is often part of the glory of the saint could not be known either. [76] Most writers have thought that this opinion of St. Thomas Aquinas is implied by the passages in Holy Scripture which speak of the revealing of past lives. [77] The result of the judgment will be the division of mankind into the saved and the lost. [78]

The Future State of the Saved

Very little in the way of detail is known about the future state of the saved. In his First Epistle St. John says it has not yet been manifested what we shall be. It is revealed that there will be the presence of Christ, [79] and the Vision of God. [80] It has been discussed whether God in His divine essence will be seen with the eyes of the risen and spiritual body; or whether in His divine essence God will be seen only by spiritual perception, and the eyes of the risen and spiritual body see only the glorified humanity of our Lord. The latter opinion has been the more usual in the Church. At one time St. Augustine, apparently following ordinary teaching, asserted it. [81] At a later time he wrote doubtfully. [82] St. Thomas Aquinas, who probably represented the usual teaching from the time of St. Augustine to his own time, says the divine essence will not be directly seen by the eyes of the body. [83] It has been revealed also that there will be the service of God, [84] fellowship with one another in the life of a city, [85] a life of continence, [86] blessedness, [87] and glory. [88] There will be special gifts of blessedness. [89] The life will be without end. [90]

The Future State of the Lost

In the case of the lost, as of the saved, body and soul will be re-united. [91] They will be banished from God. [92] The technical name for this banishment is 'poena damni,' the penalty of loss. There will be further punishment than mere absence from God. [93] The technical name for this is 'poena sensus,' the penalty of sense. Our Lord calls it worm and fire. [94] Both words have received different interpretations within the Church. Some have taken them as literal; others as metaphorical, to describe the horrors of hell without implying literal worm and literal fire, the metaphor being derived from the corruption and fires in the valley of Hinnom. St. Jerome mentions that these words were understood by many to mean the 'conscience of sinners which tortures them when under punishment.' [95] St. Ambrose so taught. [96] St. Augustine inclined towards the fire being literal and the worm metaphorical, but was careful to leave the question open. [97] St. John of Damascus, who as a rule represents the Eastern tradition, says the eternal fire is not material as our fire, but such as God knows of. [98] St. Thomas Aquinas says the worm is not literal but the fire is. [99] Both expressions have commonly been regarded as metaphorical in the East. The most usual later teaching in the West has been that at any rate the fire is literal.

It is revealed that the punishment of the lost is unending. 'These shall go away,' says our Lord, 'into eternal punishment.' [100] The etymological meaning of the word eternal (αἰώνιος) which our Lord here used is that it expresses the quality in things which is permanent, so that it denotes lasting through all ages. The use of the word in Holy Scripture corresponds to its etymology. [101] In this place, moreover, our Lord uses it in one half of the verse in reference to the punishment of the lost, and in the other half of the verse in reference to the life of the righteous. Apart from the particular word, our Lord evidently refers to a division which is final and permanent. [102]

The ordinary teaching in the Church everywhere from the first has been that the punishment of the lost is unending. Origen is often described as an exception. What Origen really taught was that after death there is still a possibility of salvation for all; and, while it is probable his own belief was that all men would ultimately be delivered from any pain of sense, he appears to think there are some who will never attain to the Beatific Vision, and will therefore always suffer the pain of loss. [103] If this is a right interpretation of what he says, he regarded the central point in the punishment as unending in the case of some. St. Jerome, St. Gregory of Nazianzus, and St. Gregory of Nyssa have also been thought to be exceptions to the general rule of teaching the eternity of punishment. In a number of places, St. Jerome very explicitly asserts the eternity of punishment; there are others in which he speaks with hesitation as to the possibility of the alleviation of the pains of the lost, or the possibility of the salvation after punishment of those who died in sin. [104] As to St. Gregory of Nazianzus, the passages in question in his writings do not necessarily deny the endless character of punishment, and elsewhere in his teaching he definitely asserts it. [105] As to St. Gregory of Nyssa, there are in his writings passages the only fair interpretation of which is that the devil and the demons and all men will finally be saved; but there are others which clearly speak of hell as unending and of those who wilfully neglect Baptism as being lost forever. There is no evidence to support a statement made in the eighth century by Germanus of Constantinople that the universalist passages had been inserted by heretics; and the probability appears to be that at times St. Gregory accepted the traditional teaching of the Church, and at other times taught speculations inconsistent with it. [106] Apart from these writers, there is a uniform tradition in all parts of the Church that the penalties of the lost are unending.

The eternity of punishment is further involved in the co-ordinate holding of the holiness of God and the free will of man. The perfect holiness of God implies that only those who have attained to righteousness can be admitted to the Beatific Vision; and, if man is free, there must be the possibility of his choosing evil as his eternal lot, a choice which must carry with it the impossibility of his character becoming good, and consequently the impossibility of his attaining to the Beatific Vision.

An opinion that, while the essential elements of hell are unending, yet the pains of hell are in the course of time alleviated, has generally been regarded as an allowable opinion. A few theologians have held it. St. Augustine is careful not to deny it. [107] At times it has had some popularity. At present, there is nothing about it in any representative teaching of the East or of the Church of England. In the Church of Borne it is regarded as allowable, though held only by few. [108]

According to the theory known as Annihilationism, all souls except the saved will cease to exist. There is nothing to support it in Holy Scripture or in the teaching of the Church; and it is contrary to the inferences which may rightly be drawn from the general belief that immortality is a natural possession of man.

According to the theory known as Universalism, all human beings, or, in its more extreme and more logical form, all rational beings, including the devil, will eventually be admitted to heaven. For this theory, support has been claimed from the phrase used by St. Peter, 'the times of restoration of all things;' St. Paul's assertion that 'all things' are to be put 'in subjection under' the 'feet' of our Lord; and the expressions used by St. Paul that it is the purpose of the Father 'to sum up all things in Christ,' and through Christ 'to reconcile all things.' [109] These passages do not mean more than that the redemption of Christ is universal, that is, He died on behalf of all men and saves them all if they accept His grace; and that finally God will be seen to be supreme by all being either conformed to His will or banished from His presence. Inferences to be drawn from these passages must be such as to be in harmony with the other teaching of Holy Scripture. They do not in themselves assert Universalism; and that theory is distinctly contrary to the express statements of Holy Scripture elsewhere and the definite teaching of the Church.

The following statements may, then, be made as to the doctrine of Eschatology:

1. It is clearly revealed that there is an unending life of blessedness for those who accept the will of God.

2. It is clearly revealed that there is a possibility of any human being remaining for ever estranged from God, and consequently absent from Him; and that this absence from God is what is central in hell. Different opinions have been held within the Church as to the nature of, and as to the possibility of the alleviation of, the pains of hell.

3. The only revealed time of probation is in this life.

4. The practical judgment of the whole Church has been that the faithful departed may be benefited by the prayers of the living. The ordinary feeling in the Church has been that the condition of the faithful departed is one of training for the Beatific Vision, and of perfecting the movements towards goodness which have begun in this life. An opinion that the extirpation of evil and the development of good will involve suffering has been held by very

many. An opinion that punishments lasting only for a time are inflicted for all sins even though forgiven, and that all such punishments not suffered in this life must be suffered in the intermediate state has been held by very many.

5. The most usual opinion in the Church is that the great saints are admitted to the Beatific Vision before the resurrection. The ordinary feeling in the Church has been that the great saints may be invoked with the object of gaining the benefit of their prayers to God, In the East and in one school of thought in the West. it has been considered that the faithful departed generally may be so invoked.

Revealed truth leaves unsolved many problems which perplex the human heart. In the recognition of these problems, it is the office of Christian faith to trust the love of God. 'Let us submit to the conditions of our state and of our knowledge, we, at least, who in the tempest and confusions of the world have as our one supreme guiding light the manifestation, the words of the Son of God. Who shall say that, though we must greatly fear, we may not also greatly hope, even if we are met by awful certainties, if we dare not say more than He has said? We cannot tell what is between the grave and the Judgment; but we know that the Living God is there, very terrible, very pitiful, very just, who leads His creatures by ways they know not to the end which only He knows. We may be sure that He will set right in His own way the in equalities of this world. We may be sure that all who seek Him in truth shall one day find Him, for He has said so. We may be sure that every one in every nation who feareth Him and worketh righteousness is accepted with Him, for His accredited Apostle has said so. Is the righteousness of God too small a thing to trust to, unless we can say in detail how it is to be carried out? Are the "multitude of His mercies," to use a favourite phrase of the Psalms, the "multitude of His mercies," to which saint and penitent must alike appeal are they too stinted, too straitened, that we cannot commit to them all the infinite issues of human life, which move our fellow-feeling, our pity, our sympathy? Can we be so compassionate and so just, and cannot we trust Him to be so, unless He shows us how? Can we not trust Him, in silent and awful expectation, with the work of His own hands, sure that He will not despise it - sure that under the shadow of His wings all the countless multitude of His creatures, from the highest to the lowest, the worst and the best, shall find His perfect truth - sure that each soul will receive what it ought to receive, and will be dealt with as it ought to be dealt with, by infinite goodness and unerring justice?' [110]

'Sorrow is hard to bear, and doubt is slow to clear,
    Each sufferer says his say, his scheme of the weal and woe:
But God has a few of us whom He whispers in the ear;
    The rest may reason and welcome: 'tis we musicians know.' [111]

---

[1] See, *e.g.*, St. Matt, xviii. 7-9; xxv. 31-46; 2 Cor. v. 10.

[2] See, *c.g.*, Eccles. xi. 3; St. Luke xvi. 26; Heb. ix. 27.

[3] St. Augustine, *Enchiridion*, 110.
[4] Origen, *De Princ.*, I. vi. 3; II. iii. 3; III. i. 21. On the other hand, see *In Rom.*, v. 10.
[5] St. Matt. xxi. 31.
[6] Luckock, *The Intermediate State*, pp. 172-196.
[7] St. Matt. xi. 24.
[8] Ps. vi. 5; xxx. 9; Lxxxviii. 5; Isa. xxxviii. 18, 19; Ps. xlix. 15.
[9] 2 St. Tim. i. 10; St. Matt. xxii. 32; St. Luke xvi. 22-31; xxiii. 43; 1 St, Peter iii. 18-20; Rev. vi. 9-11.
[10] St. Jerome, *C. Vigilantium*, 7.
[11] Council of Chalcedon, Actio xi.
[12] *Saxon Confession*, 22.
[13] St. Luke xvi. 22-31; Phil. i. 21-24.
[14] Heb. xii. 1.
[15] Westcott *in loco*.
[16] Heb. xii. 22-24.
[17] Students should consult, especially on Apocryphal and Apocalyptic literature, Charles, *A Critical History of the Doctrine of a Future Life*, a work of great learning, from many conclusions in which the author is obliged to dissent.
[18] St. Clement of Borne, *Ad Cor.*, i. 5; cf. 44.
[19] St. Ignatius, *Ad Trall*, 13; *Ad Rom.*, 7.
[20] St. Polycarp, 9.
[21] Apud Eusebius, H.E., v. 2.
[22] Tertullian, *De Resur. Carn.*, 43; *De Anim.*, 55.
[23] *S. Perpetuae Passio*, 4, 11-13.
[24] Apud Eusebius, *H.E.*, vi. 42.
[25] St. Justin Martyr, *Dial c. Tryp.*, 5.
[26] St. Irenaeus, *C. Haer.*, V. xxxi. 2.
[27] See Brightman, *Liturgies Eastern and Western*, i. 23, 40, 363.
[28] *ibid.*, i. 48, 57, 73, 74, 76, 78, 93, 94, 169, 230, 264, 330, 331, 388, 395, 406, 407, 415, 419.
[29] *ibid.*, i. 23, 57, 128, 129, 373, 387, 388, 407.
[30] *ibid.*, i. 21, 22, 128, 129, 387, 388.
[31] St. Cyril of Jerusalem, *Cat. Myst.*, v. 9.
[32] St. Augustine, *Enchir.*, 110; cf. *Serm.*, clix. 1; clxxii. 2.
[33] Pope John XXII. asserted the contrary opinion that no souls attain to the Beatific Vision before the resurrection. For the controversy which ensued, and the retractation he is said to have made, see Gieseler, *Compendium of Ecclesiastical History*, iv. 42-41 (English translation).
[34] Tertullian, *De Anim.*, 58.
[35] *S. Perpetuae Passio*, 7, 8.
[36] Clement of Alexandria, *Strom.*, vii. 6; cf. 12.
[37] Origen, *In Lev. Rom.*, xiv. 3; *In Num. Rom.*, xxv. 6; *In Jer. Rom.*, xvi. 5, 6; *In Ps. xxxvi. Hom.*, iii. 1.
[38] St. Ambrose, *In Ps. xxxvi. Enar.*, 26; *In Ps. cxviii. Expos.*, xx. 12-14.
[39] St. Gregory of Naziauzus, *Orat.*, xxxix. 9.
[40] St. Augustine, *In Ps. xxxvii.*, 3; cf. *De Civ. Dei*, xxi. 3.
[41] St. Augustine, *De Civ. Dei*, xxi. 20, § 4; cf. *Enchir.*, 69.
[42] St. Catherine of Genoa, *Treatise on Purgatory, passim*.
[43] Council of Trent, Sess. xxv., *De Invoc.*; *Deer, de Purgat*.
[44] *Catechism of the Council of Trent*, I. vi. 3.
[45] Schouppe, *Elementa Theologiae Dogmaticae*, xix. 101,
[46] Martensen, *Christian Dogmatics*, p. 457 (English translation).
[47] Council of Bethlehem, cap. xviii.
[48] See note 62 in the concluding Notes.
[49] See Blackmore, *Doctrine of the Russian Church*, pp. 98-100.
[50] 1 St. Tim. ii. 1.
[51] Origen, *De Oratione*, 14.
[52] See, *e.g.*, Luckock, *After Death*, pp. 187, 188.

[53] See Bigg, *The Christian Platonists of Alexandria*, p. 185, note 1.

[54] For a fuller treatment of this point and of the patristic evidence, see Church Quarterly Review, January, 1899, pp. 277-282, 289-295.

[55] Council of Trent, Sess. xxv., De Invoc.

[56] Catechism of the Council of Trent, IV. vi. 3, 4.

[57] Churton, *Missionary's Foundation of Doctrine*, pp. 292, 293.

[58] St. Gregory the Great, *Mor.*, xii. 26.

[59] Peter Lombard, *Sent,* IV. xlv. 6.

[60] St. Thomas Aquinas, *Sent.*, IV. xlv. 3; *Summa Theol*, Suppl. lxxii. 1.

[61] *ibid.*

[62] *Idem, Summa Theol*, II. 2 lxxxiii. 4.

[63] St. Thomas Aquinas, *Summa Theol*, II. 2 lxxxiii. 4.

[64] *ibid.*, 11.

[65] Bellarmine, *De Purgat.,* ii. 15.

[66] See, *e.g.*, Schouppe, *Elementa Theologiae Dogmaticae*, xix. 121.

[67] Khomiakoff in Birkbeck, *Russia and the English Church*, p. 216.

[68] *Theologie Dogmatique Orthodoxe*, par Macaire, traduite par un Russe, 254 (t. ii. p. 661).

[69] St. Matt. xxiv. 30; St. Mark xiii. 26; Acts i. 11; 1 Thess. iv. 16.

[70] 1 Thess. iv. 16.

[71] Rev. xx. 6.

[72] 1 Cor. xv. 35-54.

[73] St. Matt. xxv. 31; St. John v. 27-29; Rom. xiv. 10.

[74] St. Matt. xxv. 31-46; 2 Cor. v. 10.

[75] St. Matt. x. 26; St. Luke xii. 2; 1 Cor. iv. 5.

[76] Peter Lombard, *Sent.*, IV. xliii. 3; St. Thomas Aquinas, *Summa Theol*, Suppl., lxxxvii. 2; lxxxviii. 2.

[77] St. Matt. x. 26: 1 Cor. iv. 5.

[78] St. Matt. xxv. 32, 33.

[79] 1 Thess. iv. 17; 1 St. John iii. 2.

[80] Rev. xxii. 4.

[81] St. Augustine, *Ep.*, cxlvii. 52-54.

[82] Idem, *De Civ. Dei*, xxii. 29.

[83] St. Thomas Aquinas, *Summa Theol,* Suppl. xcii. 2.

[84] Rev. xxii. 3.

[85] Rev. xxi. 23, 24.

[86] St. Matt. xxii. 30.

[87] St. Matt. xxv. 34-46.

[88] Rom. viii. 18; 2 Cor. iv. 17.

[89] Rev. xiv. 3, 4.

[90] St. Matt. xxv. 46; St. Mark x. 30; Rev. xxii. 5.

[91] St. Matt. x. 28.

[92] St. Matt. xxv. 41; Rev. xxii. 15.

[93] St. Matt. xxv. 46.

[94] St. Matt, xviii. 8, 9; St. Mark ix. 48.

[95] St. Jerome, In Isa., lxvi. 24.

[96] St. Ambrose, *In Luc. Ev.*, vii. 205.

[97] St. Augustine, Enchir., 113; cf. *De Civ. Dei*, xx. 22.

[98] St. John of Damascus, *De Fid. Orth.*, iv. 27.

[99] St. Thomas Aquinas, *Summa Theol.*, Suppl. xcvii. 2, 5, 6.

[100] St. Matt. xxv. 46. Cf. St. Mark ix. 48; St. Luke xvi. 26; Rev. xiv. 11.

[101] See note 63 in the concluding Notes.

[102] Cf. St. Matt. xxvi. 24; St. Mark xiv. 21; Rev. xxii. 11.

[103] See Bigg, *The Christian Platonists of Alexandria*, pp. 284, 292 293.

[104] See note 64 in the concluding Notes.

[105] See note 65 in the concluding Notes.

[106] See note 66 in the concluding Notes.

[107] St. Augustine, *Enchiridion*, 113.

[108] See, *e.g.*, Petavius, *De Angelis*, III. viii. 18.

[109] Acts iii. 21; 1 Cor. xv. 27; Eph. i. 10; Col. i. 20.

[110] Church, *Human Life and its Conditions*, pp. 122-124.

[111] Browning, *Abt Vogler.*

Notes

1. *The angel of the Lord.*

In a number of passages in the Old Testament 'the angel of Jehovah,' 5 or 'the angel of God' is mentioned. See, *e.g.*, Gen. xvi. 7-14; xviii.; xxi. 17-19; xxii. 11, 14, 15; xxxii. 24-30. He appears to be identified with God: see Gen. xvi. 10; xxi. 18; xxxi. 11, 13; Ex. iii. 2, Q; Judg. xiii. 22. He is also distinguished: see, *e.g.*, Gen. xvi. 11; xxii. 15, 16; Num. xxii. 31. The earliest Fathers regarded this angel as God the Son Himself; in view of a misuse of the belief by the Arians, a different opinion, largely due to St. Augustine, that he was a created being who represented God, became that most usually held in the Church. See Liddon, *The Divinity of our Lord and Saviour Jesus Christ,* pp. 52-60.

2. *The phrase 'Eternal Generation.'*

The credit for this phrase, which has passed into the theology of the Church, and for greatly helping to clear Christian thought as to the relation of the Son to the Father, should, in spite of his many eccentricities and errors, be given to Origen. Thus, he says of the Son, 'There is not when He was not' (*De Princ.,* I. ii. 9; IV. xxviii.; *In Rom.,* i. 5); 'It is not the case that the Father begat the Son and separated Him from His be getting, but He always is begetting Him' (*In Jer. Rom.,* ix. 4). At the same time it must be remembered that Origen held also the eternity of Creation: see *De Princ.,* I. ii. 10, where he uses the argument that to be a lord implies rule and therefore creation must always have been, just as he argues that to be a father implies a son, and therefore the Son must always have been. See also Bigg, *The Christian Platonists of Alexandria,* pp. 159, 160, 167, 168.

3. *Eastern Fathers on the Procession of the Holy Ghost.*

The language of St. Athanasius about the procession of the Holy Ghost is of very great interest and importance. In Expos. Fid., 4, he writes, 'The Holy Ghost, being That which proceeds from the Father, is always in the hands of the Father who sends and the Son who conveys Him, through whom He filled all.' In *Orat. c. Arian.,* i. 15, he says, 'The Spirit Himself receives from the Son'. In *Ep. ad Serap.,* i. 2, 20, 24, 32; iii. 1, he calls the Holy Ghost 'the property of the Son,' 'the property of the Word and of the Godhead of the Father,' 'the image of the Son;' and says, 'As the Son is in His own image in the Spirit, so also the Father is in the Son;' 'Such a property of the Son towards the Father as we know, this we shall find the Spirit has towards the Son.' In *De Trin, et Spir.* (which however exists only in a Latin translation which may have been amplified), 19, he calls the Holy Ghost the 'spiratio' of the Son. In *De Incarn. et c. Arian.* (which, if not by St. Athanasius, is certainly Eastern), 9, the Son is called 'the fountain of the Holy Ghost.' St. Basil says that the Holy Ghost 'is called the Spirit of Christ as being His own by nature' *De Spir. S.,* 46. St. Epiphanius describes the Holy Ghost as 'proceeding from the Father and receiving from the Son,' and as the 'bond of the Trinity,' *Haer.,* lxii. 4; cf. *Ancor.,* 121. St. Cyril of Alexandria says clearly that the Holy Ghost 'is called the Spirit of truth, and Christ is the truth; and He is poured forth from Him, as certainly also from God the Father, *Ad Nest. Ep.,* iii. 10. It is difficult to see that there is any difference in essential thought between the truth which this language expresses and that conveyed by the Western phraseology when properly guarded, as, *e.g.,* in St. Augustine, *De Trin.,* xv. 29, 'And yet not in vain in this Trinity is none called the Word of God except the Son, and none the gift of God except the Holy Spirit, and none except God the Father He of whom the Word was begotten and from whom the Holy Spirit as from a source (principaliter) proceeds. Now I have added as from a source (principaliter) for this reason that the Holy Spirit is found to proceed also from the Son.' While it is probably the case that, largely through controversy, later individual Eastern and Western writers have used language which tended to exaggerate one or the other side of the truth, it may be doubted whether there has ever been an essential difference between the East and the West on this subject. In the face of the teaching of the Eastern Fathers, it is difficult to think that Easterns have meant that the Son was passive in the Procession, while Westerns have certainly not meant that there were two principia. The passages from the Fathers quoted in Pusey, *On the Clause, 'And the Son,'* pp. 108-150, will repay the study of the exact phraseology in the original languages. The student should also consult the *Reports* of the Bonn Reunion Conferences in 1874 and 1875, and the *Church Quarterly Review,* January, 1877, pp. 421-465. The possibility of real agreement, side by side with the expression of differing aspects of truth, may be illustrated by the parallel question raised by the description of the Holy Ghost as the μέσον of the Father and the Son (*e.g.,* St. Gregory of Nazianzus, Orat., xxxi. 8) and as the bond of the Trinity (*e.g.,* St. Epiphanius, *Haer.,* lxii. 4). St. John of Damascus (*De Fid. Orth.,* i. 13) says in the same sentence that the Holy Ghost is the μέσον of the Father and the Son and that He is joined to the Father through the Son. Again, it is obvious that St. John of Damascus (*ibid.*) asserts that the Holy Ghost is the image of the Son in a different sense from that in which this is denied by Richard of St. Victor (*De Trin.,* vi. 19). There is much which throws light on the misunderstandings among theologians on this subject in St. Thomas Aquinas, *Summa Theologica,* I. xxxv. 2; *C. Errores Graecorum,* i. 10, ii. 8. Some of the least satis factory statements by Easterns, together with other matter, may be found in Le Quien, *Dissertationes Damascenicae,* Diss. i. (prefixed to his edition of St. John of Damascus).

4. *Errors about God and the Holy Trinity.*

It may be convenient to give the following definitions:

Atheism. - The characteristic feature of Atheism is the denial that God exists. Atheists have accounted for the existence of the universe and man by a merely natural development of matter which either existed eternally or came into being of itself. The Greek philosopher Diagoras and the German writer Feuerbach are instances of Atheists.

Agnosticism. - The term Agnostic is due, in the first instance, to the writings of Dr. Huxley. As used by him and subsequent writers it denotes one who contends that, if God exists, nothing can be known about Him, since the knowledge of man is limited to phenomena. The same line of thought leads to the denial of possibility of any knowledge of spiritual beings or a future life.

Polytheism. - This word denotes the belief that there are many gods. It has marked many heathen religions.

Dualism. - The opinion that there are two co-ordinate and eternal Principles ruling in the world, one of good, the other of evil. It was characteristic of the early Persian religion and of the Gnostic heresies of the second century.

Tritheism. - The opinion that there are three separate Gods. The Tritheites at the end of the sixth century at any rate approximated to Tritheism.

Pantheism. - The opinion that God is identical with the universe and without personal being, and that all material objects and the souls of men are parts of God and of the same substance with Him. Thus, it distinguishes God from the world only in thought, not in reality. Pantheism formed part of ancient religious systems in India and Greece. One of the most famous of modern Pantheists was the philosopher Spinoza, a resident in the Netherlands of Jewish descent, in the seventeenth century.

Deism. - The opinion that there is a personal God who is a spiritual being who created the world, and after creating it left it partly or wholly to itself. Consequently, Deists deny revelation, and, in some cases, providence also. Deism was common in England in the seventeenth and eighteenth centuries. It was strongly marked by the system of Lord Herbert of Cherbury.

Positivism. - The opinion that there is no independent being who is called God, but the sum of humanity may rightly be called God and is to be worshipped by individual men. In a less special sense, the same word is used to denote the philosophical system which limits knowledge to the results of observation and experiment. Positivism as a system is due to Auguste Comte.

Anthropomorphism. - The heresy that God has a bodily nature like that of man. The Audians of the fourth and fifth centuries, a Syrian sect consisting of the followers of Audius, or Audaeus, were Anthropomorphites. The same heresy was held by some of the Egyptian monks at the end of the fourth century. It has been revived among the Mormons in the nineteenth century.

Sabellianism. - The heresy, prevalent from the third to the fifth century, that there are not three Persons in God, but that what are called the three Persons are only three different manifestations of the same Person. The Sabellians were sometimes called Patripassians, because it would logically follow from their theory that it was the Father who suffered in our Lord's life and death. The name Sabellian is derived from Sabellius, who nourished at Rome at the end of the second and beginning of the third century.

Arianism. - The heresy that the Son was created, and that, while He is a creature of the most exalted kind, He is not of the same essence of the Father and therefore not truly and eternally God. The name was derived from Arius. The heresy was of great influence in the fourth century.

Macedonianism. - The heresy which denied the God head of the Holy Ghost. The name was derived from Macedonius, Bishop of Constantinople. The heresy had influence in the latter part of the fourth century.

5. *The nature of the angels.*

A full discussion of the various opinions held by the Fathers on this subject is in Petavius, *De Angelis,* I. ii.-iv. A clear statement of the different sides of the teaching of the Church is in St. John of Damascus, *De Fid. Orth.,* ii. 3: 'He is the Maker and Creator of the angels, who brought them into being from having no existence; forming them in His own image, with a bodiless nature, as a spirit, or immaterial fire, as says holy David, "Who maketh His angels spirits, and His ministers a flame of fire;" thus describing their lightness, and keenness, and warmth, and penetration, and sharpness, with which they desire and serve God, and that they are borne aloft and are free from every material thought. An angel, then, is an intellectual being, ever in movement, possessing free-will, bodiless, ministering to God, by grace having an immortal nature, the form and limit of whose being the Creator alone knoweth. An angel is called bodiless and immaterial, so far as relates to us; for everything, when compared with God, the only incomparable Being, is found to be crass and material; for the Deity alone is truly immaterial and bodiless.'

6. *The time of the creation of the angels.*

Many Eastern and some Western Fathers thought that the angels were created long before the creation of the world. A discussion of their opinions is in Petavius, *De Angelis,* I. xv. It came to be the most usual opinion that they were created at the time of the creation of the world. See, *e.g.,* the sermon entitled *The existence of angels proved from reason as well as Scripture, their creation by God, the fall of some of them, the nature of the holy angels, their state and condition in reference to God,* in Bull, *English Theological Works,* pp. 193-214, especially pp. 200-203 (Oxford, 1844).

7. *A guardian angel assigned to each human being.*

A useful collection of passages from the Fathers is in Petavius, De Angelis, II. vii. The usual opinion among Catholic theologians is clearly expressed by St. Thomas Aquinas, *Summa Theologica,* I. cxiii. 4, 5: 'Man is set in the condition of this life as if in a kind of journey in which he ought to make his way to his native land. In this journey many dangers threaten man both from within and from without, as it is said, "In the way wherein I was walking they hid a snare for me." And therefore, as guards are assigned to men who walk on a road which is not safe, so also to each man, as long as he is on his journey (quamdiu viator est), an angel is appointed as a guardian.' 'Some have said that an angel is appointed to guard man from the time of Baptism; but others, from the time of birth. The latter opinion is approved by Jerome, and reasonably. For the benefits which God bestows on man, in that he is a Christian, begin from the time of Baptism, as the reception of the Eucharist, and other gifts of this kind. But those things which God provides for man, inasmuch as he has rational nature, are granted to him from that time at which, on his birth, he receives such a nature. And the protection of the angels is a gift of this kind, as is clear from what has been previously said. Where fore man has an angel appointed to be his guardian as soon as he is born.'

8. *The relation of the spirit (πνεῦμα) to the soul (ψυχή).*

There are passages in the New Testament which at first sight appear to imply that the nature of man is divided into three distinct parts, the body (σῶμα), the soul (ψυχή), and the spirit (πνεῦμα). See 1 Cor. xv. 45; 1 Thess. v. 23; Heb. iv. 12. Some writers have thought it a necessary inference that there is an actual and essential distinction between the soul and the spirit. See, *e.g.,* Ellicott on 1 Cor. ii. 15. On the other hand, other passages appear to indicate a division into two parts only. See St. Matt. x. 28 (body and soul); xxvi. 41 (flesh and spirit); St. James ii. 26 (body and spirit). A number of passages places the moral resolve, which may be regarded as the act of the spirit, in the soul. See St. Luke i. 46; Eph. vi. 6; Phil. i. 27; Col. iii. 23; Heb. vi. 19, xii. 3. This has led many writers to regard the soul and the spirit as one in essence, though distinct in function, so that the man consists of two parts, the body and the soul; and of these the soul has its lower and higher aspects, the higher aspect being called the spirit. See Delitzsch, *Biblical Psychology,* pp. 103-119 (English translation); Liddon, *Some Elements of Religion,* pp. 89-91. On the other side, see Lightfoot on 1 Thess. v. 23, in *Notes on Epistles of St. Paul from Unpublished Commentaries,* pp. 88, 89; and cf. Westcott's additional notes on 1 St. John iii. 19 (pp. 127-129), and Heb. iv. 12 (pp. 114-116).

9. *St. Justin Martyr and St. Irenaeus on the flesh of man in the image of God.*

St. Justin Martyr, *De Resur.,* 7: 'Does not the word say, Let us make man in our image and likeness? What kind of man? Plainly it means man in the flesh. For the word says, And God took dust from the earth and formed man. It is clear, then, that man was made in the image of God in the flesh. How, then, is it not absurd to say that the flesh which was made by God in His own image is dishonourable and worth nothing?' This treatise is thought not to be St. Justin's by some critics. See, *e.g.,* Canon H. S. Holland in Smith and Wace's *Dictionary of Christian Biography,* iii. 565.

St. Irenaeus, *C. Haer.,* V. vi. 1: 'By means of the hands of the Father, that is, the Son and the Spirit, man, not a part of man, is made after the likeness of God. Now the soul and the spirit can be a part of man; but they cannot possibly be the man. But the complete man is the combination and union (commixtio et adunitio) of the soul receiving the breath of the Father with flesh also joined to it, which was formed after the image of God.'

10. The accounts of Creation and the Fall in the Book of Genesis.

It has been assumed in what has been said about Creation and the Fall that the accounts given in the Book of Genesis are historical, and that they are, at the same time, susceptible of very different interpretations, according as the account of Creation is regarded as a literal chronological history or as a general representation clothed to some extent in symbolical language, and as the account of the Fall is in all details literally interpreted or taken to be of a partly or wholly allegorical character. That the accounts are historical and relate facts has been taken as the necessary outcome of a belief that, while the object of the early chapters of Genesis is religious rather than scientific, the Holy Ghost would not use substantial error as a vehicle of teaching in His revelation of truth, and because their historical character is implied in Rom. v. 12-21 and 1 St. Tim. ii. 13, 14. That they are susceptible of other interpretations than those which are verbally literal has been regarded as tenable partly because there is nothing in Holy Scripture inconsistent with such a view and partly because there appears to be sufficient authority for it in the teaching of representative Church writers. While the extreme views of Origen failed to find support among the theologians of the Church, a more moderate method of allegorical interpretation was adopted or justified by writers of unquestionable orthodoxy. The treatment of the early chapters of Genesis implied in the treatises of St. Athanasius *Contra Gentes* and *De Incarnatione* suggests an allegorical interpretation. In De Gen. ad Lit., i. 1, St. Augustine says, 'In the narrative of events which have happened, we inquire whether all things are to be accepted only in a figurative sense or whether they are also to be asserted and defended as literal occurrences (secundum fidem rerum gestarum).' His view of the account of Creation has been referred to in the text. He apparently takes the Fall as an exactly literal history; but before beginning to comment upon it says, 'If in the words of God, or of any person assumed to the prophetical office, any thing is said which cannot be literally understood without absurdity, certainly it ought to be understood to have been said in a figure for some signification; yet it is not right to doubt that it was said.' See *ibid.,* xi. 2: cf. viii. 1. St. Augustine's teaching about Holy Scripture also includes the following points: (1) It was spoken by the Holy Ghost so as to be the voice of God, the handwriting of God, the book of which, in both the Old and New Testaments, God is the author: see, *e.g., Conf.,* vii. 26; xiii. 44; *De Cons. Ev.,* iii. 28-31; *Enar. in Ps. xc.,* ii. 1; *Enar. in Ps. cxliv.,* 17; *Enar. in Ps. cxlix.,* 5; *De Util. Cred.,* 13; *C. Adim. Man. Disc.,* 4; *C. advers. Leg. et Proph.,*

ii. 13. (2) It is to be distinguished from writings outside the canon: see, *e.g.*, *Ep.*, xciii. 35; *C. Faust.*, xi. 5; *De Bapt. c. Don.*, ii. 4. (3) It has specific authority: see, *e.g.*, Conf., vi. 8; xii. 36; xiii. 16; *Ep.*, lxxxii. 5, 6; *De Civ. Dei*, xi. 3. (4) It is infallible: see, *e.g.*, Ep., lxxxii. 3, 22, 24; *C. Faust.*, xi. 5; *De Bapt. c. Don.*, ii. 4. On the allegorical interpretation of Clement of Alexandria and Origen, see Bigg, *The Christian Platonists of Alexandria*, pp. 57, 58, 131-151.

On this subject, it is of considerable importance that the ordinary traditional Christian interpretation of the Song of Songs has been allegorical: see, *e.g.*, Wordsworth, *Introduction to the Song of Solomon*, pp. 122-126; Cheyne in *Encyclopaedia Biblica*, i. 682. The significance of this fact does not depend on the interpretation being right in this particular case.

The view here rejected that the early chapters of Genesis may be popular myths which are substantially erroneous, though made to convey religious truth, is adopted and defended in *Lux Mundi*, pp. 356, 357, and (10th edition) p. 537; Driver, *Sermons on Subjects connected with the Old Testament*, pp. 1-27, 163-178; Ryle, *The Early Narratives of Genesis*.

See also note 39.

11. The Fathers on the connexion between the Fall and the Incarnation.

The following passages are those chiefly referred to: St. Athanasius, De Incar., 4: 'In speaking of the appearing of the Saviour among us, it is necessary for us to speak also of the origin of men that you may know that we were the cause of His coming down, and that our transgression called forth the loving-kindness of the Word, so that the Lord hastened to us and appeared among men;' Oral. C. Arian., ii. 54: 'The need of men precedes His becoming man, and without it He would not have put on flesh.'

St. Augustine, Serm., clxxiv. 2: 'If man had not perished, the Son of man had not come.'

St. Leo, Serin., Lxxvii. 2: 'If man, made in the image and likeness of God, had remained in the dignity of His own nature, and had not been deceived by the fraud of the devil and departed, through appetite, from the law laid down for him, the Creator of the world would not have become a creature, nor would the Everlasting have entered temporal condition, nor would God the Son, equal to God the Father, have put on the form of a servant and the likeness of sinful flesh.'

12. Duns Scotus on the connexion between the Fall and the Incarnation.

See, *e.g.*, *Opus Parisiense*, III. vii. 4 (5): 'If the Fall was the cause of the predestination of Christ' (*i.e.*, to the Incarnation), 'it would follow that the highest work of God was contingent only, because the glory of all will not be so great in degree (intensive) as that of Christ; and it seems to be very irrational to suppose that God would have left undone so great a work because of the good deed of Adam, that is, if he had not sinned.'

'I say therefore: In the first place, God loves Himself; secondly, He loves others (diligit se aliis), and His love is pure; thirdly, He wishes to be loved by another who can love Him in the highest degree, speaking of the extrinsic love of any one; and, fourthly, He foresees the union of that nature which ought to love Him in the highest degree even if no one should have fallen.'

13. St. Thomas Aquinas on the connexion between the Fall and the Incarnation.

In his earlier teaching (*Sent.*, III. i. 1) he leaves open the question whether the Word would have become incarnate if man had not sinned. In the *Summa Theologica*, III. i. 3, he wrote, 'Things which happen simply from the will of God, above all which is due to the creature, cannot be known to us except so far as they are delivered in Holy Scripture, through which the will of God is known to us. Wherefore, since in Holy Scripture the cause of the Incarnation is everywhere spoken of as proceeding from the sin of the first man, it is more fittingly said that the work of the Incarnation was ordained by God as a remedy against sin; so that, if there had been no sin, there would have been no Incarnation. Although the power of God is not hereby to be limited; for, even if there had been no sin, it would have been possible for God to become incarnate.'

14. St. Anselm, St. Bernard, St. Thomas Aquinas, and Duns Scotus on the conception and birth of the Blessed Virgin Mary.

St. Anselm, Cur Deus Homo, ii. 16 (Boso): 'The very virgin from whom His manhood was taken was conceived in iniquities, and in sins did her mother conceive her; and with original sin was she born.'

St. Bernard, Ep., clxxiv. 5, 8: 'Without doubt the Mother of the Lord was holy before she was born; Although it has been vouchsafed to a few of the sons of men to be born holy (cum sanctitate nasci), yet it has not been vouchsafed thus also to be conceived, so that the prerogative of a holy conception was kept for Him alone who was to make all holy, and alone coming without sin to accomplish the cleansing of sins...With this exception that which one confesses humbly and truly about himself applies to all who have been born in descent from Adam; In iniquities, he says, was I conceived; and in sins did my mother conceive me.'

St. Thomas Aquinas deals with this subject at length in *Summa Theologica*, III. xxvii. 1, 2, and decides, as St. Bernard, that the Blessed Virgin Mary was conceived with original sin and freed from it before birth. Thus, he says in III. xxvii. 2 ad 2, * The Blessed Virgin indeed contracted original sin; but she was cleansed from it before she was born from the womb. In passages in his earlier works (*e.g.*, *Sent.*, I. xliv. 1 (3); In *Ep. ad Gal.*, cap. iii. lect. 6), he speaks of her as being free (immunis) from original and actual sin. Whether he meant by free always without either, or freed from original sin before birth and always without actual sin, has been disputed. But his judgment in his latest

163

work, the *Summa Theologica,* is quite clear. It is fair to add that his view of the relation of life to conception is not that of modern science.

Duns Scotus, *Sent.,* III. iii. 1 (9): God was able to bring about that she was never in original sin; He was also able to bring about that she should be for one instant only in sin; He was also able to bring about that she should be for some time in sin, and at the end of that time should be cleansed from it...Now which of these three which have been shown to be possible actually happened, God knows: if not opposed to the authority of the Church or the authority of Scripture, it seems probably right to assign to Mary that which is more excellent; *ibid.,* III. xviii. 1 (13): 'The virgin Mother of God was never actually hostile by reason of actual sin, nor by reason of original sin (yet she would have been, if she had not been preserved from it).'

15. *The Papal decree of the immaculate conception.*

The 'constitutio' of Pope Pius IX., 'Ineffabilis Deus,' contained, 'Ad honorem sanctae et individuae Trinitatis, ad decus et ornamentum Virginis Deiparae, ad exaltationem Fidei Catholicae, et Christianae Religionis augmentum auctoritate Domini nostri Jesu Christi, beatorum Apostolorum Petri et Pauli, ac Nostra declaramus pronuntiamus et definimus, doctrinam quae tenet beatissimam Virginem Mariam in primo instanti suae Conceptionis fuisse singulari omnipotentis Dei gratia et privilegio, intuitu meritorum Christi Jesu Salvatoris humani generis ab omni originalis culpae labe praeservatam immunem, esse a Deo revelatam, atque idcirco ab omnibus fidelibus firmiter constanterque credendam.'

16. *The Eastern Church on the conception of the Blessed Virgin Mary.*

See, *e.g.,* Khomiakoff, *Essay on the Unity of the Church,* § 9 (in Birkbeck, *Russia and the English Church during the last Fifty Years,* p. 216): 'We glorify the Saints, the Angels, and the Prophets, and more than all the most pure Mother of the Lord Jesus, not acknowledging Her either to have been conceived without sin, or to have been perfect (for Christ alone is without sin and perfect), but remembering that the pre-eminence, passing all understanding, which She has above all God's creatures, was borne witness to by the Angel and by Elizabeth, and, above all, by the Saviour Himself, when He appointed John, His great apostle and seer of mysteries, to fulfil the duties of a son and to serve Her.' See also Pusey, *Eirenicon,* part i. p. 408.

17. *The Fathers on the Blessed Virgin Mary.*

See, *e.g.,* St. Justin Martyr, *Dial. c. Tryp.,* 100: 'We know that...by means of the virgin He was made man that the disobedience which was from the serpent might have its undoing by the same way as that from which it took its beginning. For Eve, still a virgin and inviolate, by conceiving the word which was from the serpent brought forth disobedience and death, while the Virgin Mary, receiving faith and joy, when the angel told her the glad tidings that the Spirit of the Lord should come upon her and the power of the Most High should overshadow her, and that therefore the holy thing which should be born of her should be the Son of God, answered, Be it unto me according to thy word;' St. Irenaeus, *C. Haer.*, III. xxii. 4: 'The knot of Eve's disobedience was untied through the obedience of Mary, for what Eve, a virgin, bound by her unbelief, that Mary, a virgin, untied by her faith;' V. xix. 1: 'As Eve was seduced by the word of an angel so that she transgressed the word of God and was brought to shun Him, so Mary by the word of an angel received glad tidings so that she should obey the word of God and bear Him as her son. And if the one disobeyed God, yet the other was persuaded to obey God so that the Virgin Mary might become the advocate of the virgin Eve; St. Ambrose, *In Ps. cxviii. Expos.*, xxii. 30: Uplift me not from Sarra, but from Mary, that a virgin may be undefiled, but a virgin free by grace from all spot of sin' (per gratiam ab omni integra labe peccati); Liturgy of St. James: The all-holy, undefiled, most glorious, our Lady, the Mother of God and ever-virgin Mary' in, *e.g.*, Brightman, *Liturgies Eastern and Western*, i. 40; *St. Leo, Serm.*, xxi. 1; St. Augustine, *De pec. m. et r.*, ii. 38; *De Nup. et C.*, i. 13; De Nat. et G., 42, where in dealing with the Pelagian assertion that many persons, including the Mother of our Lord, had not sinned, and that it was 'necessary to our religion to confess that she was without sin' (sine peccato), he said, 'The holy Virgin Mary excepted, about whom I am not willing, for the sake of the honour of our Lord, for any question to be discussed, when we are talking about sins; for how do we know what more grace (unde enim scimus quid ei plus gratiae: al, inde enim scimus quod ei plus gratiae, for hence we know that more grace) was bestowed on her to overcome sin in every respect (omni ex parte), who was counted worthy to conceive and bring forth Him who certainly had no sin? This virgin, then, excepted, etc.; St. Chrysostom, *In Mat. Hom.*, xliv. 1 (commenting on St. Matt. xii. 46-49): He said this, not being ashamed of His mother, or denying that she was His mother; for, if He had been ashamed of her, He would not have passed through her womb; but showing that this would not be any benefit to her unless she did all things that are right. For that which she was then taking in hand was excessively ambitious; for she wished to show to the people that she rules and governs her Son, imagining, as yet, nothing great about Him. Therefore she came to Him at a wrong time. See, then, her madness and theirs. See Turrecremata, *Tractatus de Veritate Concep. B. Virginis*; Petavius, *De Incar.*, XIV. ii.; Perrone, *De Imm.* B. V. *Mariae Conceptu*; Pusey, *Eirenicon*, part ii.

18. Kenotic theories of the Incarnation.

The kenotic theory of the Incarnation, which has been due to the influence of Lutheran theology, has taken the following, among other, forms: -

1. The Son of God on becoming incarnate altogether ceased to live the life of Godhead alike in his divine functions in the Holy Trinity, His cosmic functions in the universe, and His human acts.

2. The Son of God on becoming incarnate abandoned in all relations His physical attributes, *i.e.*, His omnipotence, omniscience, and omnipresence; but retained in all relations His ethical attributes, *i.e.*, his truth and love.

3. The Son of God on becoming incarnate retained all His divine attributes in His divine functions in the Holy Trinity and in His cosmic functions in the universe, but abandoned them within the sphere of the Incarnation. In this, its most moderate form, the kenotic theory has been advocated in Gore, *The Incarnation of the Son of God,* pp. 157-159, 266; *Dissertations on Subjects connected with the Incarnation,* pp. 71-225.

The central objections to even the most moderate form of the theory are grounded upon the immutability of the divine nature; the impossibility of separating the divine attributes from the divine nature except in thought; and the fact that the theory was practically unknown until the sixteenth century. The attempt to distinguish between the metaphysical and moral immutability of God and deny the first while asserting the second will not bear examination. It is admitted by the advocates of the theory that there is no support for it in any Father except St. Irenaeus, Origen, and St. Gregory of Nyssa; and it is very doubtful whether any one of these held it or any similar view. See *Church Quarterly Review,* January, 1896, pp. 304-326.

19. *The Councils of Constantinople* (A.D. 381) *on the completeness of the humanity of Christ.*

Council of Constantinople, canon 1: 'The confession of faith of the three hundred and eighteen Fathers, who were assembled at Nicaea in Bithynia, shall not be abolished but shall remain in force, and every heresy shall be anathematized, especially that of...and that of the Apollinarians.'

20. *The Council of Constantinople* (A.D. 680) *on the will of Christ.*

The decree passed in the eighteenth session of the Council affirmed, 'We also declare that there are two natural wills in Him and two natural energies, indivisibly, inconvertibly, inseparably, inconfusedly, according to the teaching of the holy Fathers... We will not allow that there is one energy only in God and His creature (*i.e.*, the humanity of Christ), that we may not introduce that which is made into the divine essence (οὐσία) or bring down the excellence of the divine nature into the place which is suitable for the creatures. For we recognize the miracles and the sufferings as being of one and the same Person in one or the other of the natures of which He is and in which He exists... We confess two natural wills and energies going together harmoniously for the salvation of the human race.'

21. *St. Cyril of Alexandria and the Council of Ephesus* (A.D. 431) *on the unity of the Person of our Lord.*

St. Cyril of Alexandria, Ad. Nest. Ep., ii. For the ratification, see the first session of the Council of Ephesus (Hardouin, *Concilia,* i. 1363-1387).

22. *The word Θεοτόκος applied to the Blessed Virgin Mary.*

The passages read at the Council of Ephesus may be found in the proceedings of the first session of the Council (Hardouin, *Concilia,* i. 1399-1410). Among the more important references for this use of the word before the fifth century are St. Athanasius, *C. Arian.,* iii. 14, 29, 33; iv. 32. See also Socrates, *Hist. Eccl.,* vii. 32; Constantine, *Orat. ad Sane. Coet.,* 11: Apart from marriage there was conception; there was childbirth as well as chaste virginity; and a maiden was the mother of God;' Eusebius, *De Vit. Const.,* iii. 43; 'The most pious empress adorned with splendid memorials the travail of the mother of God.'

St. Ambrose, *Hexaemeron,* v. 65, calls the Blessed Virgin Dei mater.

St. Leo, *Serm.,* xxi. 1, calls her 'Dei genetrix:' *Cf. Ep.,* clxv. 2.

23. *Human knowledge of Christ*

The following opinions have been held by theologians who asserted the infallibility of our Lord both as man and as God:

1. His human knowledge, by reason of the union of His divine nature and His human nature in one Person, and the complete illumination of His human nature by the Holy Ghost, embraced everything which a human mind is capable of receiving without exception, although His human mind could not have the infinite knowledge which is characteristic of the divine nature alone. This opinion was held by most of the Fathers and by the schoolmen generally. See, *e.g.,* St. Thomas Aquinas, *Summa Theologica,* III. x. 1. It is stated with great accuracy by Hooker, *Laws of Ecclesiastical Polity,* V. liv. 7, in his summing up of his inferences from the single Personality of Christ. Cf. Wilberforce, *The Incarnation of our Lord Jesus Christ,* chapter iv.

2. The human knowledge of Christ ordinarily embraced all which a human mind is capable of receiving, but to this complete knowledge there was one exception, namely, our Lord for a special purpose withheld from His human mind the knowledge of the time of His second coming. See Liddon, The Divinity of our Lord and Saviour Jesus Christ, pp. 461-480, especially pp. 472, 474.

3. Our Lord was habitually ignorant in his human mind of everything which He did not learn by the ordinary use of His human faculties or receive as a special revelation from the Father for the purpose of revealing it to man. His supernatural knowledge was due not to the union of His human mind with His deity, but to revelation through the Holy Ghost, and may be compared with the knowledge of the prophets and other inspired men. See Gore, *The Incarnation of the Son of God,* chapter vi. (cf. note 18 on page 291).

The passages in Holy Scripture which bear on this subject are -

1. There are many passages which indicate our Lord's supernatural knowledge, that is, instances of His knowing something which could not be known by the natural faculties of man. The student should work through the following groups: (1) St. Matt. ix. 4; xii. 15, 25; xxvi. 21-25; St. Mark ii. 8; xii. 15; xiv. 18-21; St. Luke vi. 8; vii. 39, 40; xxii. 21, 22; St. John ii. 24, 25; vi. 70, 71; xiii. 21-26. (2) St. Matt. xvi. 21; xvii. 22, 23; xx. 18, 19; xxvi. 2; St. Mark viii. 31; ix. 9, 31; x. 33, 34; St. Luke ix. 22; xviii. 32, 33; St. John ii. 19-21; xii. 32, 33; xiii. 1-3; xviii. 4. (3) St. Mark v. 30-32; St. Luke viii. 45, 46. (4) St. John xi. 11-14. (5) St. John i. 48-50. (b) St. John iv. 17, 18. (7) St. Matt. xvii. 27. (8) St. Matt. xxi. 2; St. Mark xi. 2; St. Luke xix. 30. (9) St. Mark xiv. 13; St. Luke xxii. 10. (10) St. Matt. xxvi. 34; St. Mark xiv. 30; St. Luke xxii. 34, 61; St. John xiii. 38.

The different interpretations of these passages which may be noticed are

(a) The knowledge existed by reason of the union of our Lord's human mind with His deity. See Liddon, *ibid.,* pp. 472-475.

(b) The knowledge existed by means of revelation to our Lord. See Gore, *ibid.,* pp. 146, 147.

2. St. Luke ii. 52. The following interpretations may be noticed:

(a) It refers to the acquiring of knowledge by human processes, although what was thus gained was from the first known in His human mind through union with His deity. See Wilberforce, *ibid.;* Liddon, *ibid.,* pp. 464-466.

(b) It refers to the acquiring of knowledge previously altogether unknown to our Lord. See Gore, *ibid.,* p. 145.

3. St. Mark xiii. 32. The following interpretations may be noticed:

(a) Our Lord whether as God or as man knew the time of His second coming by the gift of the Father only, in the same way in which everything which the Son possesses is received by Him from the Father. Thus, this passage is parallel to St. Matt. xx. 23, where our Lord says that the places on His right hand and on His left hand were not His to give, while in another sense they were His to give, the explanation being afforded by the last words in the verse, which show that they were His to give only as had been appointed by the Father. There is a similar way of speech in St. John vii. 16, where our Lord says that His teaching is not His, when in another sense it was His, the explanation being here afforded by the following words, showing that His teaching was His only by the appointment of Him who sent Him, that is the Father. So in St. Mark xiii. 32, according to this interpretation, the explanation of the saying that the Son does not know is given in the last words of the verse, which indicate that He knows only by the appointment of the Father. See Burgon, Sermon on St. Mark xiii. 32, following St. Basil, Ep., ccxxxvi.

(b) Our Lord, though He knew the day in His human mind through its union with His Godhead, did not know it by the exercise of His human faculties. See Wilberforce, *ibid.*

(c) Our Lord did not know the day as part of that sphere of knowledge which it was the work of His incarnate life to reveal, that is, He did actually know it in His human mind but not as part of what He came to teach. See Newman, *Select Treatises of St. Athanasius,* pp. 461-469.

(d) Our Lord did not know the day at all in His human mind, this ignorance being exceptional for a special purpose; that is, while our Lord's divine Person communicated to His human mind knowledge generally, the same divine Person withheld from His human mind this particular point. See Liddon, *ibid.,* pp. 466-472.

(e) Our Lord did not know the day, this ignorance of all which was not specially revealed to Him or learnt by experience being His normal condition. See Gore, *ibid.,* p. 149.

4. The questions and prayers of our Lord and the Fourth Word from the cross. The following interpretations may be noticed: -

(a) These are not signs of ignorance. The questions were means of working out circumstances which were required or were rebukes. The prayers were acts of using the ordinary methods whereby man leans upon the divine working. The Fourth Word from the cross was the sign that our Lord was then without the joy of union with God, not that He had lost the knowledge of union with God. This interpretation is implied in Liddon, *ibid.,* pp. 21, 22. It is worked out in the *Church Quarterly Review,* January, 1892, pp. 298-300.

(b) These are signs of ignorance. The questions show ignorance of facts. The prayers show ignorance of the future. The Fourth Word from the cross shows ignorance that our Lord was not forsaken by the Father. See Gore, *ibid.,* p. 148.

24. *The Council of Chalcedon* (A.D. 451) *on the distinction of the natures of our Lord.*

The decree affirmed in the fifth session of the Council included the passage, οὐδαμοῦ τῆς τῶν φύσεων διαφορᾶς ἀνῃρημένης διὰ τὴν ἕνωσιν, σωζομένης δὲ μᾶλλον τῆς ἰδιότητος ἑκατέρας φύσεως, καὶ εἰς ἓν πρόσωπον καὶ μίαν ὑπόστασιν συντρεχούσης.

25. *Errors about the distinction of the natures of our Lord*

The Eutychians in the fifth century asserted that the human nature was converted into the divine nature, so that, after the union between God and man, our Lord only possessed one nature, and this one nature was divine. Some forms of Monophysitism in the fifth century asserted that there was only one nature and that this one nature was intermediate between the nature of God and the nature of man, the two natures being intermingled as two liquids are mingled together, as, for instance, wine and water. Bishop Pearson mentions foreign Anabaptists of whom he says that they asserted that the divine nature was converted into the human nature, so that, after the union between God and man, our Lord had only one nature and this one nature had come to be wholly human. See his *Exposition of the Creed,* Article iii.

26. The theory of a ransom to Satan in the death of Christ.

One or another form of this theory was held by very many until the end of the eleventh century. See, *e.g.*, St. Irenaeus, *C. Haer.,* V. i. 1; Origen, *In Rom.,* iv. 11. The rejection of it by St. Gregory of Nazianzus is in *Orat.,* xlv. 22: 'To whom was the blood which was on our behalf offered, and why was it shed, the great and famous blood of our God and High-priest and Sacrifice? We were held in bondage by the evil one, having been sold under sin, and having received pleasure in exchange for wickedness. Now, if the ransom is to no one else than to him who holds in bondage, I ask to whom was this offered and for what cause? If it was to the evil one, alas for the outrage, if the robber receives a ransom not only from God, but even God Himself, and such splendid pay for his tyranny on account of which it was just that he should spare us! But, if it was paid to the Father, in the first place how can this be? For it was not by Him that we were held in bondage. And in the second place, what is the reason that the blood of the only-begotten should be a delight to the Father, who did not even accept Isaac when offered up by his father, but changed the sacrifice and gave a ram instead of the offering of a rational being? Is it not clear that the Father receives it, not because He asked for it or needed it, but because of the dispensation of His dealings with man, and because it was right that man should be sanctified by that which is human in God, that it should be He who should deliver us by violently conquering the tyrant, and that He should bring us back to Himself through the mediation of the Son who orders this also to the honour of the Father, to whom He seems to concede all things?' In *Orat.,* xxxix. 13, however, St. Gregory of Nazianzus speaks of the devil as being ensnared. The general sense of the teaching of St. Athanasius in, *e.g.*, *De Incar.,* 6-10, is against the idea of a ransom to Satan. So also are parts of the teaching of St. Augustine: see, *e.g.*, *Conf.,* x. 69. St. Leo strongly emphasizes the idea of the death of Christ as a sacrifice offered to the Father: see, *e.g.*, *Serm.,* lxiv. 3; lxviii. 3. The extent to which the theory of the ransom to Satan prevailed has been exaggerated by many writers. On the other hand, the idea is minimized in Mill, *Five Sermons on the Temptation of our Lord in the Wilderness,* pp. 165, 166. See, also, Bigg, *The Christian Platonists of Alexandria,* pp. 290, 291, note 1.

27. The Fathers on the descent into hades.

The following are some of the most important passages on this subject:
St. Ignatius, *Ad Magn.,* 9: 'Whom also the prophets, being His disciples, in the Spirit expected Him as their teacher; and, for this reason. He for whom they rightly waited, when He came to them, raised them from the dead.' On this passage Bishop Lightfoot comments, 'Here our Lord is assumed to have

visited the souls of the patriarchs and prophets in hades, to have taught them the truths of the Gospel, and to have raised them either to paradise or to heaven.' See his *Apostolic Fathers*, II. ii. 131.

St. Justin Martyr, *Dial c. Tryp.*, 72: 'They' (*i.e.*, the Jews) 'cut out this in like manner from the words of the same Jeremiah, The Lord God remembered His dead people of Israel who slept in the earth of the grave, and He went down to them to preach to them His salvation.'

St. Irenaeus cites the same passage as St. Justin Martyr, without mentioning its omission from the text of the Old Testament, in *C. Haer.*, III. xx. 4 (as from Isaiah); IV. xxii. 1 (as from Jeremiah); xxiii. 1, 12 (without any author); V. xxxi. 1 (as from the 'prophet'). In each place there is the addition to the passage as quoted by St. Justin of 'ut salvaret eos,' or 'ad salvandum eos,' or 'uti erueret eos,' or 'uti erigeret, ad salvandum illos,' or 'extrahere eos, et salvare eos.' St. Irenaeus also says in C. Haer., IV. xxvii., that he 'heard from a certain presbyter, who had heard from those who had seen the Apostles and had been taught by them,' that 'the Lord descended into the parts under the earth, preaching to them the Gospel of His coming, there being remission of sins to those who believe on Him. But all those believed on Him who hoped for Him, that is, who foretold His coming and served His dispensations, just men and prophets and patriarchs, to whom He remitted sins in like manner as to us, which we ought not to impute to them unless we despise the grace of God.'

Tertullian, *De Anima,* 55: Christ 'did not ascend to the heights of heaven before He had descended to the lower parts of the earth, that there He might make patriarchs and prophets possessors of Himself (compotes sui).' It is not clear whether, later in the same chapter, he means to reject the view that 'the patriarchs and prophets have gone from the lower world' to 'paradise' as 'a sequel to the resurrection of the Lord' by putting this sentence in the contention of an opponent that the faithful departed Christians generally, not only the martyrs, have left the lower world. The treatise is Montanistic.

Clement of Alexandria, *Strom.*, vi. 6: Christ descended to preach the Gospel, and the Apostles similarly preached after death: cf. ii. 9, and also Hernias, *Pastor, Sim.*, ix. 16.

Origen, *C. Celsum*, ii. 43: 'Having His soul without His body, He held converse with the souls which were without bodies, turning unto Himself those of them who were willing or whom He saw, for reasons which He knew, to be fitting;' In *Gen. Hom.*, xv. 5: 'His only -begotten Son, for the salvation of the world, descended even to the lower regions and brought from thence our first parent. For know that the words to the robber, "To-day shalt thou be with Me in paradise," were spoken, not only to him, but also to all the holy ones for whom He descended into the lower regions;' In *Luc. Hom.*, iv.: He (*i.e.*, St. John the Baptist) 'died before Him that, going down to the lower regions, he might foretell' (or 'proclaim,' praedicaret) 'His coming;' *Comm., in Joan.*, ii. 30: 'Everywhere is John the witness and forerunner of Jesus, anticipating His birth and dying a little before the death of the Son of God, that, coming before Christ, not only to those in life, but also to those who were waiting for freedom from death through Christ, he might everywhere make ready a people prepared for the Lord:' cf. *In Lib. Beg. Hom.*, ii., *ad fin.*

St. Athanasius, *Ep. ad Epict.*, 6: 'He Himself went to preach' 'to the spirits in hades.'

St. Hilary of Poictiers, *Tract, in cxxxviii.* Ps., 22: 'It is a law of the necessity common to man that, when bodies are buried, souls descend to the lower regions. And the Lord, in the perfection of His true manhood, did not refuse this descent.'

St. Basil *Hom. in Ps. xlviii.*, 9: 'The true shepherd, who laid down His life for the sheep, and thus raising them up with Himself and bringing them out of the prison of hades against the morning of the resurrection, delivered them to the upright, that is, His holy angels, to tend them;' 'Plainly he foretells the descent of the Lord to hades, who with the rest will deliver also the soul of the prophet himself, so that he may not remain there.'

St. Ambrose, *De Fide*, iv. 8: 'The Lord by the pledge of His resurrection loosed the chains of the lower world and raised the souls of the holy;' De Exces. Frat. sui Sat., ii. (De Fid. Res.) 102, 103: 'Although as man He died, yet in the lower regions themselves He was free. Do you wish to know how He was free? "I have become as a man with out help, free among the dead." And well was He free who could raise Himself, according as it is written, "Destroy this temple, and in three days I will raise it up." And well was He free who had descended to redeem others.'

St. Cyril of Jerusalem, *Cat.*, vi. 11: 'He went down to the parts under the earth, that from thence He might set free the righteous. For do you wish, tell me, that the living should enjoy grace, and that too when very many of them are not holy, but that those who from Adam had been shut up for a long time should not now obtain freedom? Isaiah the prophet loudly proclaimed so great things of Him. Would you not wish that the King should go down and set free the herald? David was there, and Samuel, and all the prophets, and John himself, who said through his messengers, "Art Thou He who is to come, or are we to look for another?" Would you not wish that He should go down and set such men free?' Cf. xiv. 18, 19.

This collection of passages, which might be greatly extended, is sufficient to show that, though the Fathers differed as to some questions in relation to the descent into hell, there was a general agreement in the early Church that our Lord accomplished a work in the hidden world, and that some of the souls of the departed received benefit through it.

28. *St. Bernard on the progress in the resurrection of Christ.*

In Die Sane. Pasch. Serm., 14: 'Nempe resurrectio, transitus et transmigratio. Christus enim, fratres, non recidit hodie, sed resurrexit: non rediit, sed transiit; transmigravit, non remeavit.'

29. St. Clement of Rome on the resurrection.

Ad Cor., i. 24-26: 'Let us understand, dearly beloved, how the Master continually shows unto us the resurrection which shall be hereafter, whereof He made the Lord Jesus Christ the firstfruit, when He raised Him from the dead. Let us behold, dearly beloved, the resurrection which happens at its proper season. Day and night show us the resurrection. The night falls asleep, and the day arises; the day departs and night comes on. Let us mark the fruits, how and in what manner the sowing takes place. The sower goes forth and casts into the earth each of the seeds; and these, falling dry and bare into the earth, rot; then out of their decay the greatness of the providence of the Master raises them up, and from being one they increase manifold and bear fruit. Let us consider the marvellous sign which is seen in the regions of the East...There is a bird which is named the phoenix. This, being the only one of its kind, lives for five hundred years...As the flesh rots, a certain worm is engendered, which is nurtured from the moisture of the dead creature and puts forth wings... Do we then think it to be a great and marvellous thing, if the Creator of the universe shall bring about the resurrection of them who have served Him with holiness in the assurance of a good faith, seeing that He shows us even by a bird the magnificence of His promise? For He saith in a certain place, "And Thou shalt raise me up, and I will praise Thee; and I went to rest and slept, I was awaked, for Thou art with me." [1] And again Job saith, "And Thou shalt raise this my flesh which has endured all these things."' [2]

[1] See Ps. iii. 5; xxiii. 4; xxviii. 7.   [2] Joh xix 26 (note the reading).

30. Pseudo-Clement of Rome on the raising of the flesh.

Ad Cor., ii. 9: Let not any one of you say that this flesh is not judged, nor that it does not rise again. Understand ye. In what were ye saved, in what did ye recover your sight, if ye were not in this flesh 1 We ought therefore to judge the flesh as a temple of God; for in like manner as ye were called in the flesh, ye shall come also in the flesh. If Christ the Lord who saved us, being first spirit, then became flesh, and so called us, in like manner shall we also in this flesh receive our reward.

31. The promise of the Holy Ghost.

This phrase in Acts ii. 33 means the 'gift of the Holy Ghost which had been promised,' as may be seen by comparing the parallel phrase, 'the promise of my Father', in St. Luke xxiv. 49.

32. The word ἐκκλησία in the New Testament.

Ἐκκλησία is used in the New Testament in the following ways: -

1. A congregation: Rom. xvi. 5; 1 Cor. xi. 18, 22; xiv. 4, 5, 12, 19, 23, 28, 33, 34, 35; xvi. 19; Col. iv. 15; Philem. 2.

2. The union of congregations in one place (singular): St. Matt, xviii. 17 (probably); Acts v. 11; viii. 1, 3; xi. 22, 26; xii. 1, 5; xiii. 1; xiv. 23, 27; xv. 3, 4, 22; xviii. 22; xx. 17, 28; Rom. xvi. 1, 23; 1 Cor. i. 2; iv. 17; vi. 4; x. 32; 2 Cor. i. 1; Phil. iv. 15; Col. iv. 16; 1 Thess. i. 1; 2 Thess. i. 1; 1 St. Tim. iii. 5; v. 16; St. James v. 14; 3 St. John 6, 9, 10; Rev. ii. 1, 8, 12, 18; iii. 1, 7, 14.

3. The union of congregations in a city or country (plural): Acts xii. 5; xv. 41; xvi. 5; Rom. xvi. 4, 16; 1 Cor. vii. 17; xi. 16; xiv. 33; xvi. 1, 19; 2 Cor. viii. 1, 18, 19, 23, 24; xi. 8, 28; xii. 13; Gal. i. 2, 22; 1 Thess. ii. 14; 2 Thess. i. 4; Rev. i. 4, 11, 20; ii. 7, 11, 17, 23, 29; iii. 6, 13, 22; xxii. 16.

4. The whole Christian society: St. Matt. xvi. 18; Acts ix. 31; 1 Cor. xii. 28; xv. 9; Gal. i. 13; Eph. i. 22; iii. 10, 21; v. 23, 24, 25, 27, 29, 32; Phil. iii. 6; Col. i. 18, 24; 1 St. Tim. iii. 15; Heb. xii. 23.

A more elaborate classification, in which some passages are taken differently from the interpretation in the above list, of the use of the word in the Epistles and the Revelation, is in Hort, *The Christian Ecclesia*, pp. 116-118.

33. The Fathers on the Church as one body

The general teaching of the Fathers is represented by Tertullian's words, 'We are a body,' in Apol., 39. See, also, *e.g.*, St. Cyprian, Ep., lv. 20: 'One Church throughout the whole world has been divided into many members;' *De Unit. Eccl,* 4: 'Although to all the Apostles after the resurrection He gives His power equally and says, "As the Father hath sent Me, I also send you. Receive ye the Holy Ghost: whosoever's sins ye remit, they shall be remitted to him; whosoever's ye retain, they shall be retained," yet, that He might manifest unity, by His authority He appointed the origin of the same unity beginning from one. The other Apostles also were what Peter was, endowed with an equal share both of honour and power; but the beginning sets out from unity, that the Church of Christ may be shown to be one. This one Church also in the Song of Songs the Holy Ghost, speaking in the person of the Lord, describes and says, "One is my dove, my undefiled; she is the only one of her mother, the choice of her who bare her." Does he who holds not this unity of the Church believe that he holds the faith? Does he who opposes and resists the Church trust that he is in the Church, when the blessed Apostle Paul teaches this very thing and shows the mystery of unity (sacramentum unitatis), saying, "One body and one spirit, one hope of your calling, one Lord, one faith, one Baptism, one God"?'

34. The word 'Catholic.'

This word is used to denote the true Church throughout the world in communion with the Bishops, in contrast, not only to particular bodies of Christians, but also, as the context shows, to heretical sects out of communion with the Episcopate, by St. Ignatius, *Ad Smyrn.,* 8. It is used for the true Church throughout the world in the *Martyrdom of Polycarp,* init., 8, 19. According to one reading (al. holy), it is used to denote the Church in a particular place which is in communion with the true Church throughout the world in *ibid.,* 16. It denotes the true Church as opposed to heretical bodies in the Muratorian fragment and in Clement of Alexandria, *Strom.,* vii. 17. It is used for the true Church throughout the world and the Church in any particular place in communion with it by St. Cyprian in, *e.g.,* Ep., xliv., xlv., xlvi., xlvii., xlviii. 2; lv. 1; lxvi. 8, and St. Athanasius in, *e.g., Ep. Encycl.,* 5; *Apol. c. Arian.,* 28; *Hist. Arian.,* 81; *Ep. Heort.,* xi. 11. It denotes the true Church in canons 8, 9, 19 of the Council of Nicaea (A.D. 325). St. Cyril of Jerusalem uses it as St. Cyprian and St. Athanasius: see *Cat.,* xviii. 23, 26. So do St. Gregory of Nazianzus in *Exemp. Test,* and St. Augustine in, *e.g.,* Ep., lii. 1; C. *Ep. Fundam.,* 5. Thus, throughout the Christian use of the word, there were two ideas connected with it, (1) universality, and (2) orthodoxy in communion with the Episcopate. In the passage referred to in the text, St. Cyril of Jerusalem draws out what is implied in the two ideas. He does not add anything which is fundamentally new.

(Since the above was written, a very useful note on the word 'Catholic,' by Dom Rottmanner, has appeared in *Revue Bénédictine,* January, 1000, pp. 1-9.)

35. *The Fathers on Episcopacy.*

Besides the passage quoted in the text, see, *e.g.,* St. Ignatius, *Ad Smyr.,* 8; Hegesippus in Eusebius, *H.E.,* iv. 22; St. Irenaeus, *C. Haer.* IV. xxvi. 2, 5; Tertullian, *De Praesc. Haer.,* 32; St. Cyprian, *Ep.,* xxxiii 1; lxvi. 8; St. Athanasius, *Ep. ad Dracon.,* 3, 4; St. Augustine, *C. Faust.,* xxviii. 2, 4; *C. Lit. Petil.,* ii. 118. On the whole subject, see Gore, *The Church and the Ministry. The Canons of Hippolytus,* canon vi., 43, say that one who has been tortured for the faith may be ranked with the presbyters, but not with the bishops, without ordination. On this, see Gore, *ibid.,* pp. 134-137 (fourth edition). Cf. *Testament of our Lord Jesus Christ,* i. 39; *Egyptian Church Ordinances,* 34. Contrast *Apostolical Constitutions,* viii. 23.

36. *St. Jerome and the See of Home.*

There is a strong passage in *Ep.,* xv. 2: 'I, following no one as first but Christ, am associated in communion with Your Blessedness, that is, with the chair of Peter. I know that the Church is built upon that rock...Whosoever shall eat the lamb outside this house is profane. Whoever does not gather with thee, scatters, that is, he who is not of Christ is of Anti-Christ.' This expression of opinion does not appear to represent St. Jerome's own permanent belief. It was written before he had attained to the wide know ledge of Christian thought which he afterwards possessed and in a tune of difficulty and confusion which would be almost maddening to a person of St. Jerome's vehement and passionate temper. There is nothing like it in the multitude of voluminous writings of his later years; and in one of his later epistles, when he is attacking a practice of the Church at Rome, he asks indignantly, 'Why do you cite to me the practice of one city?' 'the world is greater than the city,' language which, if too much has sometimes been made of it, does not look as if he at that time held to the strong statements of his earlier letter. See *Ep.*, cxlvi. For the date, see Vallarsi's preface in his edition of St. Jerome, tom. i. p. lxiv. Cf. Puller, *The Primitive Saints and the See of Rome*, pp. 170, 171, 392-395.

37. The word Apostolic.

The ordinary sense of this word appears to have been 'associated with the Apostles' or 'descended from the Apostles.' See Tertullian, *De Praesc. Haer.*, 32: 'If any dare to connect themselves with the apostolic age that they may appear to have descended from the Apostles (ab apostolis traditae) because they are under the rule of the Apostles (sub apostolis), we can say, Let them then declare the origins of their churches, let them unfold the succession (ordinem) of their bishops so coming down from the beginning with continuous steps (per successiones) that the first bishop may have had as his consecrator (auctorem) and predecessor one of the Apostles or of apostolic men (apostolicis viris) who remained in the communion of the Apostles (cum apostolis perseveraverit). For in this way the apostolic churches (ecclesiae apostolicae) bring down their accounts, as the church of the Smyrnaeans goes back to Polycarp, who was appointed by John, and as the church of the Romans to Clement, who was consecrated by Peter. Cf. St. Ignatius, *Ad Trall.*, init.; *Mart. Polyc.*, 16; St. Irenaeus, *C. Haer.*, I. iii. 6; Clement of Alexandria, *Strom.*, ii. 20; Origen, *Comm. in Joan.*, v. 4; *Antiochene Acts of the Martyrdom of St. Ignatius*, 1. Cf. Lightfoot, *Apostolic Fathers*, II. ii. 152, 153, 474, 475.

38. God the author of Holy Scripture.

This phrase appears to have been used originally to deny the heretical idea that the Old Testament was the work of a power other than the true God. Thus, in the first canon of the so-called 'Fourth Council of Carthage' (probably Gallican at the beginning of the sixth century), it is affirmed that the one true God is the 'auctor' of both the Old and New Testaments. The phrase may be found in, *e.g.*, Second Council of Lyons (A.D. 1274); St. Thomas Aquinas, *Summa Theologica*, I. i. 10; Council of Bethlehem (A.D. 1672), cap. 2; Council of Trent, Sess. iv.; Sarum Pontifical, Consec. in Episc. (see, *e.g.*, Maskell, *Monumenta Bitualia Ecclesiae Anglicanae*, iii. 251); Roman Pontifical, Consec. in Episc.; Vatican Council, Sess. iii. cap. 1, quoted in note 41 on page 316; Encyclical Letter of Pope Leo XIII., 'Providentissimus Deus.'

39. The canon of Holy Scripture.

The canon of the Old Testament was inherited by the Christian Church from the Jews. The Hebrew form of this canon contained (1) the Law, *i.e.*, the five books of the Pentateuch; (2) the Prophets, consisting of (*a*) the earlier prophets, *i.e.*, Joshua, Judges, Samuel, and Kings, (*b*) the later prophets, the greater, *i.e.*, Isaiah, Jeremiah, Ezekiel, and the less, *i.e.*, the twelve minor prophets; (3) the Writings, *i.e.*, (*a*) the Psalms, Proverbs, Job, (*b*) the Song of Songs, Ruth, Lamentations, Ecclesiastes, Esther, known as the five rolls, (*c*) Daniel, Ezra, Nehemiah, Chronicles. The history of the Jewish canon is obscure; but in our Lord's time it was at any rate practically settled that all these books were within it. [1] The Greek books used by the Hellenistic Jews included also the deutero-canonical books of the Old Testament sometimes described as the 'Apocrypha.' It has been thought that a clear distinction between these books and the proto-canonical books is implied in the Prologue to Ecclesiasticus; and Josephus, writing in the first century A.D., distinguishes the authority of the two sets of books: see *C. Apion.*, i. 8. In the New Testament, no passage appears to be quoted from the deutero-canonical books; but there may be indications of the writers familiarity with and use of them. *E.g.*, Wisd. xv. 7 may be in view in Rom. ix. 21; Wisd. v. 17-20 in Eph. vi. 13-17; Ecclus. v. 11 in St. James i. 19; 2 Macc. vi. 18-vii. 42 in Heb. xi. 35. Reference may also be made in the New Testament to books called Pseudepigrapha, *i.e.*, books altogether apart from the canon: cf., *e.g.*, Jude 14, 15 with Enoch ii. In the Fathers both proto-canonical and deutero-canonical books are extensively quoted as Scripture. St. Augustine classed together the proto-canonical and deutero-canonical books: see, *e.g.*, *De Doct. Chr.*, ii. 12, 13. St. Jerome sharply distinguished between them: see, *e.g.*, *Prol. Gal., In Lib. Sal.* Cf. Origen in Eusebius, H.E., vi. 25; St. Hilary of Poictiers, *Prol. in Lib. Psalm.*, 15; St. Cyril of Jerusalem, Cat., iv. 35. The Council of Carthage (A.D. 397), canon 47, put Wisdom, Ecclesiasticus, Tobit, Judith, and the First and Second Books of the Maccabees with the proto-canonical books. The Council of Laodicea (probably between A.D. 343 and 381), canons 59 and 60, limited the canon to the proto-canonical books, with the addition of Baruch and a book which is probably the Epistle of Jeremiah. St. John of Damascus very clearly distinguishes between the proto-canonical and deutero-canonical books: see *De Fid. Orth.*, iv. 17. St. Thomas Aquinas speaks doubtfully as to the authority of the deutero-canonical books: see *Summa Theologica,* I. lxxxix. 8, ad 2. The Council of Trent put all the books together, but apparently without any adequate consideration of the question. The Council of Bethlehem (A.D. 1672) put all the books together as canonical and Holy Scripture. Here, again, it is probable that there was no adequate consideration. The Russian Church, in accepting the decisions of the Council of Bethlehem, omitted the passage on the canon; and in the *Longer Catechism* enumerated the proto-canonical books as the books of the Old Testament, and answered the question how the 'Book of the Wisdom of the Son of Sirach and certain others' were to be regarded by saying, 'Athanasius the Great says that they have been appointed of the Fathers to be read by proselytes who are preparing for admission into the Church:' see Blackmore, *The Doctrine of the Russian Church,* pp. 38, 39. The English Church has continued to read some of the deutero-canonical books in public services. They are sharply distinguished from the proto-canonical books in the sixth Article of Religion. It is obvious that the question had not been adequately considered in the Church of England when this Article was drawn up, since it uses the phrase 'of whose authority was never any doubt in the Church' with regard to the books of the Old and New Testament accounted canonical, while there certainly has been 'doubt in the Church' about some of them, for instance, the Revelation.

The formation of the canon of the New Testament by the Christian Church was a work of time and was marked by some hesitation. The settlement of it affords a striking instance of the assertion of the mind of the Church. By the end of the fifth century, the present books had come to be universally regarded as the New Testament canon. The judgment of later ages, in the face of searching criticism and investigation, has, in a very remarkable way, ratified what the sense of the Church at large then did.

Questions of extreme difficulty are raised by the recent discoveries and study of Jewish and Christian apocryphal writings, and by comparison of these with the protocanonical and deutero-canonical books. In most matters of this kind, there is, at present, need for investigation rather than assertion. But, it is well within the limits of what is clear to say, that the whole Christian Church is committed to the belief that the New Testament and the proto-canonical books of the Old Testament are such a revelation of the nature and purpose of God and the condition and needs of man as involves the trustworthiness of the teaching which they contain. It would be rash to add to the positive statements about these books for which there is good ground, speculations as to the relations of other books to them.

See also note 10.

[1] For doubts and discussion among the Jews in the first century A.D. about Ecclesiastes and the Song of Songs, and for the work of the Jewish Synod of Jamnia at the end of the first century A.D., see, *e.g.,* Buhl, *Canon and Text of the Old Testament,* pp. 27-29; Robinson in *Encyclopaedia Biblica,* i. 670, 671.

40. The number of the Oecumenical Councils.

The Anglican divines have generally allowed six Oecumenical Councils, namely, Nicaea (A.D. 325), Constantinople (A.D. 381), Ephesus (A.D. 431), Chalcedon (A.D. 451), Constantinople ii. (A.D. 553), Constantinople iii. (A.D. 680). The Second Council of Nicaea (A.D. 787) should also be reckoned as oecumenical. The oecumenicity of this Council has sometimes been questioned on the ground that, though its decisions have always been accepted in the East, they were rejected in the West at the Council of Frankfurt in A.D. 794. As a matter of fact, that which the Council of Frankfurt rejected was not what the Second Council of Nicaea affirmed, and the decisions of the latter

Council were eventually generally accepted in the West as well as in the East. The affirmation at Nicaea was that reverence of honour, as distinct from worship of adoration, should be accorded to images (see the decree of the Council, Actio vii., Hardouin, *Concilia,* iv. 456). The denial at Frankfurt was of the lawfulness of giving service (servitium) or adoration (adoratio) to images in such a way as to the Holy Trinity (see the Council, canon 2, Hardouin, *Concilia,* iv. 904). See a paper read by Mr. W. J. Birkbeck at the Church Congress of 1895 (*Guardian,* October 16, 1895), and the *Church Quarterly Review,* July, 1896, pp. 448-476.

41. The Church of Home on Scripture, tradition, and reason.

It may be worthwhile to point out that the official teaching of the Church of Rome recognizes the offices of Scripture, tradition, and reason; and lays stress on their harmony. The Council of Trent was careful to emphasize that the traditions affirmed were those which were derived from the Apostles and had been permanent in the Church. See Sess. iv.: 'The most holy Oecumenical and General Council of Trent...in order that by the removal of errors the very purity of the Gospel may be preserved in the Church, setting this continually before its eyes, which, promised before through the prophets in the Holy Scriptures, our Lord Jesus Christ the Son of God first proclaimed by His own mouth, and then ordered to be preached to every creature by His Apostles as a fount of all saving truth and discipline of morals; and perceiving that this truth and discipline is contained in the written books and in the unwritten traditions which, received by the Apostles from the mouth of Christ Himself, or, as it were, handed down by the Apostles themselves at the dictation of the Holy Ghost, have come even unto us; following the examples of the orthodox Fathers, receives and venerates with like pious regard and reverence all the books of both the Old and the New Testament, since the one God is the author of both, and also the traditions themselves which pertain to faith and morals as having been dictated either by word of mouth by Christ or by the Holy Ghost and preserved by a continual succession in the Catholic Church.' The Tridentine Confession of faith known as the Creed of Pope Pius IV. emphasizes that interpretations of Holy Scripture must have permanence and universality: 'I also admit Holy Scripture according to that sense which Holy Mother Church has held and does hold, to whom it belongs to judge of the true sense and interpretation of the Holy Scriptures, nor will I ever take and interpret it otherwise than in accordance with the unanimous consent of the Fathers (*Bulla Pii IV. super forma jur. prof, fidei*). The Vatican Council declared the value of the processes of reason, and, in repeating the decision of the Council of Trent on the subject of Holy Scripture and tradition, asserted also the need of interpreting Holy Scripture so as not to be contrary to the unanimous consent of the Fathers. See Sess. iii. cap. 1: 'The same Holy Mother Church holds and teaches that God, the source and end of all things, can be known from created things by the natural light of human reason; for "the

179

invisible things of Him since the creation of the world are seen, being perceived through the things that are made:" yet that it has pleased His wisdom and goodness to reveal Himself and the eternal decrees of His will to the human race in another, that is, a supernatural, way, as the Apostle says, "God, who spoke in time past to the fathers in the prophets in diverse fashion and many ways, hath, last of all, in these days spoken unto us in His Son"...This supernatural revelation, according to the faith of the universal Church as declared by the holy Council of Trent, is contained in written books and unwritten traditions which, received by the Apostles from the mouth of Christ Himself, or, as it were, handed down by the Apostles themselves at the dictation of the Holy Ghost, have come even unto us. And these complete books of the Old and New Testament with all their parts, as they are set forth in the decree of the said Council and are contained in the old Latin Vulgate version, are to be received as holy and canonical. Now these the Church holds as holy and canonical, not because having been compiled by human industry alone they were afterwards approved by her authority, nor merely because they contain revelation without error; but because, being written by the inspiration of the Holy Ghost, they have God as their author and have been delivered as such to the Church herself. But, since those declarations which the holy Council of Trent soundly affirmed about the interpretation of divine Scripture so as to restrain wayward minds are badly explained by certain people, we, re-enacting the same decree, declare its meaning to be that, in matters of faith and morals for the building up of the things which pertain to Christian doctrine, the true sense of Holy Scripture is to be held to be this which Holy Mother Church has held and does hold, to whom it belongs to judge of the true sense and interpretation of the Holy Scriptures; and therefore that it is lawful for no one to interpret Holy Scripture contrary to this sense, or, likewise, contrary to the unanimous consent of the Fathers.' Among the statements of the Vatican Council on the relation of faith and reason it was said (Sess. iii. cap. 4), 'Although faith is above reason, yet there never can be any true dissension between faith and reason, since the same God, who reveals mysteries and bestows faith, has given to the human mind the light of reason; and God cannot deny Himself, nor can truth ever contradict truth.' If the principles thus laid down were fully carried out, the process which would result would hardly differ substantially from that threefold appeal to Scripture, tradition, and reason insistence on which was the characteristic feature of Hooker's *Laws of Ecclesiastical Polity*. For an admirable treatment of Hooker's teaching in this matter, see Paget, *An Introduction to the Fifth Book of Hooker's Treatise on the Laws of Ecclesiastical Polity*.

42. St. Luke xxii. 32.

Tertullian, *De Fug. in Persec.*, 2, takes this passage as showing that the power of Satan in temptation is under the control of God. St. Cyprian, *Ep.*, vii. 5; *De Orat. Dom.*, 30, uses it as a proof that Christ prays for our sins. St. Hilary of Poictiers, *De Trin.,* x. 38; St. Basil, *Hom. de Humil.,* 4; St. Ambrose, *In Ps.* xliii., 40; and St. Augustine, *In Ps. cxviii.,* xiii. 3, quote it as illustrating the general dealings of God with men. St. Augustine, *De Grat. et Lib.* Arb., 9; and St. Jerome, *Dial. c. Pelag.,* ii. 16, refer to it as illustrating human need of divine grace. PseudoIgnatius, *Ad Smyrn.,* long recension, 7, and the *Apostolical Constitutions,* vi. 5, take it as referring to all the Apostles. St. Leo, *Serm.,* iv. 3, 4, refers it specially to St. Peter. Cf. St. Gregory the Great, Ep., v. 20; vii. 40; St. Bernard, *De Error. Abael.,* praef. The passages in St. Chrysostom referred to in the text are *In Act. Ap. Rom.,* iii. 3, and *In S. Mat. Rom.,* lxxxii. 3. There is a defence of the Roman interpretation in Bellarmine, *De Verb. Dei,* iii. 5; *De Rom. Pontif.,* i. 20; iv. 3, 6. It will not bear examination.

43. *The word 'Sacrament.'*

For the pre-Christian use of 'sacramentum,' see, *e.g.,* Gaius, *Inst.,* iv. 16; Caesar, *De Bell. Civ.,* i. 23; Horace, *Carm., II.* xvii. 10. Pliny, *Ep.,* x. 96, seems to show that at the beginning of the second century the word was in use among the Christians in Bithynia. Pliny's statement that they bound themselves by a sacrament may be a reference to either Baptism or the Eucharist, or simply to the obligation by which Christians believed themselves to be bound in consequence of their being Christians. See Lightfoot, *Apostolic Fathers,* II. i. 51, 52.

The word is used to denote the Incarnation in, *e.g.,* St. Leo, *Serm.,* xxii. 1; *Ep.,* xxviii. 3, 5; the Atonement in, *e.g.,* St. Leo, *Serm.,* liv. 1; Holy Baptism in, *e.g.,* St. Augustine, *Serm.,* ccxxviii. 3; De Doct. Chr., iii. 13; De Bapt. c. Don., v. 28; St. Leo, *Serm.,* xxi. 3; the Holy Eucharist in, *e.g.,* St. Augustine, *Serm.,* ccxxviii. 3; *De Bapt. c. Don.,* v. 28; the chrism and the imposition of hands in, *e.g.,* St. Augustine, *De Bapt. c. Don.,* v. 28; the Lord's Prayer and the Creed in, *e.g.,* St. Augustine, *Serm.,* ccxxviii. 3; the blessed salt given to catechumens in, *e.g.,* St. Augustine, *De Cat. Rud.,* 50; and the ordinances of the Jewish religion in, *e.g.,* St. Augustine, *Ep.,* cxxxvii. 15; *C. Faust.,* xix. 17. Cf. Bright, *Select Sermons of St. Leo the Great on the Incarnation,* p. 136.

For the restricted use of the middle ages, see, *e.g.,* St. Thomas Aquinas, *Summa Theologica,* III. lx. 2; *Catechism of the Council of Trent,* II. i. 8.

44. *The number of the Sacraments.*

Gregory of Bergamo, *Tract, de Ver. Corp. Christi,* 14: In the Church we have three Sacraments, which not undeservedly are thought more worthy than the other Sacraments, Baptism, Chrism, the Body and Blood of the Lord... There are besides certain others, which seem as it were more ancient Sacraments, namely, priestly ordination, lawful marriage, and sometimes we speak of the Sacraments of the Scriptures and the Sacrament of an oath.

The passages referred to in the Sentences of Roland Bandinelli are on pp. 157, 194, 212, 214, 237, 261, 262, 264, 269 of Gietl's edition (Die Sentenzen Rolands, Freiburg im Breisgau, 1891).

Peter Lombard, *Sent.*, IV. ii. 1.

Decretum Eugenii Papae IV. (Hardouin, *Concilia,* ix. 438-440).

Council of Paris, *Decreta Fidei,* cap. 10 (Hardouin, *Concilia,* ix. 1940-1942).

Council of Trent, Sess. vii., *De Sacr. in Gen.,* canon 1 (Hardouin, *Concilia,* x. 52).

Council of Constantinople, cap. 15 (Hardouin, *Concilia,* xi. 174).

Council of Bethlehem, cap. 15 (Hardouin, *Concilia,* xi. 247).

The English Homilies referred to are *A Sermon against Swearing and Perjury,* part i.; *Homily wherein is declared that Common Prayer and Sacraments ought to be ministered in a tongue that is understood of the hearers.* The passages are quoted in the volume Holy Baptism, pp. 91-93, in the *Oxford Library of Practical Theology.*

45. *The baptismal formula in the Acts of the Apostles.*

Different views on this subject than that expressed in the text, with which compare *Holy Baptism* (*Oxford Library of Practical Theology*), pp. 22, 23, may be found in, *e.g.,* Dr. Armitage Robinson's article 'Baptism' in *Encyclopaedia Biblica,* i. 473-475. The objection to them is that they require it to be supposed that St. Matt, xxviii. 19 was not spoken by our Lord. The fact of our Lord having used the words there recorded supplies the explanation of the references to the Holy Trinity in the Epistles mentioned on page 22.

46. *The sacramental 'character.'*

'Character' is the technical term which denotes an indelible impression on the soul which permanently distinguishes all who have received it from those who have not received it. The Sacraments which confer character are Baptism, Confirmation, and Orders. Consequently, since character is indelible, these three Sacraments cannot be repeated. To attempt to repeat them is sacrilegious. Therefore, in cases where there is a doubt as to the validity of any of them, the administration of the Sacrament which thereby becomes necessary must always be conditional. The character in Baptism is that the baptized person receives the Christian sonship to God and is therefore put in a position to receive the graces which are bestowed through the ministrations of the Church. The character in Confirmation is that the confirmed person is made the servant and soldier of God, is strengthened with the special Confirmation gift of the Holy Ghost, and has therefore greater fitness to receive other Sacraments. The character in Orders is that the ordained person is made the authorized minister of God, with the special gift of the particular Order.

The effect of the reality of character is that a baptized person can never become an unbaptized person, a confirmed person can never become an unconfirmed person, and an ordained person, *e.g.,* a priest, can never become an unordained person, *e.g.,* not a priest.

47. Roman theologians on the blessing of the chrism for Confirmation.

As this is a point on which misapprehension exists widely, it may be well to quote the statements of several representative Roman theologians about it.

Liguori, *Theol. Mor.*, vi. 163: 'There is a question whether the chrism must of necessity be blessed by a bishop. The first and more common opinion says that it must; and this is held by St. Thomas, III. lxxii. 3. ... This is laid down also in the decree of Eugenius IV., where the matter of Confirmation is said to be chrism blessed by a bishop. But the second opinion, which is held by Tournely...says that it need not be so blessed; and Suarez, Dist. xxxiii. sect. 2, ...rightly (speaking speculatively) thinks the latter the more probable. The reason is that, as the Pope can grant authority for administering Confirmation to any one who is only a priest, ...so also he can allow him the blessing of the chrism...I have said, speaking speculatively, for in practice, since the matter is very doubtful, the first opinion, as the safer, ought certainly to be maintained.'

Gury, *Theol. Mor.*, ii. 268: 'There is a question whether the Pope can delegate to one who is only a priest authority to consecrate the chrism. The point is in dispute. Not a few say that he can ...; but others, more in number, say that he cannot.'

Schouppe, *Elem. Theol Dogm.*, xii. 21: 'The blessing of the chrism by the ordinary rule pertains to bishops only; yet, according to the more probable opinion, it can be allowed also to one who is only a priest by the delegation of the Pope.'

Lehmkuhl, *Theol. Mor.*, ii. 93: 'It appears it must be said that the Pope can delegate one who is only a priest to consecrate the chrism. For there are some instances of such a faculty being given; but at present, although the faculty for administering Confirmation is not seldom given, the use of chrism consecrated by a bishop is always ordered, since there is no difficulty in procuring it.'

48. The Council of Nicaea (A.D. 325) on deacons and the Holy Eucharist.

Canon 18 of the Council says, 'It has come to the know ledge of the great and holy synod that in some places and cities the deacons give the Eucharist to the presbyters, whereas neither the rule nor custom have handed down that those who have no authority to offer should give the Body of Christ to those who do offer...Let all this, then, be done away.' Cf. Council of Aries (A.D. 314), canon 15.

49. The two parts in the Holy Eucharist after consecration.

St. Justin Martyr, *Apol.*, i. 66: 'This food we call the Eucharist, of which no one is allowed to partake unless he believes our teaching to be true, has been bathed with the washing which is for the remission of sins and unto regeneration, and lives as Christ ordained. For we do not receive this as common bread or common drink; but as Jesus Christ our Saviour, having been made flesh by the word of God, had both flesh and blood for our salvation, so also we have been taught that the food, from which our blood and flesh are nourished as it is transformed, after being blessed by the prayer of His word, is both the flesh and blood of that Jesus who was made flesh.'

St. Irenaeus, *C. Haer.*, IV. xviii. 5: As the bread which is earthly, on receiving the invocation of God, is no longer common bread, but a Eucharist, consisting of two things, the earthly and the heavenly, so also our bodies, by partaking of the Eucharist, are no longer mortal, having the hope of the resurrection to eternal life.'

Gelasius, *De Duabus Naturis in Christo:* 'The Sacraments which we receive are the divine reality (divina res) of the body and blood of Christ, wherefore it comes to pass both that we by them are made partakers of the divine nature, and that nevertheless the substance or nature of the bread and wine does not cease to be (esse non desinit substantia vel natura panis et vini). And certainly the image and likeness of the body and blood of Christ are celebrated in the performance of the mysteries. It is therefore shown us clearly enough that we are to think in the case of the Lord Christ Himself that which we confess, celebrate, and receive in His image, so that, as the elements pass into this, that is the divine, substance, by the operation of the Holy Ghost, yet remain in the peculiarity of their own nature, so they show that the chief mystery Himself, whose efficacy and power they truly represent to us, remains one Christ because whole and true, while those natures in which He participates remain in their proper being (sicut in hanc, scilicet in divinain, transeunt, Sancto Spiritu pernciente, substantiam, permanente [al. perma nent; al. permanentiaj tamen in suae proprietate naturae, sic illud ipsum mysterium principale, cujus nobis efficientiam virtutemque veraciter representant, ex quibus constat permanentibus, unum Christum, quia integrum verumque, permanere demonstrant). The treatise is in De la Bigne's *Bibliotheca SS. Patrum,* V. 467-476. This passage is on col. 475. It is quoted in Routh, *Scriptorum Ecclesiasticorum Opuscula,* ii. 493. It may be seen also in Pearson, *An Exposition of the Creed,* article iii. p. 162 of folio edition of 1723.

It has been questioned whether this treatise is by Gelasius, Bishop of Rome (A.D. 492-496): see Bellarmine, De Sacr., Euch., ii. 27; Migne, *Patrologia Latina,* LIX. 11, 12 (b). The most obvious meaning of the passage is against both the popular and the technical ideas of Transubstantiation. It has been contended that it is not contrary to the technical doctrine on the ground that the substance or nature of the bread or wine means the nature and essence of the accidents: see Bellarmine, *ibid.;* Migne, *ibid.* The probability is that this exact question was not in the mind of the writer.

50. *Modern Lutherans on the Holy Eucharist.*

Dorner, *System of Christian Doctrine,* iv. 308, 311, 312, 319, 320 (English translation): 'In the Supper...believers are to be made directly partakers of the body and blood of Christ as the true Paschal Lamb, and there with of His personality, His merit and life;' 'The meaning then certainly is: The bread is a figure of my body;' 'The symbolism denotes a present gift offered to be partaken of; the elements are aliments. But that which is offered under the symbolic veil of the elements is described by Christ in the words "My body" and "My blood," by which, in opposition to anything merely ideal or merely material, is meant the entire reality of His personality, Christ Himself with body and blood; The view taken by the Lutheran Church of the connexion of Christ with the elements is not so rigid...that it makes a material imprisonment of Christ (*impanatio*) take place. Further, the *unio sacramentalis* with the elements is not made so indissoluble as to take place also *extra usum*. The presence of Christ is not to be conceived after the manner of the presence of the elements (not locally), but a *modus supernaturalis* of the presence obtains: and the view is earnestly to be repudiated, that the *manducatio oralis* is a *Capernaitica* one, for only the elements, not Christ's body and blood, experience a *lacerari dentibus*;' 'Not merely does the universal Lutheran doctrine affirm that the unworthy do not receive the spiritual blessing attached to faith, although the sacramental contents are objectively present to man along with the elements, and are presented, *i.e.*, offered, to every one, but a difference is made between the spiritual and material eating.

Martensen, *Christian Dogmatics*, pp. 436, 439, 440, 441 (English translation): The Lutheran doctrine is opposed not only to the doctrine of transubstantiation, but to the Calvinistic separation of heaven and earth likewise. Christ is not in a literal manner separate from His believing people, so as that they must go to heaven in order to find Him. Christ is on the right hand of God; but the right hand of God is everywhere. *Dextera Dei ubique est.* And therefore He is present wholly and entirely (totus et integer) in His Supper, wherein He in an especial manner wills to be. There are not in the ordinance two acts, one heavenly and one earthly, distinct from each other, but the heavenly is comprehended in the earthly and visible act, and is organically connected therewith, thus constituting one sacramental act. The heavenly substance is communicated in, with, and under the earthly substances. And as the sacramental communion is not a partaking of the corporeal nature of Christ apart from His spiritual nature, no more is it a mere partaking of the spiritual nature of Christ apart from His corporeity. It is one and undivided, a spiritual and corporeal communion; It is the communion of the body and blood of Christ; for in the blessed bread is *His* power who called Himself the "corn of wheat" (John xii. 24), and like the corn of wheat He implants Himself in human nature, in order to germinate and to grow, to take form and to bear fruit; in the cup of blessing is His power who has called Himself the Vine" (John xv. 1), and whose undying life will glow through our natural life, that we may grow up together with Him. The act here in question is not a literal eating of Christ, according to the notion of the Jews at Capernaum (John vi. 52, 59), but it is one whereby we are made partakers of Christ, as the *princi-*

ple of the entire new creation of man, and of the future humanity of the resurrection which shall be revealed in that day. Here we have to do not with a presence of Christ literally defined according to the category of place, but with a presence in which the higher heavenly sphere invisibly penetrates the lower and the earthly; a presence in power, in working, in gift; for in His gifts He gives Himself. "Take, eat, drink, this is I, in this I give you what is the inmost power of life in Myself! If ye eat not My flesh nor drink My blood, ye have not life in you!" It follows from what has now been unfolded that the Calvinistic notion, that Christ is present only for the faithful, must be rejected;' 'As we oppose the Calvinistic principle that the presence of Christ is conditional upon faith, we equally reject the Romish representation that the consecrated bread and the consecrated wine are the body and blood of Christ *apart from the partaking thereof.* For the presence of Christ in the Eucharist extends only so far as the words of institution extend; but the words of institution are inseparable from the *distribution* and the receiving of the bread and wine. The Lord has instituted His supper as one undivided act, and to separate one single element from the ordinance for a holy use is arbitrary and without promise;' 'The Lutheran doctrine regarding the Lord's Supper rests neither upon a Dualism between nature and grace, nor upon a transformation of the one into the other, but upon an inner *marriage* of the heavenly and the earthly substance.' For Luther's teaching, see his *Short Cat., Greater Cat., Bab. Capt.*

51. The word ἀνάμνησις.

In the Septuagint ἀνάμνησις occurs in Lev. xxiv. 7; Num. x. 10; Ps. xxxvii. (Heb. xxxviii.) 1; lxix. (Heb. lxx.) 1, in the sense of a memorial before God. For the use in Lev. xxiv. 7, cf. vers. 6, 7, 8; and for that in Num. x. 10, cf. vers. 9, 10. The only other place in the Septuagint where it occurs is Wisd. xvi. 16, where it is used for a reminder to man.

52. St. Augustine on the reception of the body and blood of Christ by the wicked.

The ordinary teaching on this subject is very clearly put by St. Augustine in several passages. See, *e.g., De Bapt. c. Don.,* v. 9: "He who receives the Sacrament of the Lord unworthily does not bring about that because he himself is evil the Sacrament becomes evil, or that because he does not receive to salvation he has received nothing, for the Sacrament was none the less the body and blood of the Lord in the case of those even to whom the Apostle said, "He who eats unworthily eats and drinks judgment to himself."' A question has been raised as to what St. Augustine really held on this point. Besides such statements as that which has been quoted, which state in the clearest possible way that all communicants receive the body and blood of Christ, but that those who receive unworthily do not receive the benefit, there are also passages which are expressed differently. See, *e.g.,* In *Joan. Ev. Tract.,* xxvi. 18: 'In this way he who does not remain in Christ and in whom Christ does not remain without doubt neither eats His flesh nor drinks His blood, but rather eats and drinks the Sacrament of so great a thing to his own judgment.' This passage was interpolated in the middle ages with a view to make it clear that, while denying benefit to the wicked, it asserted that they receive the body and blood of Christ; and it is quoted in the interpolated form in the English Article xxix. There is strong reason for thinking that the meaning of the second set of passages is that the reception of the body and blood of Christ is not beneficial to those who receive it unworthily, because the second set of passages can be so interpreted without straining them, whereas the first set of passages cannot mean anything else than that all communicants receive the body and blood of Christ. This also is the belief which is in harmony with St. Augustine's general teaching about the Sacraments and the Church. There is no probability that his teaching on this point varied at different points, because in the *Retractations,* a treatise he wrote near the end of his life, he mentioned in detail the subjects upon which he had at various times taught what he afterwards saw to be mistaken, or on which he had at different times taught different opinions, both of which he thought tenable, and no reference is made to this point, and it is not likely that he would have been silent on a matter of so great importance if his opinion about it had varied.

53. Roman view of the jurisdiction required for giving Absolution.

The present theory of the Church of Rome is that a priest cannot validly absolve unless in addition to the power of Orders which is given at Ordination, he has also the power of jurisdiction which is given by the Bishop's license to hear confessions, and extends only to the district for which it is granted, that in the case of a dying person any priest can validly absolve, but that in any other case the absolution of a priest without a license which covers the case is invalid. See Council of Trent, Sess. xiv., *De Poen.,* cap. 7; Addis, Arnold, and Scannell's *Catholic Dictionary,* pp. 5, 538 (fifth edition). A certain amount of power of delegation by those who have a license for a particular district is recognized, and some general licenses to hear confessions are given. This view is based on the Roman theory that the power of jurisdiction is something additional to the power of Orders, so that one merely ordained priest and not having a license for confessions is without a gift which is necessary for the giving of valid Absolution. About this view it may be said that it appears inconsistent with the offices of Ordination which appear to mean that at Ordination and apart from anything future the person ordained priest receives all the power of for giving and retaining sins. It is probably inconsistent also with the teaching naturally inferred from the history of the Church, since the evidence points to this view about Absolution being a part of the whole system of Church government which has been developed by the Papacy as the distinctively Papal system, which differs in important respects from the doctrine of the Church found in the Fathers generally which has been continuously preserved in the East. Moreover, the view of jurisdiction as to the Sacraments upon which it is based is probably mistaken in regarding jurisdiction as an added gift, the truth probably being that jurisdiction is, properly speaking, a restriction, not an addition, that is, the priest's license does not confer on him any gift which he did not before possess, but simply assigns the sphere in which he can lawfully use the powers which by his ordination he possesses. It may be thought also that doubt is cast upon the Roman view by the admission that any priest can validly absolve a dying person, on the ground that if has the power in such a case he must have it in any other case, however wrong it may be for him to exercise it. It is possible that on this last point there is something in the ordinary Roman argument that the Church by her regulations implicitly confers jurisdiction for this particular case upon the priest, whoever he may be, who has to deal with it. On the other points, there does not appear to be any sufficient answer to what has been said here.

54. *Bishop Cosin on Absolution in the Church of England.*

Cosin, *Notes on the Book of Common Prayer,* First Series, On the Order for the Visitation of the Sick (*Works,* Oxford, 1855, v. 163, 164); 'The Church of England, howsoever it holdeth not confession and absolution sacramental, that is, made unto, and received from, a priest, to be so absolutely necessary as without it there can be no remission of sins; yet by this place it is manifest what she teacheth concerning the virtue and force of this sacred action. The confession is commanded to be special. The absolution is the same that the ancient Church and the present Church of Rome useth. What would they more? Maidonate, their greatest divine that I meet with, *De Poenit.,* p. 19, saith thus: "Ego autem sic respondendum puto, non esse necesse, ut semper peccata remittantur per sacramentum poenitentiae, sed ut ipsum sacramentum natura sua possit peccata remittere, si inveniat peccata, et non inveniat contrarium impedimentum." And so much we acknowledge. Our "if he feel his conscience troubled" is no more than his "si inveniat peccata;" for if he be not troubled with sin, what needs either confession or absolution? Venial sins, that separate not from the grace of God, need not so much to trouble a man's conscience; if he hath committed any mortal sin, then we require confession of it to a priest, who may give him, upon his true contrition and repentance, the benefit of absolution; which takes effect according to his disposition that is absolved...The truth is, that in the priest's absolution there is the true power and virtue of forgiveness, which will most certainly take effect "nisi ponitur obex," as in Baptism.'

55. *The Council of Trent on marriages not contracted before a priest.*

A decree of the Council of Trent declares that marriages which are not contracted before a priest and two witnesses are invalid. This was part of the action taken by the Council to put a stop to clandestine marriages. The Council provided that the invalidity of such marriages, being set up by the disciplinary power of the Church and not being theologically necessary, only exists where the decree has been published. See *Conc. Trid.,* Sess. xxiv., Decretum de reform, mat. Consequently, according to the teaching of the Church of Rome, a marriage of this kind is regarded as invalid in, *e.g.,* Belgium, where the decree was published, and as valid in, *e.g.,* England, where the decree was not published.

56. *Deuteronomy xxiv.* 1-4.

The right translation of this passage is: 'When a man taketh a wife and marrieth her, and it cometh to pass, if she find no favour in his eyes, because he hath found in her some unseemly thing, that he writeth her a bill of divorce, and delivereth it into her hand, and sendeth her out of his house, and she departeth out of his house, and goeth and becometh another man's wife, and the latter husband hateth her and writeth her a bill of divorce, and delivereth it into her hand, and sendeth her out of his house; or if the latter husband, which took her to be his wife, die; her former husband, which sent her away, may not take her again to be his wife, after that she is defiled.' See, *e.g.,* Driver, *Deuteronomy (International Critical Commentary),* p. 270. The importance of the accurate translation of this passage is that it shows that the divorce and re-marriage were merely tolerated in the Mosaic Law.

57. *St. Matthew* xix. 9.

Other interpretations of this verse are: (1) πορνεία is used in its strict sense of the sin of an unmarried person, and our Lord refers to Jews, not Christians, and simply contemplates the regulation of the Jewish law of His time according to which, if an unacknowledged act of fornication on the part of the woman had preceded the marriage, the contract in the marriage was void from the first because of the deception, and consequently the husband was at liberty to put away his wife and marry another. This interpretation has the advantage of taking πορνεία in its proper sense. It is against it that it is difficult to take the passage as referring to Jews only. (2) This passage, while it forbids the re-marriage of a divorced wife, sanctions re-marriage in the one case of a husband who has divorced his wife for adultery. On this interpretation, it has to be supposed that in St. Mark and St. Luke our Lord was simply stating a general law, and meant an exception to exist in the case of an innocent husband of a guilty wife, and that the exception which was passed over in those passages is specified in this passage.

The MSS. contain variations which look as if there was some corruption in the text going back behind the existing MSS. The Vatican MS. omits the reference to remarriage.

58. *The unworthiness of the minister.*

It was said by, *e.g.*, the Novatians in the third century, and the Donatists in the fourth century, that a bad man cannot minister a valid Sacrament. A similar view was held by Wiclif in the fourteenth century. One of the propositions selected from his writings and condemned was 'that if a bishop or priest be in mortal sin, he cannot ordain, consecrate, or baptize.' This opinion appears to have formed part of his 'doctrine of dominion,' according to which a person in a state of sin lost all his spiritual and temporal rights. See, *e.g.*, Perry, *History of the English Church,* i. 433, 441; A. L. Moore, *History of the Reformation,* p. 469. In opposition to such teaching, it has always been the teaching of the Church that the unworthiness of the minister does not affect the grace of the Sacrament; that the grace of the Sacrament necessarily follows from the objective character of God's gifts in the Sacraments; and that this is the only safeguard of the certainty of God's gifts being found in the appointed channels, since, as the heart is known to God only, it would otherwise be impossible for persons to know where they could find the objective grace of God. The whole subject is dealt with in St. Augustine's treatises against the Donatists. See, *e.g.*, *De Bapt. c. Don.,* iv. 5, where he speaks of various types of bad men forgiving sins 'by the power of the Sacrament of God' (*i.e.* Baptism), 'for the Sacrament is known to be the Sacrament of Christ, even in evil men;' *ibid.,* vi. 43; 'When a bad man baptizes, he gives nothing else than a good man gives.'

59. *Intention.*

This word has been and is used in many senses. The doctrine of intention most usual in the middle ages is probably that stated by St. Thomas Aquinas in the *Summa Theologica,* III. lxiv. 8: 'When anything has a relation to many things, it is needful that it be in some way limited to one thing, if that is to be accomplished. Now these things which are done in the Sacraments can be done in different ways, as, for example, the washing of water, which takes place in Baptism, can be directed either to clean the body, or to give health to the body, or in sport, or in many other ways of this kind; and therefore it is necessary that it be limited to one end, that is, to effect the Sacrament, by means of the intention of the person who performs the washing; and this intention is expressed by means of the words spoken in the Sacrament, as when he says, I baptize thee...The minister of the Sacrament acts in the person of the whole Church of which he is the minister. Now in the words which he utters, the intention of the Church is expressed, which is sufficient for the perfection of the Sacrament unless there be a contrary expression externally made.' The same writer in the *Summa Theologica,* III. lxiv. 10, says, 'The intention of the minister can be perverted in two ways, in the first way, so far as the Sacrament itself is concerned, as when any one does not intend to confer a Sacrament but to do something in the way of mockery; and such a perversion destroys the reality of the Sacrament, especially when he shows his intention outwardly. The other way in which the intention of the minister can be perverted is as regards the purpose which is aimed at in the Sacrament, as if a priest should intend to baptize some woman, in order that he might violate her, or if he should intend to consecrate the body of Christ to use it for sorcery; and, because that which is earlier does not depend on that which is later, therefore such a perversion of the intention does not destroy the reality of the Sacrament.'

The official doctrine of intention in the Roman Church was defined by the Council of Trent, Session vii., *De Sac. in Gen.,* canon 11: 'If any one shall say that in ministers, when they consecrate and confer Sacraments, there is not required the intention at least of doing what the Church does, let him be anathema.' This canon leaves the phrase the intention of 'doing what the Church does' undefined. The ordinary explanation given by Roman writers of authority is that this may be a general intention which does not require any specific idea of what the Church does, or necessitate a true view of the Church. Schouppe, *Elementa Theologicae Dogmaticae,* x. 113, says, 'There is not required an intention of producing the effect of the Sacrament, nor of celebrating the rite as something sacred, nor of doing that which the Roman Church does; but it is sufficient if there is a general intention of doing what the Church does.' At an earlier date, Bellarmine, *De Sacr. in Gen.,* i. 27, wrote, 'There is no need to intend what the Roman Church does, but what the true Church, whatever it may be, does, or what Christ instituted, or what Christians do; for these come to the same thing. You will ask, What if one intends to do what some particular Church, and that a false Church, which he thinks true, even the Genevan Church, does, and does not intend to do what the Roman Church does? I answer, Even that is enough. For he who intends to do what the Church of Geneva does, intends to do what the universal Church does. For he intends to do that which such a Church does because he thinks it to be a member of the true Universal Church, though he is deceived in his idea about the true Church. But it is not error on the part of the minister about the Church, but lack of intention which makes the Sacrament void.'

Similar statements to these may be found in nearly all standard Roman books on the subject. Thus, the doctrine taught by St. Thomas Aquinas, and the usual explanations given of the decree of Trent, require that, if a Sacrament is to be valid, it must be administered as a Church Service with an outward indication of what is meant, so that, for example, a Sacrament ministered in mockery would not be valid; but that no further intention than this on the part of the minister is necessary. In addition to this, a further doctrine has been taught by Roman Catholics and was affirmed by Pope Leo XIII. in his Bull on Anglican Orders. According to it, the intention of the particular Church in which any ministration takes place is required to include a true belief about the Sacrament in question, so that if, for example, a particular part of the Church had abandoned the true doctrine of the priesthood, and therefore did not mean its offices of Ordination to confer the powers of the priesthood, all such ordinations would be invalid. This doctrine is not supported by the teaching of St. Thomas Aquinas, and is not involved in the interpretation of the canon of the Council of Trent which has hitherto been customary in standard Roman theology.

This question does not seem to have been raised in the patristic period; and there is nothing in the Fathers which bears directly upon it. The general tendency of what the Fathers say about the requirements of valid Sacraments goes against the view of intention which has been mentioned last; and the natural inferences from the teaching of the Church on the parallel question of the unworthiness of the minister are also against it.

60. *Thomist and Scotist theology.*

Some of the chief differences between the Thomist and Scotist theology were as follows:

THOMIST.

1. Man was created in grace. See, *e.g.*, St. Thomas Aquinas, Summa Theologica, I. xcv. 1.

2. By the Fall the nature of man was in itself weakened and wounded so that an evil element was introduced into it.

See, *e.g.*, *ibid.*, II. 1 Lxxxv. 3.

3. The Incarnation was designed by God to remedy the Fall.

See note 13 in the concluding Notes.

4. The Blessed Virgin Mary had the taint of original sin at her conception, though she was freed from it before her birth.

See note 14 in the concluding Notes.

5. The merit of the death of Christ was superabounding, so that it was more than sufficient to atone for the sins of mankind.

See, *e.g.*, *ibid.*, III. xlviii. 2.

6. The predestination of man to both grace and glory is absolute by the will of God.

See, *e.g.*, *ibid.*, I. xxiii.

7. Infused virtue is bestowed by God on man without his cooperation, though not without his assent.

See, *e.g.*, *ibid.* II. 1 Iv. 4.

SCOTIST.

1. Man was not created in grace; but was placed in grace after his creation.

See, *e.g.*, Duns Scotus, Sent., II. xxix.

2. By the Fall the nature of man, though deprived of the super natural gifts, was not injured by the introduction of any element of evil.

See, *e.g.*, *ibid.*, II. xxix; xxxii.

3. The Incarnation would have taken place, even if man had not sinned.

See note 12 in the concluding Notes.

4. The Blessed Virgin Mary was free from original sin at the time of her conception.

See note 14 in the concluding Notes.

5. The merit of the death of Christ, being in His manhood, was finite; and the sufficiency of it lay, not in the act of Christ, but in the acceptance by God.

See, *e.g.*, *ibid.*, III. xix.

6. The predestination of man is a divine act in view of foreseen merits.

See, *e.g.*, *ibid.*, I. xl.

7. The will of man by the help of God assists in the reception of virtue.

See, *e.g.*, *ibid.*, III. xxxiv.

These differences deeply marked the theology which was characteristic of the Dominicans and the Franciscans respectively. The study and comparison of the two schools of thought will well repay much consideration. Their influence in the controversies of the sixteenth century was perhaps greater than is commonly supposed.

61. Technical terms in connexion with the doctrine of grace.

Habitual or sanctifying grace denotes the gift of God which is bestowed in the Sacraments, and inheres in the soul, by means of which men are made holy, and well-pleasing to God, and capable of performing acts of righteousness.

Actual grace denotes the movement of God's power in the soul, whereby it is impelled towards sanctification or directed and aided in the process of sanctification. The occasions of it are innumerable, and may be of almost any kind, from a time of prayer to some seemingly trivial circumstance of daily life. It can exist in the unbaptized and can produce in them supernatural acts.

Exciting, Operative, or Prevenient Grace denotes that form of actual grace which leads men in the direction of sanctification before the reception of the Sacraments.

Assisting, Co-operating, or Concomitant Grace denotes that form of actual grace which assists man in the work of sanctification.

Merit denotes that quality in good works done through the grace of God, which moves God towards the giving of what He of His free liberality has promised as reward, that is, increase of grace here, and eternal glory here after.

Merit *de condigno* is the phrase used when there is said to be equality between the reward and the merit, according to a right estimation.

Merit *de congruo* is the phrase used when a work, though it is not equal to the reward, has a certain fitness to receive the reward, not of right, but of the liberality of the donor.

Essential merit is in the work of Christ, and there alone.

Merit by participation is in man when he is in union with Christ.

62. The Church in Russia and the Council of Bethlehem on the state of the departed.

The alterations in the decree of the Council quoted in the text made by the Russian Church were (1) 'which the Catholic Church has from the beginning rightly called satisfaction,' was altered to 'which the Catholic Church from the beginning has acknowledged as pleasing to God and befitting;' (2) 'sustain the just punishment due to their sins, but know that they shall by' was altered to 'endure discipline for the sins they have committed, with out, however, being deprived of hope of refreshment from them by;' (3) 'and the good deeds of their relatives, and to this nothing contributes so much as the unbloody sacrifice which each person severally offers for his departed relatives' was altered to 'and works of mercy which are wrought on behalf of the dead; and particularly by the virtue of the unbloody sacrifice which the servant of the altar offers in behalf of each Christian in particular and for his connexions;' and (4) 'But we know not the time of this deliverance, only we know and believe that they shall be freed from their pains before the general resurrection and judgment, but when that shall be we know not' was omitted. See an article entitled *The Russian Church and the Council of Trent,* signed W. J. B., in the *Guardian,* March 31, 1897.

63. The word αἰώνιος in the New Testament.

Of the seventy-one places in the New Testament in which αἰώνιος is used, in sixty-four it refers to that which is necessarily permanent. The only one of these sixty-four places in which any question could be raised as to its denoting that which is permanent is Philemon 15, where St. Paul uses it to describe the new and abiding relation of Onesimus; and there the point appears to be that this relation will never cease. The remaining seven passages refer to fire, punishment, destruction, and sin against the Holy Ghost (St. Mark iii. 29). It is natural to take the word in these seven passages so that its meaning corresponds with that in the sixty-four passages. See Pusey, *What is of Faith as to Everlasting Punishment,* pp. 38-46. For the use of αἰών and αἰώνιος in classical Greek, see a note by the Rev. J. Riddell in Pusey, *University Sermons,* iii. 32-35.

64. St. Jerome and Universalism.

St. Jerome speaks explicitly of the eternity of punishment in *In Jonam,* iii. 6, 7; *In Dan.,* iii. 96; *In Isa.,* v. 14, 15; xxvii. 1; lxv. 20; *In Matt.,* xxv. 46. In In Isa., lxvi. 24, he (1) explicitly asserts the eternity of punishment; (2) explicitly asserts that the devil and those who deny God will suffer this eternal punishment; (3) speaks doubtfully on the subject of alleviation ('refrigeria') for Christians who undergo it. In *Dial c. Pelag.,* 28, he (1) explicitly asserts the eternity of the punishment of the devil; (2) says about Christians, 'si in peccato praeventi fuerint, salvandos esse post poenas,' a sentence which appears

194

to mean that if Christians die in a state of sin they may be saved after suffering punishment. It is possible, though there is nothing to show that this is the meaning, that the sin referred to is of such a kind as would not be thought to shut out grace. In *In Eph.,* ii. 7; iv. 16, there are statements which appear to contemplate the restoration of the devil and the evil angels. This commentary was written in A.D. 388. In *C. Ruff.,* i. 27, he repudiates the idea of the restoration of the evil angels expressed in *In Eph.,* iv. 16, as having been a reference, not to his own belief, but to an heretical opinion. This treatise was written in A.D. 402.

An interesting passage is *In Isa.,* xxiv. 22: 'This seems to favour friends of mine who allow repentance to the devil and the demons, that after long time they will be visited by the Lord. But let them consider that Holy Scripture does not say openly, They shall be visited by the Lord, or, They shall be visited by angels, but simply, They shall be visited. This ambiguity of the word suggests both a remedy and a rebuke, so that, after the just have received their rewards, these will be visited in everlasting penalties (in poenis perpetuis). Nevertheless, it must be recognized that the weakness of man cannot know the judgment of God or pass sentence about the greatness and measure (magnitudine atque mensura) of the punishments, which is left to the will (arbitrio) of the Lord.' See Petavius, *De Angelis,* III. vii., viii.; Pusey, *What is of Faith as to Everlasting Punishment,* pp. 232-236; Fremantle in Smith and Wace's *Dictionary of Christian Biography,* iii. 40, 43.

65. St. Gregory of Nazianzus and Universalism.

Passages which are capable of a Universalistic interpretation are *Orat.,* xxxix. 19; xl. 36; *Carm.,* II. i. 1, 543546. Passages which are clearly opposed to Universalism are *Orat.,* xvi. 7-9; *Carm.,* I. ii. 8, 191-196.

See Petavius, *De Angelis,* III. viii. 8; Pusey, *What is of Faith as to Everlasting Punishment,* pp. 209-213.

66. St. Gregory of Nyssa and Universalism.

St. Gregory of Nyssa asserts the ultimate salvation of (1) all men in *Catech. Orat.,* 35; (2) the devil in *ibid.,* 26; (3) the lower evil spirits in *De Anim. et Resur.* Yet, he appears to regard those who wilfully postpone Baptism and die without it as eternally lost in *Adv. eos qui differunt Bapt. Cf. In Diem Nat. Christi.*

See Petavius, *De Angelis,* III. vii. 1-5; Pusey, *What is of Faith as to Everlasting Punishment,* pp. 213-216. For the view of Germanus of Constantinople, see Petavius, *ibid.,* 6; Venables in Smith and Wace's *Dictionary of Christian Biography,* ii. 767; Sinclair in *ibid.,* ii. 659. See also Alzog, *Patrologie,* p. 300; Fessler, *Institutions Patrologiae* (Jungmann's edition), i. 575, note 2.

www.ingramcontent.com/pod-product-compliance
Lightning Source LLC
LaVergne TN
LVHW091254080426
835510LV00007B/256